Healing the Hospital Environment

P9-DUM-804

WITHDRAWN
UTSA LIBRARIES

Frontispiece *Ancoats Hospital Outpatients' Department*, L.S. Lowry, 1952

Healing the Hospital Environment

Design, management and maintenance of
healthcare premises

Sarah Hosking and Liz Haggard

London and New York

First published 1999 by E & FN Spon
11 New Fetter Lane, London EC4P 4EE

Simultaneously published in the USA and Canada
by Routledge
29 West 35th Street, New York, NY 10001

E & FN Spon is an imprint of the Taylor & Francis Group

© 1999 Sarah Hosking and Liz Haggard

Typeset in Bembo by Keystroke, Jacaranda Lodge, Wolverhampton
Colour separation by Tenon & Polert Colour Scanning Ltd
Printed and bound in China

All rights reserved. No part of this book may be reprinted or reproduced
or utilised in any form or by any electronic, mechanical, or other means,
now known or hereafter invented, including photocopying and
recording, or in any information storage or retrieval system, without
permission in writing from the publishers.

The publisher makes no representation, express or implied, with regard
to the accuracy of the information contained in this book and cannot
accept any legal responsibility or liability for any errors or omissions
that may be made.

British Library Cataloguing in Publication Data
A catalogue record for this book is available from the British Library

Library of Congress Cataloguing in Publication Data
Hosking, Sarah.
      Healing the hospital environment: design, management and
      maintenance of healthcare premises / Sarah Hosking and Liz Haggard.
            p.   cm.
      Includes bibliographical references and index.
      1. Health facilities–Design and construction. 2. Hospitals–
Planning. I. Haggard, Liz. II. Title.
      [DNLM: 1. Hospital Design and Construction.   2. Environment
Design.   3. Health Facility Environment–organization &
administration.   4. Health Facility Planning–organization &
administration.   WX 140 H816h 1999]
RA967.H584 1999
362.1′1′068–dc21
DNLM/DLC
for Library of Congress   98–42212
                                                                             CIP

ISBN 0–419–23170–6

Library
University of Texas
at San Antonio

To those who founded the NHS, to all those who work for it, use it and
wish it well, this book is dedicated.

Contents

Foreword

During the thirty years and more that I have been a doctor, I have worked in a relatively small number of hospitals. The first, St Vincent's Hospital in Dublin, where I spent a brief time as a patient during my teens, and a somewhat longer period as a medical student at the beginning of the 1960s, started out life as a hospital in 1834. It was a warm, friendly and compact hospital, little more in fact that a great town house with a handful of operating theatres, easy to get around and to get to know, until it closed at the end of the 1960s and moved to a massive, purpose-built reinforced-concrete edifice on the southern edge of the city. After a year at a small community hospital attached to the State University in Syracuse, New York State, I returned to Dublin to start training to be a psychiatrist at St Patrick's Hospital. This hospital has a distinguished history. It was founded by Jonathan Swift, Dean of St Patrick's Cathedral. When the author of *Gulliver's Travels* died in 1745, he left all his monies to the buying of land and the building of a hospital for 'fools and the mad' – the first hospital to be built specifically for the mentally ill in Ireland and one of the first in Europe. St Patrick's still functions on its original site – surely the oldest European psychiatric hospital to do so – and I am now its medical director. Over its two and a half centuries, it has been transformed from a rather grey, grim, intimidating institution into a bright, modern, well-equipped and furnished hospital which, amongst other features, boasts a remarkable collection of attractive and striking prints, posters, portraits and pictures which adorn the walls of wards, lounges, corridors and recreation and treatment facilities. My time there and my other working life as a doctor in a number of distinguished hospitals – the Maudsley, St Bartholomew's and Hackney Hospitals in London – have reminded me again and again of the enormous impact, for good and ill, on the morale, confidence and emotions of patients and staff of a hospital's environment, its design, its space, its wards, passages, rooms, casualty department, treatment areas, its colours, smells and sounds.

The origins of the modern hospital, like those of medicine itself, are rooted in the fusion of religion and healing which characterised the civilisations of Egypt, Greece and Rome. The Bethlem Royal Hospital in London, the oldest psychiatric hospital in the world, like so many hospitals in the Western world, began as a monastery. In pre-Christian times, Romans who sought a cure went to a temple on an island in the Tiber dedicated to Aesculapius, the healer of men. The Christians transformed this temple into a church dedicated to St Bartholomew but the sick continued to come and pray for healing. It was to this island that the ailing monk Rahere journeyed from London and it was there that he had his vision of St Bartholomew which led him on his return to Britain to found St Bartholomew's Hospital in 1123 which, having survived the efforts of Henry VIII and Margaret Thatcher to close it, thrives to this day. These old, great hospitals of Europe, characterised by cloisters and squares, atria and gardens, emphasised space and light and tranquillity and the need for rest and relaxation. With the dawn of scientific medicine and the rise of medical technology, the hospital atmosphere, like the bedside manner, seemed to become redundant. Through the historical evolution of the hospital, the patient has become, in the words of two American critics of hospital design, 'more an object on the scene than the focus of design' (Carpman and Grant 1993). It has meant that patients increasingly feel alienated and anonymous in a complicated, dehumanised and intimidating environment.

Iden Wickings in his important monograph from the King's Fund, *Improving Hospital Design*, challenges the view that there is an inevitable choice to be made between providing a technically efficient hospital and an environment focused upon patient needs. He quotes research work which indicates that poor hospital design can have such negative consequence for patients as anxiety, delirium, elevated blood pressure and increased intake of pain-relieving drugs. This book by Sarah Hosking and Liz Haggard serves to put the environment of the modern hospital right back into centre stage of the discussions concerning the development and maintenance of a reassuring, inviting and friendly environment for people who are acutely as well as chronically ill. From the hospital's earliest designs to its actual erection, from its grounds and entrance through its corridors and wards to its specialised units, there is a need for attention to be paid to such factors as light, colour, interior design, furnishings and maintenance. The two authors throughout remind us what hospitals primarily are for – they are for people, human beings, in varying stages of distress, anxiety, depression and fear and not for staff, technology or administrative convenience. For anyone who is involved with the planning, building and maintenance of a modern hospital, this book is a must and it wonderfully responds to Iden Wickings's ringing endorsement of the importance of hospital design when he writes:

> Patients, of course, give the highest priority to obtaining the very best available treatment; but they are also individuals who merit respect, who may be frightened and need reassurance, and who are people with eyes, ears and other senses who need and deserve to receive pleasure from their environment.
>
> (Wickings 1994)

The best hospitals in which I have worked have had a soul, have exuded some tangible sense of the humanity, the compassion and the dedication of their staff, have suggested more a home than a workplace. No one of course will ever feel completely at home in a hospital but the best hospitals by their very atmosphere and ambience indicate to their patients that they are the nearest thing to home. At a time when modern medical and nursing care are subject to the straitjackets of accountancy and accountability, it is vitally important that a voice is heard on behalf of patients and their most human of needs. In arguing for the aesthetics of health care, both authors are arguing on behalf of one of the most crucial linchpins in the whole argument for a more human and a more humane health service.

Professor Anthony Clare

REFERENCES

Carpman, J.R. and Grant, M.A. (1993) *Design that Cares – Planning Health Facilities for Patients and Visitors*. American Hospital Publishing Inc., Chicago.

Wickings, I. (1994) *Improving Hospital Design*. King's Fund, London.

Preface

This book is written for all those who support and admire the National Health Service (NHS) and wish it well, but whose heart often sinks at the reality of the appearance of their local hospital, clinic or surgery.

Everyone who reads this book will almost certainly have had some experience of the health service, whether as a patient, visitor or staff member. Our book is not about the clinical quality of that experience; we and other patients entrust our health to the skills and commitment of doctors, nurses and therapists and we take it for granted that our safety is their paramount concern.

We are writing instead about the aesthetic qualities of those experiences. Aesthetics are not an obscure, elitist discipline concerned with art, expensive interior design or abstract discussion about the meaning of beauty; our use of the word 'aesthetic' is about the quality of the total experience our surroundings give us, as perceived by our senses and intellect.

We believe that a gap exists between people's admiration of the NHS's high ideals and our disappointment with the appearance of its buildings and their entrances, reception areas, corridors and wards. Any built environment and the way it is presented give a message but too often the NHS presents a negative message and implies that no one cares about either the building, its surroundings or those who use them. It may be that the NHS is so lacking in money that it cannot provide aesthetic delight and normal standards of comfort and this, if true, undermines the confidence of all who use it. Or, as we suggest, this may be only a small part of the several reasons that have allowed this shabby state of affairs to develop and remain unattended.

There is a strong national culture of gratitude for the NHS and sympathy for its staff who are seen as working hard without enough money to do all they want. We feel grateful for the NHS and we know the pressures and strain of providing safe health care in a system which demands that an ever larger number of patients are treated to ever more exacting standards without any corresponding increase in resources. Countries can only get the public services they are willing to pay for and Britain pays less for health care than other European countries; our politicians are apparently convinced that when the public say that they are willing to pay higher taxes for better health care they do not really mean it.

But most health care does not take place in hospitals. There are thousands of GP surgeries and clinics and a comparatively small number of hospitals and, throughout an average lifetime, most people spend only a few days in a hospital. However, hospitals as large buildings are the most visible part of the NHS and have a powerful symbolic value in a community: the sense that there is a well-run local hospital is an important part of the mosaic of our local town. For most people this sense will come not from direct experience as an in-patient, but from visiting other patients, going to an out-patient clinic, talking to people about the hospital, local news stories and the general impression given by the hospital buildings and entrance.

Since the last world war, most groups of public buildings have received professional design treatment for their interiors and surroundings as an integral part of their professional image. The Post Office enjoyed major refurbishment during the 1960s; since then the railways, major stores, banks, offices and workplaces, whether private or public sector, have generally benefited from professional handling of their environment. It has gradually become generally accepted that design qualities need to be addressed on behalf of the general public as a reasonable expectation of modern society.

We believe there are many reasons why hospitals and NHS premises generally have not consistently benefited from this attention to their premises, presentation and image, and we discuss these, besides offering specific solutions, during the course of this book.

When clinicians and managers feel they have to choose between spending money on treating patients safely or improving the quality of buildings, we would of course want them to opt for the former. The appearance of most hospitals with their legacy of backlog maintenance and shabby decoration shows how often that choice has been made. However, we believe that this choice is not always necessary and that even within its existing limited resources the NHS can achieve some measure of aesthetic success within and around its premises.

Our central theme is that real improvement can be made by making a small financial investment in design expertise and then allowing those experts to use existing resources in the best possible way. While this sounds easy and obvious, if it really was easy and obvious we would not have needed to write this book.

Our book is not intended as a DIY guide. Because of our insistence on the need for professional design advice, we devote the whole of Chapter Nine to the appointment of a design team. All sectors of the health service employ the appropriate professionals for the job, whether pharmacy, surgery or laundry, and design and decoration should not be left to the amateur. The traditional lack of design professionalism within the NHS leaves a lasting legacy in disappointing premises which do not do justice to the commitment and quality of the health care given there.

However, just to employ a professional designer is not enough. The NHS and its leaders have to take an intelligent interest in the issues which are the concern of design professionals if they are to be effective in leading, managing and monitoring real improvements in aesthetic delight and standards of comfort. This book should equip the NHS with enough knowledge of design issues and solutions to create a satisfying and productive working relationship with appropriate designers.

Because the range of topics we include is so wide, our data has come from several sources. We have drawn on a number of excellent, detailed studies of the history of medicine and of hospital buildings and the evolution of the welfare state to set our comments in a context of continuing health service evolution. We have also referred to other substantial studies – on the development of twentieth-century design, Western art, plant life,

landscape and so on – as required, as the combined bibliographies of the ten chapters illustrate.

Another important source has been journalistic comment from newspapers and many professional magazines covering nursing and medical matters, hospital management, art and design besides architecture and landscape issues. These have had the honesty of 'short shelf-life' data and the quality of library and internet searches have led us to some excellent unpublished material. Our final source has been our own combined personal experiences and those of many friends and colleagues.

The sources for our illustrations have been equally varied. We intended initially to use only contemporary photographs but we decided to include some historical material for two reasons. First, historic pictures can include people; for sensible reasons of privacy, modern photographs carefully have to avoid showing patients and this can lead to an illusion of premises devoid of people. Also, period pictures often remind us that the aesthetic qualities we advocate are not new; old pictures of wards often show good-quality furniture well maintained, pictures and decorative items such as lace and cushions, flowers and plants, pets such as dogs and birds, and large windows offering peaceful views (see Figs P.1 and P.2).

For these historic pictures, the national medical and architectural libraries and archives have been our main sources but other material has sometimes become available when someone, most typically a retired hospital librarian, kept a box of oddly assorted pictures and brochures and fate

Figs P.1 and P.2 'Bethlem' The Royal Hospital of Bethlehem, Gallery for men (top); Gallery for women (bottom). Woodcut, *The Illustrated London News*, 1860.

While these wards look comfortable and well appointed, they are obviously the 'public view' of the hospital. The reality of care in the privacy of wards away from public gaze was too often cruel and squalid.

These two illustrations show how 'perceptions' of mental illness in men and women were, and perhaps still are, inconsistent. Even though they are mentally ill, the men are shown displaying normal and dignified behaviour with even a hint that they may be 'officers and gentlemen'. The women are shown displaying agitated behaviour or sunk in catatonic vacancy.

Wellcome Institute Library, London

suddenly made these available to authors like us. Finally, there are our own pictures taken discreetly during our many years working in and visiting numerous hospitals.

We have had to make a decision about naming pictures and particular buildings, gardens or interior and art schemes cited as examples. We decided to opt for generalised locations and avoid named instances, because these initiatives are often subject to rapid alteration and we did not want to send people in search of examples which had disappeared or were no longer exemplary. There are instances where we believed it appropriate to give a place-name, but these are the exception.

Hospitals and the organisations that run them tend to change their names; in Chapter One, for example, Figs. 1.10, 1.11 and 1.12 show three photographs of the same site separated by fifty years and with three different names. Therefore, where we do identify an example, we have used the hospital name as it was when the picture was taken or the undertaking completed.

One problem of such research is that the NHS has no central archive. In the past, hospitals tended to retain their own data but, since the recent reforms, archives have been amalgamated and relocated with national or county archives and record offices, with museums and libraries or even with pharmaceutical and healthcare companies. The NHS Estates conducted a survey of their whereabouts in 1998 and this disparity of access was apparent. There appear to be no significant records of the appointment and furnishings of hospitals which may suggest that the subject has never been considered important. Hence this book.

Many prospective readers may riffle through our illustrations and subject lists or index and feel that many urgent and popular topics have been omitted. All authors have to make choices and we selected our subjects on the following basis: we visualised visits to any typical hospital and have considered those aesthetic elements that offer comfort and delight as people work, walk, wait or occupy a bed.

On this basis, we have not included discussion of stores, computer rooms, engineering and boiler houses, sluices or staff facilities. We have not written about access for the disabled, nor have we discussed clinical standards or factors such as cleanliness and specialist furniture. We do not deal either with public relations or printed material and some non-visual factors such as libraries and shops are hardly mentioned. Matters that pertain more to long-term care such as the various therapies and entertainment are similarly left out. Current issues such as waiting lists and choice of hospital have had ample coverage elsewhere and are not within our remit.

The book is arranged so that most chapters are in two parts. The first discusses the issues and the second part, called 'Chapter Information', gives the associated professional data. Some of the best cookery writers offer an informed essay about their ingredients before giving the recipes and we have adopted a similar plan. It is after our 'essay' that we give the 'recipes' which in our case include a bibliography, appropriate addresses, identification of materials, codes and symbols, explanation of relevant terms, names and addresses of suppliers, relevant professional and voluntary agencies and organisations, printed and published data and any other material relevant to the text.

Our book is written for staff in the health service and especially senior management and board members who may understandably feel defeated by their inheritance of shabby buildings. It is equally addressed to members of the various art and design professions with the anticipation that they may be invited to participate to a greater degree in the visual quality of their local general or distant specialist hospital.

We know that politicians and lobby groups, the voluntary sector, the media and the public all care about the NHS and its future and it is also to them we have addressed ourselves. But above all, we have written this book for patients whose justified gratitude for the clinical treatment they receive from the NHS may be too often clouded by the poor environment in which it is delivered.

Sarah Hosking
Liz Haggard

Acknowledgements

FINANCIAL ACKNOWLEDGEMENTS

For financial support during the research and preparation of this book, thanks are extended to:

The Helen Hamlyn Foundation

King Edward's Hospital Trust Fund for London

The Lankelly Foundation

The Nuffield Foundation

The Office for Public Management.

Support for the inclusion of colour illustrations has been generously donated by:

Forbo-Nairn Ltd

Margaret Houston

The Nuffield Foundation.

ACKNOWLEDGEMENTS FOR RESEARCH ASSISTANCE

Staff in many institutions have been invariably reliable and helpful and deserve commendation: the King's Fund, the Royal Commission for Historic Monuments in England, and the London Metropolitan Archives and the MARU Library at the South Bank University, the Wellcome Institute. We would also like to thank many NHS staff countrywide who have answered queries and given us access to premises and to archives.

PERSONAL ACKNOWLEDGEMENTS

Sarah Hosking wishes to acknowledge the many staff at Basingstoke Health Authority and the Special Hospitals Service Authority, in particular Charles Kaye, Chief Executive of both of them; also Annette Clayson and Alan Simpson, nurse/managers 'extraordinary'.

Liz Haggard wishes to thank Southern Derbyshire Community Health Services Trust and Nottingham Community Health Council for their work for patients and the education they gave her.

Thanks are due to The Whitworth Art Gallery, The University of Manchester, for permision to reproduce *Ancoats Hospital Outpatients' Department* by courtesy of Mrs Carol Ann Danes, the copyright owner of the work.

Line drawings and logos interspersed in the text by Sarah Hosking.

The legacy and appearance of hospital buildings

CHAPTER

1

I think it frets the saints in heaven to see
How many desolate creatures on the earth
Have learnt the simple dues of fellowship
And social comfort, in a Hospital.
(Elizabeth Barrett Browning, *Aurora Leigh*, 1856)

INTRODUCTION

An analogy

Hospitals are like garages where people are taken to be checked and repaired before being sent off to resume their journey. Diagnosis and treatment are achieved by a combination of scientific and machine calculation balanced by human wisdom and experience; sometimes it has to be accepted that the whole journey is over and discreet disposal is made of the chassis after those parts deemed to be still able to function elsewhere on another vehicle are removed. There are often piles of old jalopies with no further use, sad crash victims or just worn-out bodies, piled at the back out of sight so as not to distract customers. New deliveries are always being made, of course, and these pristine models are taken off by their unhabituated owners with the warranty promising professional attention if they are found deficient in performance.

This analogy is, unfortunately, rather too close for comfort. It is the aspect of hospitals acting as if they are garages and believing that brisk repair of the physical parts is all that needs to be done that is the basis of our concern and the subject not only of this chapter but of this book.

We assume that cars do not have feelings and that a car repaired in a chaotic, dark, unpainted garage with broken windows will have as good a chance of emerging 'healed' as a car repaired in a glistening and newly appointed garage; the skill of the mechanic is all that matters. But people are not cars; while the clinical and technical skills of those who treat patients are the highest priority, we know that people's judgements and feelings about their environment have a strong impact. In too many of our health service buildings this impact is not a positive contributor to confidence, or healing and happiness.

The 'social comfort' of a hospital

CHARACTERISTICS AND QUALITIES

Size and complexity

Hospitals are amongst the largest and most complex of all modern institutions. They require a huge bureaucratic structure to run them and this is subject to political pressure, financial circumstance and public scrutiny. They are at once scientific laboratories and refuge asylums, they are hotels and offices quite apart from their rather messy 'garage' functions of diagnostic and repair workshops; they incorporate advanced technological resources which are guided by intellectual and scientific enquiry. None of these varied elements are static for, as technology develops, as medical understanding progresses and their combined application expands, so do social demand and expectation. The country's political mandate can also dramatically alter medical and managerial policies as the last decade of the twentieth century demonstrates.

There are many reasons why hospitals are difficult to plan and build, to run and maintain. This chapter considers hospital buildings from one point of enquiry: that of the human comfort that well-designed and -maintained buildings can give, or, to use the more formal term, the 'aesthetics' of hospitals.

Comfort and the 'aesthetic'

In a recent internet search using the word 'comfort' under the subject heading 'hospitals', only two items transpired; one was for air cushions to be used after rectal operations and the other was for evangelical Christianity and the 'comfortable words of Christ'. This suggests that modern use of the word is limited and perhaps devalued by advertising usage, whereby most people now asked to think of 'comfort' visualise towels washed with a particular product.

Our use of 'aesthetics' includes comfort with all its snuggly, cosy implications but has more profound implications linked to spiritual comfort. We use the word 'aesthetic' many times in this book, as a noun and as an adjective and its qualities play a major role throughout. So, what is it?

The 'aesthetic' quality: a definition

'Aesthetic' means appreciation of our surroundings as they are perceived by our senses but it is not simply a sensory matter of distinguishing hot from cold, clear air from a stink, silence from a cacophony but more, much more.

For it also implies discriminating appreciation of our surroundings as they are understood by our higher senses in the following twelve ways:

- the psychological aesthetic includes happiness, joy and pleasure
- the spiritual aesthetic suggests hope, contentment and peace
- the physical aesthetic implies well-being, ease and convenience
- the intellectual aesthetic inspires humour, interest and contemplative delight.

All these are desirable qualities; while the spiritual aesthetic is perhaps attributable mainly to a person's state of mind which depends on other factors, the other three forms can be stimulated, encouraged, maintained or extinguished to a considerable extent by those complex factors we call our surroundings.

We believe this general listing of 'aesthetic' qualities worth making because whatever inspires twelve such reactions should surely be taken into account in a hospital environment. Nevertheless, we know that it is a limited definition because the factors that prompt, for example, interest and contemplation in a person will depend on their culture and expectations; of course each of us has vastly different experiences and assumptions which shape our reactions; ask any volunteer hospital librarian about people's responses to the books on the trolley. Also, while 'well-being, ease and contentment' may be prompted by a comfortable ward with thoughtful pictures to look at and a well-managed outlook, it is no consolation for poor medical or nursing care.

So, how far do architects and planners take such needs into account? There is an established classical precedent.

The third part of a good building

The Roman architect Vitruvius, writing in the first century BC, wrote that all successful public buildings must be built with due reference to these three parts:

Durability will be assured when foundations are carried down to the solid ground and materials are wisely and liberally selected.

Convenience when the arrangement of the apartments is faultless and presents no hindrance to use.

Beauty when the appearance of the work is pleasing and in good taste.

Vitruvius was the most practical and chatty of men, but even he had problems with what constituted 'beauty' and deplored the decadence of contemporary fresco painting: 'We now have fresco paintings of monstrosities rather than truthful representations of definite things . . . and it is this new taste that has caused bad judges of poor art to prevail over true artistic excellence' (Vitruvius, *The Ten Books on Architecture*, trans. by Morris Hicky Morgan, Dover Publications 1960). His annoyance echoes across two millennia and we can at least agree that, still, 'beauty' is notoriously hard to define.

A definition of 'delight'

We shall therefore combine this ancient exhortation to 'beauty' with our own understanding of the 'aesthetic' and call the two 'delight' both here and for the remainder of this book.

Current popular opinion would probably say that 'delight' is not associated with most modern architecture and, on the face of it, this is the case. Why is this? Recent architectural history presents part of the answer.

The 'Modern Movement'

Early in the twentieth century, architects allied themselves with artists and other intellectuals to establish a universal Modern Movement for visual and design arts. Painting led the way with Cubism which fragmented familiar objects and sited them in apparently infinite space; abstract art then repudiated all representation in exploring the universal qualities of purity of proportion, light and colour.

It was a gift to opportunity that New York Manhattan was being built during the 1920s and 1930s on its rocky substrata and that the Americans were not hidebound by tradition in architecture, in government, in films or in any other way; for example, what other nation could have produced Mickey Mouse? It is an outrageous portrayal of a mouse . . . nothing like.

Within this culture of visual and engineering adventure, architects were able to build their visionary city of huge abstract shapes, formally interrelated, surrounded by sea and reaching clouds to make the biggest sculpture park ever built. Inside, these buildings used the new technology for highly functional efficiency and the influence of this great enterprise has become the universal 'trademark' of the twentieth century.

While Vitruvius' 'durability' and 'convenience' were integral to the Modern Movement, 'delight' was not apparent except in a highly intellectualised form. The London South Bank Festival Hall is perhaps the one such building held to be delightful, which is why it remains popular, but this may also be due to the fact that its interior design and detailing have been well maintained

Fig. 1.1 Finsbury Health Centre, London; architect Bertold Lubetkin 1938. This innovative building with its wall of glass bricks is now surrounded by mature trees and bushes, but the inappropriate signs and notices and the condition and colour of the railings do not do justice to its architecture. At the end of the 1990s it is due for renovation. 1998

and not messed about by passing fashion changes. Another such building which can very reasonably be called 'delightful' (though less well maintained) is the Finsbury Health Centre, designed in 1938 by Bertold Lubetkin and still in use in the late 1990s, with its wall of glass bricks illuminating the interior, and the mature surrounding trees suggesting a 'healing' green oasis (Fig. 1.1).

The point in explaining this is that hospitals built during and since the 1920s and 1930s are largely derived from this 'modernist' language (see Fig. 1.2). There were and are many eminent European architects who developed these basic modernist theses and some built hospitals, such as Alvar Aalto's tuberculous sanatorium in Finland (Fig. 1.3). The introduction of reinforced concrete, steel supports and large glass sheets made possible such developments as the 'verandah ward', used for the care of lung disease. But this change experienced by architecture in the early part of the twentieth century had two universal, fundamental concepts:

Internal rather than wall-bearing strength
Structural strength depended on internal uprights and beams, in themselves forming rectangular, modular shapes and spaces wherein the pipes and cabling could be concealed. This influenced the internal appointment which was suitably basic and abstract. Walls were not weight-supporting so glass and coloured cladding could be used. This meant that the exterior was inevitably an abstract, rectilinear façade.

Decorative ornamentation was banned
Previous architecture had throughout centuries decreed that the degree and complexity of ornament declared the importance of a building. This was totally rejected by the Modern Movement and the whole vocabulary of architectural decorative ornamentation was for decades unused and unacceptable.

There are, of course, many other late twentieth-century architectural trends, of which brick and later concrete 'brutalism' is one of the most unpopular. One reason for this may be their use in unsuitable places, like hospitals. Stratford-upon-Avon Memorial Theatre (brick 'brutalism' of the 1930s) and the National Theatre (concrete 'brutalism' of the 1960s) declare their inheritance from fortified, 'brutal' castles which we laud and admire. Theatre 'happens' in the evening, so the public arrive, often in the dark, to see this

Fig. 1.2 Aerial photograph of St Helier Hospital, Carshalton, Sutton, London. 1930s, RCHME

Fig. 1.3 Entrance to the Paimlo Sanatorium, Paimlo, Finland (1929–33) designed by Alvar Aalto. This asymmetrical canopy is known to the nurses as 'Alvar's lung'. 1996 Photograph, Sino Rista

powerful building, brilliantly and imaginatively lit up inside and out, bustling with people, and the worse the weather the greater the anticipation; marvellously suitable for a theatre but possibly not for a hospital.

The other reason for the unpopularity of much modernist architecture is that it was often badly built, shoddily equipped and remained ill-maintained.

Schemes such as Corbusier's Unité d'Habitation, which provided the model for many post-war projects, included a wide range of communal facilities to serve the needs of their inhabitants, from creches to laundries to proper maintenance. In Britain, after the war, similar schemes were given the go-ahead, but minus these essential humanising elements. Poor standards of construction, lack of maintenance and cost-cutting on every turn set the seal on their failure. It is interesting to note that where attempts have been made to salvage some of these tower blocks, the simple expedient of putting a 'concierge' at the entrance – putting a human face on the building – has made them desirable places to live.

(T. Conran, *Terence Conran on Design*, Conran Octopus, 1996)

Hence the current trend of high-quality refurbishing of even the most vilified, brutalist office blocks into luxury flats. Restore these buildings to the intended level, furnish them appropriately and the 'white elephant' becomes the 'desired residence'. Of all those who deal in delight, estate agents are the best assessors.

Post-modernist architecture

Since the 1950s there have been attacks on Modernism, based in part on its lack of 'delight'. The high-tec approach has been eroded by a demand for architecture once again to be a human language, a cultural signifier of place and populace. Architecture largely abandoned its one, international style and diversified, introducing elements from vernacular, national and regional architecture of which decoration was a part (Fig. 1.4). Social demands for more and cheaper homes introduced 'self-build' kits for houses and other forms of self-sufficiency housing, while temporary dwellings and the occasional tree house show the influence of protest groups. The so-called 'vernacular' style is also popular, as seen in many an out-of-town supermarket with its clock tower and chalet-type pitched roofs.

Fig. 1.4 Entrance to St Mary's Hospital, Isle of Wight, opened 1991. This entrance canopy and the 'towers' behind reflect the island's maritime environment.

'**I am wild about technology, but not technology run wild.**'
Richard Rogers

At the other end of the scale, galloping technical advances have permitted buildings of marvellous invention: using concrete and titanium in shapes like sails and wings, buildings with the usual internal working parts placed outside in transparent structures, dazzling suspensions of steel, roofs that can fold and regular geometry shattered into irregularities.

These changes in architecture have affected hospitals, so let us now look at their historical development.

HISTORIC HOSPITAL PROVISION

What they could do with round here is a good war . . . You know what the trouble with peace is? No organisation. And when do you get organisation? In a war . . . That's the story; no organisation, no war.
(Bertolt Brecht, *Mother Courage*, 1939)

Brief history to 1800

Warrior nations tend to be well organised so it was axiomatic that the ancient, classical world had hospitals, including military hospitals, built with understanding of human requirements whereby the beds were arranged on an east–south–west basis to receive the maximum sun wherever possible.

During the dark ages it can be assumed that people only had one serious illness, their last, before the late medieval centuries started the long tradition of hospital foundations, for which there are written records and actual remains of the buildings.

At the basis of hospital foundation lay the understanding that separation of the sick from everyday life was necessary . . . Hospitals were founded at the entrances to towns, in areas unsuitable for settlement, on the sidelines of a town's business and social centre.
(Lindsay Granshaw and Roy Porter, *The Hospital in History*, Routledge, 1989)

This was due to fear of contagion, which was real enough and the first significant attempt by any state to care for public health was as a result of contagious diseases. The horror of leprosy coupled with the biblical connotations meant that the disease had special attention, and specific hospitals were founded outside towns, beside streams, secluded. It is now thought that people

with eczema, psoriasis and skin cancer were lumped together in the 'leprosy' category.

Leper hospitals, small hospital almshouses and a plethora of lay and monastic houses with hospitals attached were founded and evolved during the four centuries that most people call the Middle Ages. What did they offer?

Basically, they gave asylum to those lucky enough to be admitted; many hospitals had strict criteria for admission so that, sadly, some people had to be turned away. The 'frenzied' or 'silly' were no-one's favourite; pregnant 'lewd' women were often refused care besides those carrying any hint of contagion or suggestion of idleness. This policy of selection was in force even in the more enlightened eighteenth century when the new infirmaries would often not admit the same categories: pregnant women, children and the unsavoury mad, contagious or dying.

Little is known about the furnishings or appointments of medieval hospitals except for Henry VII's Savoy Hospital in which they were unusually lavish.

The hundred beds in the dormitory were furnished with flock mattresses and featherbeds, bolsters and pillows, a linen coverlet, and a green and white tapestry counterpane with a red rose at the centre. Each bed also had green and white curtains that could be pulled to screen it. The dormitory was lighted all night by wheel-lamps, and earthenware chamberpots were provided for the use of the inmates.
(Robert Somerville, *The Savoy*, London, 1960, quoted in *The Hospital in History*)

The lack of medical care was striking: 'One often deals with quite a full hospital archive covering hundreds of years and yet encounters not one mention of purchase of drugs or payments to physicians or surgeons' (*The Hospital in History*). Apart from crude surgery that sometimes worked by chance rather than design, and general bone setting, bleeding and lancing, there was little to be done except to offer 'placebo' benefits, skilful and palliative care, hygiene, warmth, peace and food and the solace of religion, which the proximity of the chapel often provided.

The Dissolution of the Monasteries during the late 1530s was a blow to the nations' medical care as so many of the 'hospitals' and asylums vanished. However, many had suffered from maladministration and performed their functions poorly. It was, after all, alleged and actual monastic and clergy corruption that was one of the many tinders that sparked the Reforming conflagration.

This hotch-potch of hospitals, almshouses, leper hospitals, religious fraternities, guild foundations and charitable institutions was founded and run locally. But during the sixteenth century there was developing in the Italian states a fine tradition of hospitals which even Martin Luther praised: 'Regal buildings, with the finest food and drink, attentive service, very learned physicians and clean beds' (*The Hospital in History*). Clearly, these must have been 'comfortable' places.

Such a city-state with a large population developed the 'new learning', the Renaissance, that began to regard man not as an ill-gotten son of Adam's sin, forever lower than the Angels and likely to stay there, but as a personable and personal creature. 'What a piece of work is a man!' exclaimed Hamlet, expressing this new self-confidence. Such a creature deserved to be physically investigated and, before the middle of the seventeenth century, Harvey had understood and explained that 'The heart of animals is the foundation of their life, the sovereign of everything within them' and responsible for blood circulation. 'This Book alone declares the blood to course and revolve by a new route, very different from the ancient and beaten pathway trodden for so many ages' (William Harvey, *Circulation of the Blood*, 1628). This was the finest achievement of Renaissance medicine and it laid the foundation for the belief that medical knowledge would be advanced by probing ever more deeply into the body. Doctors and people of like mind needed buildings in which to conduct such serious and adventurous work, so the tradition of fine medical architecture was established.

The five great monastic foundations in London had been taken over by Henry VIII and Edward VI and they had become the five London Royal Hospitals (three of them teaching hospitals) during the seventeenth century, and three of them are (just about) with us still. The eighteenth century then saw the building of several infirmaries around the country in the major towns which broke with much tradition in care of the sick.

The new 'infirmaries' were of a specifically medical nature and not concerned just with housing indigent mendicants as formerly. Also, there was a voluntary aspect whereby people chose to be admitted for care and cure rather than being forcibly confined, either because of fear of contagion or because, in the case of the poorhouse, there was nowhere else for them to go. While it was still the lower classes who were so accommodated (the wealthy being nursed by their servants), the Georgian infirmaries were a significant development architecturally, in medical care and in 'comfort' (see Fig. 1.5).

Hospitals from 1800 to 1948

Over the last two hundred years, these hospitals and infirmaries still served only a minority of the population but had evolved into a fragile network of institutions dedicated to those aspects of health care that are now familiar to us. Hospitals gradually became centres for medical training, clinical laboratories for research and eventually institutions concerned for the welfare of the entire population.

Until 1948 when hospitals were nationalised, the word 'hospital' had very diverse meanings. There were the cottage hospitals (Fig. 1.6) but also the workhouse infirmaries and special

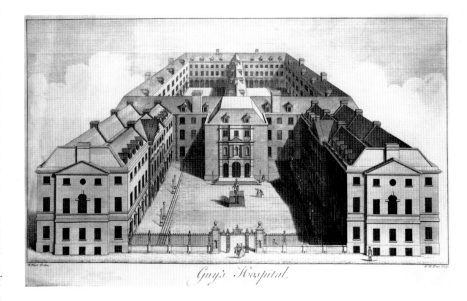

Fig. 1.5 Guy's Hospital, London. Print made between 1722 and 1770.

Prints and illustrations of all periods showing newly completed hospitals tend to illustrate them in a schematised manner. New hospitals, whether built in 1700, 1800 or 1900 or even 1990, are characteristically illustrated sitting pristine in their site, surrounded by trees, countryside, even clouds or in a modernist colour-haze. People of the period on horseback, in crinolines or driving a Morris Minor are passing their new hospital and discussing it, pointing at it and clearly proud of it as an expression of civic pride and architectural modernism meant to house scientific advances for humanitarian benefit. RCHME

Fig. 1.6 Early nineteenth-century cottage hospital, High Wycombe, Buckinghamshire.

This cosy little building was intended for the lucky ones amongst local people to receive such palliative care as was then available. RCHME

Fig. 1.7 Royal Northern Sea Bathing Infirmary, Scarborough.

Sea bathing at Scarborough had been promoted as 'healthful' since 1660 but this Italianate villa was not built until 1860. RCHME

hospitals such as spa and sea-bathing infirmaries (Fig. 1.7). Philanthropist foundations were sometimes set up and run by doctors treating particular complaints and there were hospitals for infectious diseases; there were also convalescent homes, the lunatic asylums after the 1840 act requiring local authorities to 'contain' the insane, and finally the municipal and voluntary hospitals. All these were generally small by later standards and had few technical or clinical requirements to meet.

Throughout this period, hospitals appear to have been designed and built by an association of engineering surveyors and architects, using each other's completed work as models, with strict criteria for economy while nodding briefly at the current architectural style, often incorporated in a glamorous façade. There were exceptions, but this was the pattern. Hospitals generally were surprisingly free from the influence of doctors although the developments of medicine had an inevitable effect on planning. The realisation in the late nineteenth century that many infections are spread by water led to better plumbing and this enabled the old 'sanitary annexe', once separated by a 'ventilation lobby', to be built adjacent to a ward. The introduction of chloroform in the 1840s and the steam-powered carbolic spray in the 1870s led to the increased use and therefore development of the operating theatre (usually on

the north side of a hospital) which remained basically unchanged until the 1950s.

The point of briskly running through this historical development is because many of those aspects of care that engender 'comfort' derive from this history, while other factors may have set the precedent for its neglect. One of these is the mid-nineteenth-century development of ward design.

The pavilion or Nightingale ward was developed from 1858 in response to the Sanitarian movement; it consisted of a long ward with beds on each side between opposing series of windows for cross-ventilation. How comfortable these wards were, and indeed still are, is discussed in Chapters Four and Eight. One of the country's grandest hospitals designed with Italianate flamboyance by Henry Currey (no mere engineering surveyor here) and built on a prime site opposite the Houses of Parliament was St Thomas's (Fig. 1.8). Six blocks of pavilion wards were built at right angles to the river and the long, narrow site prohibited courtyards but offered the opportunity of riverside balconies for 'verandah' treatment (Fig. 1.9).

The lunatic asylum

After the 1840 act which required local authorities to 'contain' the insane, there was a

Fig. 1.8 Queen Victoria opening the new St Thomas's Hospital 1872.

The original St Thomas's Hospital was a thirteenth-century monastic foundation, named after the English progenitor of healing miracles, Thomas Beckett. The foundation was dissolved in the 1540s but Edward VI re-endowed it and retained its name albeit with the subtle, Protestant attribution to St Thomas the Apostle. *Illustrated London News*; London Metropolitan Archives

Fig. 1.9 The opportunity of the St Thomas's Thames-side site was used by the architect and used later for patients requiring 'verandah' treatment, which was common until the 1960s. 1948, London Metropolitan Archives

tremendous burst of building activity and the large 'lunatic asylums' were built on what were then green field sites. Lunatics had had a rough time throughout history; possession by the devil was a condition to be exorcised, demons had to be physically controlled and punitive care was generally the rule. The Quakers and several individual philanthropists established centres of humane care in contrast to this but the number of 'lunatics' seemed to increase in Victorian times.

This was probably due to many factors; the rise in population, the stresses caused by migrations from country to town, the dissolution of family and neighbourhood ties, unregulated capitalism causing social distress, a fear of social unrest caused by malcontents all combined with the Victorians' enthusiasm to identify and categorise things and make appropriate organisations to contain them, whether an asylum or a cabinet of shells.

These asylums lasted nearly a century, but by the 1960s they were falling out of fashion. 'There they stand, isolated, majestic, imperious, brooded over by the gigantic water-tower and chimney combined, rising unmistakable and daunting out of the countryside – the asylums which our forefathers built with such solidity.' These, said Enoch Powell in 1961, were 'the defences we have to storm' and he talked of setting 'the torch to the funeral pyre' of the mental hospitals (Nicholas Timmins, *The Five Giants*, Fontana, 1996). Figures 1.10, 1.11 and 1.12, three shots of one site separated by fifty years, reveal many of these qualities and changes.

Was this justified or did the asylums offer any sort of 'comfort and delight'? The best ones had something of these endearing qualities and several staff reminiscences are of a happy environment, but it was not by any means always so. Patient voices are usually silent, but a patient speaks by proxy in the novel *Comforts of Madness* (1988) by Paul Sayer:

Ah this place, this huge solid place. What mind, what hands designed it? These stone arches and pillars thicker than a man's length, the bolted metal window frames, the great wide doors that slam like bombs, the awesome weight of this place, holding me in its shiny-white proper angles, a tiny thing now, a little piece of meat cradled in a hard shell – who, what philosophy, what science caused such a monstrous construction?'

In Chapter Two we discuss some of the landscape and garden appointments these hospitals enjoyed and which are now envied. The farm and greenhouses offering open-air tasks (Fig. 1.13), the social tasks in the laundry and kitchens, the comfort of a community geared for their disabilities were all very 'comfortable'; the disadvantages were the lack of alternative or cure, the opportunities for mistreatment, poor redress and to be simply forgotten. Young women felt to be in need of 'moral guidance' could be detained for the rest of their lives.

Pre-war voluntary and municipal hospitals

By the 1930s, the voluntary hospitals for physical illnesses had become the better 'class' of hospital and depended for their income on gifts and investments and increasingly on patients' payments, donations and legacies. They ranged in size from the large teaching hospitals to the hundreds of small, local 'cottage' hospitals.

Municipal hospitals were run by local authorities.

Many of them had grown up as appendages to the 1834 workhouses and some were still called 'workhouse infirmary' . . . They were regarded generally as being grossly inferior to the voluntary hospitals, certainly outside the big cities, and real stigma attached to many. They comprised a mix of old Poor Law institutions, the great mental illness 'bins', and the 'fever' and 'TB' hospitals . . . They ranged in quality from the excellent to the awful . . . Access to their beds was means tested, although on one estimate only about 10% of costs were recovered from patients . . . The stigma of the old Poor Law hospitals . . . left many reluctant to resort to them.

(*The Five Giants*)

The King Edward VII Memorial Chest Hospital at Hertford Hill near Warwick must surely have been one of the 'awful' ones. Thankfully it is now closed, but in the 1930s, Jess – the daughter of the posthumously famous George Dillen – was taken there with TB. Her sister Mary visited her and was told at the gate:

'Er'll be at the top in cowsheds.' That's what they called them . . . It *was* a hut, right at the very top and all open. They'd each got a little

Fig. 1.10 Park Prewett Asylum, Basingstoke, Hampshire.
Aerial view 1942

Fig. 1.11 Park Prewett Psychiatric Hospital and Basingstoke District Hospital, Hampshire.
Aerial view of the same site 1994

Fig. 1.12   Parkland Hospital, Lodden Community NHS Trust and the North Hampshire Hospitals' Trust, Hampshire.
Aerial view of the same site. 1998

These three photographs of the same hospital complex, separated by over fifty years, offer much information. The original asylum was built at the beginning of the twentieth century and was a self-contained community for hundreds of patients and staff with its own farm and domestic services, serviced by a small single-track railway, visible here. The grounds were extensive and secluded and the formality of the paths and planting are clearly seen, including the Rooksdown Hospital in the lower right-hand corner (Fig. 1.10).

Thirty years later, Rooksdown Hospital has been demolished (out of the picture) and the large general hospital has been built on the southern edge of the site. The railway has gone, farmland has been absorbed by roads and development of the nearby town (Fig 1.11).

A modern photograph shows the asylum being demolished and land sold, a smaller psychiatric hospital has been built and the emphasis is on the general hospital and its services. One building has also been turned into a hospice.

These three photographs reveal many changes in medical and psychiatric provision, besides land usage. Seclusion and the charm of countryside peace have gone and with it the disadvantages of possible secret ill-treatment and the then hopelessness of mental illness. The modern rapid growth in the successful treatment of many physical conditions and the mobility of people arriving to be treated is revealed by the obvious importance of the general hospital and the large car parks. The current high value of land is apparent; also, the disregard for period architecture of this type and the readiness to demolish rather than adapt and convert fine buildings for modern needs, is revealed in the most recent of these photographs.

wooden hut, 'bout the size of a garden shed. There was no door, no glass in the windows, the wind and the rain blowed through. I looked at Jess . . . She'd got no life. She was skin and bones, she just lay there . . . There was a plate of cold taters on the side, with a number on it, number fourteen, and some gravy. You could see she hadn't touched it . . . And when I left her, I felt I was helping to kill her, going . . . but it was like being *with* death.

(Angela Hewins, *Mary, after the Queen – Memories of a Working Girl*, OUP, 1986)

Some cities had, before the war, commissioned purpose-built hospitals but, in general, the state of the nation's hospitals in 1939 was deplorable, inherited from this historical patchwork of provision.

Fig. 1.13 Greenhouse in the grounds of a psychiatric hospital where patients tend plants. 1997

NATIONAL HEALTH SERVICE HOSPITALS

And when do you get organisation? In a war.

(Bertolt Brecht, *Mother Courage*, 1939)

After the Munich crisis in 1938 and in expectation of the Blitz, a national survey of hospitals was conducted in 1937–8, which showed how deficient hospital services were, not only for the existing population but in expectation of war. The 'Emergency Medical Service' (the 'EMS') was therefore instigated by the Government and, by October 1939, nearly one thousand new operating theatres had been installed in purpose-built hutted annexes and tens of thousands of beds provided (Fig. 1.14).

At first, free medical treatment was for the forces and direct war casualties but it filtered down to firemen, child evacuees and war workers generally. Gradually, a growing section of the population was treated and so enjoyed, in effect, the first truly 'national' health service.

One aspect of this was the free dental treatment given to the Royal Air Force staff. Up in the air, the low air pressure meant that tooth cavities were aggravated and dental treatment was especially necessary. When these men were demobbed, they knew the benefits of free dentistry and wanted them for their families.

So it was that wartime showed that a health service for everyone could indeed be run, and that what was in effect the nationalisation of the hospitals had occurred, and succeeded.

The new NHS and its inherited buildings

When the National Health Service was launched in July 1948, it nationalised nearly four thousand hospitals. These included all those descended from the chequered history we described above, and included also were the great lunatic asylums and the work-houses that had been swallowed up by the municipal hospitals but which, even in the 1990s, retained their 'poor-house' stigma, besides hundreds of the temporary 'pre-fabs' thrown up during the war.

In his book *The Five Giants* Nicholas Timmins describes the planning and implementing of the new NHS. The complex system of health care was taken over by this one authority, the government-created NHS, thereby inheriting a system of gross differentiation of standards, of access, even of aims and medical opportunity. But while systems can be reformed by act of parliament, buildings take years to construct or reorganise.

The post-war NHS building programme

Fourteen new towns were built in the war's aftermath and these included new schools but, even in 1955, no new hospitals; they were sacrificed to acres of housing and many schools.

Instead, existing buildings were adapted and many new extensions built but it remained 'make do and mend' time, prompting the then Minister for Health, Enoch Powell, to say in 1960: 'I am landlord to the biggest slums in the world.'

In 1962 the great 'Hospital Plan' was launched and this intended, over a ten-year plan, to build 90 new hospitals, remodel 134 and provide 356 improvement schemes.

It was a laudable intention but the cost was to be borne by the local authorities and this they were reluctant to do. At the same time, the old lunatic asylums were politically condemned and the 'care in the community' ideal launched. This meant that the old asylums were 'run down' but, until the late 1980s and early 1990s when they were actually sold so that capital money could be released, little funding was available for the new ideal and new scandals of 'comfort's lack' were in the making.

There were some new hospitals built and there was more spent on hospital building between 1961 and 1963 than in the previous thirteen years. But it is a long gestation process for a hospital: depending on size, an average of ten years at least from design commission to completion. So while, amongst others, hospitals at Greenwich and Basingstoke opened in the 1960s, the Nottingham Queen's Medical Centre in the 1970s, the Isle of Wight St Mary's, Hammersmith, Poole and many others during the 1980s and 1990s, they were not part of a large-scale development that covered the country as, for example, the motorway network.

Our current political and financial state

Many of the changes in the nature and the quality of health care are due to political change; the Labour government of 1945 and the Conservatives of the 1980s being two of the most influential.

At the end of the 1990s, the NHS appears financially to be in a continuing time of austerity rather than affluence. It is unlikely that even a government totally committed to the NHS will ever launch a massive countrywide rebuilding programme. There will continue to be a small number of new hospitals and this may be convenient in the light of the expectation that some schemes, like the earlier 'cottage hospitals' which were run by doctors for the working people nearby, may be revived. These were popular because they were community-based and may reappear for some of the same reasons. But, in general, for the massive technological hospitals that we now expect, we shall have to make the most of what we have. There is quality there if we can find the way to utilise it, and that is one of the central themes of this book.

Fig. 1.14 Hydestile Hospital, Essex. Nissan huts erected during the 1940s and used as a 'country' hospital by St Thomas's Hospital until 1968. London Metropolitan Archives

Can the NHS deliver comfort and delight?

From the handling of buildings, whether period masterpieces or 'modern movement' infill, to their interior design and the planning of surrounding roads and gardens, it appears to be acknowledged that most NHS hospitals are a mess.

From the evidence of contemporary journalism, from our experience of working in hospitals and from conversations with many health professionals, there is persistent dissatisfaction with buildings and their surroundings. There are, of course, areas of excellence both in terms of care and decor but they are always reported just as they have been completed, opened, finished and one wonders what they will be like in five or ten years' time.

The reasons why our hospitals lack these 'aesthetic' qualities can be summarised as follows:

- national attitudes; our visual aesthetic is not generally well developed
- poor architectural procedures
- the nature of the health profession
- design expertise not used.

NATIONAL ATTITUDES

The British are not seen as a sophisticated nation in terms of architecture and town-planning during the twentieth century. As regards literature, the filmic and theatre arts it is another matter but generally we do not traditionally give high priority to the quality of our public buildings or townscapes, or to visual matters generally. One reason for this is the manner of our appointment of architects, which other nations handle differently.

POOR ARCHITECTURAL PROCEDURES

French architectural policy

Richard Rogers, one of our most distinguished contemporary British architects, recently described the French approach to modern architecture.

The late President François Mitterand stated that 'culture' and, in particular, 'architecture' was the fourth most important voting issue in France . . . In France, there is a competition for each and every new government building, be it a public housing project, a school, a post office, a local square, a park or an entire new town.

All competitions of any significance are decided by a jury comprised of the mayor, a representative of the users, members of the local community, technical experts and architects. There are small competitions and large ones, all designed to ensure that France is home to the best of international architecture.

Contrast this to the situation in Britain where the taxpayer spends 4 billion on public buildings and yet the government has no architectural policy. In 1992 we held 10 public design competitions compared to France's 2,000.

(Richard Rogers, *Cities for a Small Planet*, Faber & Faber, 1997)

Fig. 1.15 The classical eighteenth-century Addenbrooke's Hospital in Cambridge was remodelled by Matthew Digby Wyatt in 1866 and used as a hospital until 1984. The 'listed' façade prevented its demolition so this was retained and achieved startling renovation by John Outram Associates in association with Fitzroy Robinson Ltd during the early 1990s. The façade uses strong colour to emphasise the shape of the building and the immaculate forecourt is sadly unlike any hospital equivalent, the cars and bicycles being cleverly hidden and the paving slabs used imaginatively in conjunction with the gravel, grass and new trees. This extraordinary building now houses the Judge Institute of Management Studies, University of Cambridge. 1998

These, then, are some of the reasons why our new hospitals are not more successful, but there are others.

THE NATURE OF THE HEALTH PROFESSION

The NHS will end up building the slums of the future unless it gets its act together.
(Stella Yarrow in *Health Service Journal*, October 1992)

There are occasionally exciting new hospitals opened which receive glowing reports because they have paid special attention to visual aspects, art and design and patient delight, or old ones that have been magnificently refurbished. St Mary's on the Isle of Wight belongs in the first category, Old Addenbrookes Hospital in Cambridge to the second but, significantly, this is no longer a hospital and its renovation was not directed by any health authority (Fig. 1.15). But these are the exception, not the rule, and it is the handling of the ordinary site that is our main concern. Why is it not better done?

The recruitment of health professionals

The NHS incorporates many professions but they tend to be from the scientific and technical disciplines. Our education system demands specialisation early in teenage years so the managers and doctors, financial, pharmaceutical, nursing and engineering staff who comprise the NHS may know that some hospitals look and feel more delightful than others, but will probably not be able to assess why or specify how to achieve this.

Managerial responsibilities

Modern healthcare management is not a soft option and this may be another reason why the comparatively simple matters of comfort and delight get overlooked. Hospital management is required to keep buildings and equipment functioning at an acceptable level despite strong budget pressures and frightening levels of backlog maintenance. This, besides the increasing emphasis on health and safety, absorbs the full attention of most managers and their estates department staff.

The estates staff are the ones who keep the buildings and the technical services in operation; however, because usually no other staffing provision is made, they are also often required to select items such as paint colours and furnishings and to specify room layout, garden design and so on, and this sort of task they are generally not qualified to do. Since the disbandment of regional design teams (see Chapter Three) there has been no assistance in this work and this is another reason why the average hospital finds its 'aesthetic' neglected.

Are 'hospital environment' issues forgotten?

The subject is neither forgotten nor neglected: seminars are held about patient comfort, about art in hospitals and presenting a friendly environment, indeed all the factors we call 'delight'. Next, reports are circulated, articles of criticism, of analysis and possible solution appear in the specialist and the general press and books are written. The books tend to be 'booklets' and of a rather transient nature but there are some qualities which characterise all these efforts and we would describe them as follows.

- These papers and booklets imply that they have been written by an 'academic' mind, one which is used to policy appraisal and definition but which, the writing being done, implies that the job is complete. Suggestions are all vested in the far future, in impossibly distant schemes of re-education and reorganisation.
- There are generally no immediate, practical solutions offered; suggestions are esoteric and based in the future, to take place only after yet more appraisals and consultations. Suggestions are not made as to what a hospital manager could do that very afternoon, within existing facilities. Never is it suggested that simple improvements could be implemented immediately.

Changing work patterns

The care and attention which hospital buildings traditionally received were linked to a pattern of working which has changed. In times past, staff stayed in one hospital for much of their career so that the estates, maintenance and cleaning staff were part of an established order and identified with the hospital. Often, many members of one family worked in a hospital, lived in a hospital house and identified closely with it. Hospitals tended to look old-fashioned but well maintained and this was before pressure on costs had eliminated these staff teams and contracted out many of the polishing, cleaning and tidying services.

Directors are nowadays appointed for services, such as physiotherapy, rehabilitation and so on, but often there is no one to run the building itself. It is not unusual to find even three separate trusts running one building. The Griffiths Report, commissioned and written in 1983 under very different political circumstances, offered the central, specific message that remains chillingly relevant: 'If Florence Nightingale were carrying her lamp through the corridors of the NHS today, she would almost certainly be searching for the people in charge.'

Department of Health guidance publications

The Department of Health has, for some years, produced under the 'NHS Estates' label a series of guide publications intended to assist managers in raising environmental standards. Certainly, they started off as a good idea but they became too prescriptive, presenting a limited and strictly utilitarian view of possibilities. We quote here from Health Building Note 51: 'Some spaces contribute to the well-being of patients, for example, a patients' library, but this is not essential to the smooth running of a hospital.'

This series presents technical data well and on such issues as the legal and technical requirements of spacing, safety, public liability, fire precautions and so on they are very good and required reading and reference for anyone working in this field. Yet they purport to represent a high standard of advice and encourage chief executives and chairs of trusts to commission quality buildings without any guidance as to how to do so. For example, it is suggested in these guides that 'art' is a good thing but it is not explained how to acquire it; that 'gardens' are peaceful, but not how to achieve them.

Sometimes there is a suggestion that all is not well and the publication *Demonstrably Different* (HMSO 1991) addresses this by selecting five hospitals that have refurbished some part of their premises and describing the transformation. A selection of advisers were involved in this and one of these cautions estates teams: 'Beware of thinking of projects purely in estates terms. Environment issues need to be addressed as a part

of an overall strategy for a quality service.' This is one of the occasional signs that the impact of buildings is recognised by the NHS profession as important. However, note must have been taken of this, since the environmental primer circulated in 1997 says its aim is:

> To provide a practical means to enable trusts to specify, and architects and designers to design, new healthcare facilities or refurbish schemes for existing facilities, that positively contribute to the promotion and maintenance of human health and well being by means of incorporating the best possible environmental quality.

State-supported, not income-generating

Whether you regard the NHS as a profession or as an industry, it is destined to spend money, never to make it. Like education, its 'income' is not from the sale of goods but the perceived and actual health and welfare of the nation's people. Love and culture, religion, health and education are all as hard to evaluate as they are to deliver but we believe we need them so we go on trying to put a price on the priceless.

PROFESSIONAL DESIGN TEAM

There is seldom any suggestion, let alone encouragement, that hospital management should appoint a design team who can become acquainted with hospital life and oversee the aesthetic aspects of all design decisions. We suggest that the single most effective way to improve the hospital environment is to make appropriate design appointments. Assuming that a good architect is employed on all building work, an 'in house' design team should include:

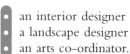

- an interior designer
- a landscape designer
- an arts co-ordinator.

Such a team working together would be able to transform any average hospital in five years and make real improvements in one. The cost of the team will depend on the size of the organisation and the resources. Management's role would be to make sure that good people are appointed and that their first task is to look for quick improvements within their budget and give expert practical advice whenever money is being spent

'It is a sad but inescapable fact that the interiors of most NHS buildings are depressing and dreary. This applies as much to new ones as old. There are numerous reasons for this . . . but the real underlying cause is absence of professional interior design input.'
(John Haddock in *Hospital Equipment and Supplies*, May 1987)

on maintenance, decoration, refurbishing and changes in buildings and land. Because this suggestion is central to our argument, it is dealt with in detail in Chapter Nine, 'Professional appointments: the "design team"'.

Is beauty in the eye of the beholder?

NATIONAL TRUST PROPERTIES

Most people who visit a house or garden owned by the National Trust or some similar venerable institution will say that it is 'beautiful'. What constitutes this opinion?

- *Age.* An old building, tree, landscape is comforting because it shows human life is enduring, that such things can survive the turbulence of time and history and we relate to the people that have been before us and will come after.
- *Appointment.* This is usually of a consistent and high quality in a cherished building or garden; you are unlikely to see plastic door-knobs in a castle or fibre-glass gnomes in an old garden. Consciously and unconsciously we respond to excellence in both large-scale and small detail.
- *Exclusivity invaded.* The property may once have been created for the wealthy, the princely or a particular group (like monks) but us 'plebs' can now march up the grand staircase and picnic on the lawn in the knowledge that each and every one of us represents a many millionth part of our state ownership.
- *The awfulness of times past.* The castle dungeons with the scold's bridle or the grassy lumps and humps of a plague village, now 'enclosed' as part of the estate, can make any who survey them grateful for modern civil rights and public-health procedures.
- *The comfort of time present.* The inviting tea room, the ramps for wheelchairs and the buggy-ride round the grounds should similarly persuade most of us that to be alive today is preferable to the frequently nasty, brutish and short life of yesteryear.

The twelve qualities that we earlier suggested constituted 'the aesthetic' are pretty well all fulfilled by this. The psychological, spiritual, physical and intellectual aesthetic could all be met by, for example, a sunny day at a great cathedral, a tour with an informative guide, then a cheese sandwich and cup of tea in the refectory before a walk around the cloisters and into the watermeadows beyond.

Can hospitals compete?

Most hospitals have the opportunity to fulfil some or all of these qualities, perhaps not to the same extent, but to a considerable degree.

Many hospitals have something of age, if only they would present, preserve and use it; quality appointment can be achieved if management is determined and it depends less on money and more on organisation than is usually supposed. Exclusivity in health care was banished by the very fact of the NHS; the awfulness of times past can be evoked by a display case of last-century surgical instruments and the humane convenience of time present should be apparent to anyone given one of a multitude of modern treatments under a general or local anaesthetic.

Part of the 'beauty' of our hypothetical National Trust property relates to its grounds, gardens and surrounding land and this is the same for hospitals. Very few are surrounded only by tarmac, for even in an inner-city hospital there will be a few struggling self-seeded buddleia trees and the odd tub of geraniums, so in the next chapter we shall consider the landscape aspect of our average hospital.

CHAPTER ONE INFORMATION

The legacy and appearance of hospital buildings

Any well-established hospital estates department will have quantities of information about the necessary technical elements of maintaining buildings and making them operable, but there will probably be less about their historic and aesthetic aspects. Most of this brief and selective section refers to those relevant organisations, libraries and archives that deal with these issues and which have been of help during the writing of this chapter, but there are many other agencies which could be found, as and when required, from these key contacts.

Quotations in the text are accompanied by their reference, and the bibliography at the end of this section includes further books that we have used but from which we have not quoted directly. We also include those magazines to which we have consistently referred or which might generally be helpful, and finally we include (as in all 'Chapter information' sections) details of copyright owners of illustrations and photographers.

RELEVANT ORGANISATIONS

English Heritage
23 Saville Row
London W1X 1AB
(0171 973 3000)
This is the government's official adviser on all matters pertaining to conservation of the historical built environment. It is the major source of public funding for research, rescue archaeology, conservation and repairs.

King's Fund
11–13 Cavendish Square
London W1M OAN
(0171 307 2423)
This is an independent charity (founded by Edward VII) that offers a wide range of expertise and services in health matters and social care. It works to raise standards and promote good practice in medicine from working with doctors and associated staff to providing grants for health-related initiatives in London. It is also an independent publisher carrying over 150 titles on health care and associated matters. Its publications are available in the bookshop at the same address.

NHS Estates
Department of Health
1 Trevelyan Square
Boar Lane
Leeds LS1 6AE
(0113 254 7000)
The NHS Estates is an Executive Agency of the Department of Health and is involved with all aspects of health estate management, development and maintenance. It publishes booklets and guides to which we refer towards the end of Chapter One under 'Department of Health guidance publications'. It also provides software programmes on selected subjects and runs a Consultancy Service. A full list of its publications, products and services is available from the address above.

Royal Institute of British Architects
66 Portland Place
London W1N 4D1
(0171 580 5533)
Information line for members, 0891 234444; for non-members, 0891 234400.
The RIBA is an independent body for architectural study and research, housing historical archives, and for the encouragement of architecture. It also has an excellent bookshop for new publications and magazines.

The Georgian Group (1700–1837)
6 Fitzroy Square
London W1P 6DX
(0171 387 1720)

The Victorian Society (1837–1915)
1 Priory Gardens
London W4 1TT
(0181 994 1019)

The Twentieth Century Society
70 Cowcross Street
London EC1M 6BP
(0171 250 3857)

The Wellcome Institute
183 Euston Road
London NW1 2BE
(0171 611 8888)

The Wellcome Institute for the History of Medicine forms part of the Wellcome Trust, the bio-medical research charity. It provides library and archive resources, research and teaching facilities for all those interested in the history of medicine and allied subjects. The Wellcome Library is a major study and archive centre: medicine forms the central core, along with the allied sciences, particularly botany and chemistry. There are other important and wealthy archives including oriental material and the iconographic collections besides unique historical and modern material.

SURVEYS AND ARCHIVES

MARU Health Buildings Research and Policy
    Centre
Faculty of the Built Environment
South Bank University
Wandsworth Road
London SW8 2JZ
(0171 815 8395)
(0171 815 8338)

MARU is an integrated research and post-graduate teaching unit with a special interest in the planning, management and design of health buildings. Established over thirty years ago, MARU has undertaken commissioned research and consultancy, contributed to formal health service guidance, developed databases for buildings, compiled literature and professional contacts internationally, drawn together students from over fifty countries and has over seventy publications currently available. The MARU Resource Centre is a unique and specialist collection of books and papers on all matters relating to the built environment of hospitals.

Royal Commission for Historical Monuments in England (RCHME Hospital Survey)

The changes in the health service during the 1980s and 1990s have led to a great many hospital buildings of merit being made redundant or being subjected to adaptation, at the same time as fresh regard for period and twentieth-century architecture has developed.

The Royal Commission for Historical Monuments in England therefore instigated and commissioned a survey in 1994 whereby every hospital building in England from about 1660 to the foundation of the NHS in 1948 has been recorded. Three thousand such buildings were located; half of these have been visited and recorded and the result is now published in *English Hospitals 1660–1948: A Survey of Their Architecture and Design*, ed. Harriet Richardson, HMSO 1998.

The full documentation of photographs and other data from this survey is available to the public at the National Monuments Record Centre in two locations.

For all buildings in Greater London, material is at:

National Monument Records Centre
55 Blandford Street
London W1H 3AF
(0171 208 8200)

All material on buildings elsewhere and including all aerial photography and archaeological data is at:

National Monument Records Centre
Great Western Village
Kemble Drive
Swindon
Wiltshire SN2 2GZ
(01793 414600)

GENERAL BIBLIOGRAPHY

The Architect and the Pavilion Hospital: Dialogue and Design Creativity in England 1850–1914, Jeremy Taylor, Cassell, 1998.

Book of Twentieth Century Design, Catherine McDermott, Design museum, 1997.

'Delight in the Public Domain: Design Quality in Public Areas of Health Buildings', Christopher Richards, MA dissertation, session 1994–5, unpublished paper in the MARU Library, South Bank University (see above).

Environmental Design Quality in Health Care, a discussion paper by Peter Scher, Visiting Research Fellow for Arts for Health, 1992. Published by Arts for Health, Manchester Polytechnic, All Saints, Manchester M15 6BY.

The Greatest Benefit to Mankind: A Medical History of Humanity From Antiquity to the Present Day, Roy Porter, HarperCollins, 1998.

Hospital and Asylum Architecture 1840–1914, Jeremy Taylor, Mansell, 1992.

'Hospital City', Jonathan Hughes, *Architectural History; the Journal of the Society of Architectural Historians of Great Britain*, vol. 40, 1997.

Hospital Interior Architecture, J. Malkin, Chapman & Hall, 1992.

A Social History of Madness: Stories of the Insane, Roy Porter, Weidenfeld & Nicholson, 1987.

RELEVANT MAGAZINES

Medical and hospital matters

A reliable guide to UK magazines is given in the annual publication Writers' and Artists' Yearbook.

British Medical Journal
published by the British Medical Association
Tavistock Square
London WC1H 9JR
(0171 387 4499)

The Health Service Journal and *Nursing Times*
Porters South
4 Crinan Street
London N1 9XW
(0171 843 3600)

Hospital Development and *Hospital Equipment and Supplies*
Wilmington Publishers Ltd
Wilmington House
Church Hill
Wilmington
Dartford
Kent DA2 7EF
(01322 277788)

Nursing Standard
Nursing Standard House
17–19 Peterborough Road
Harrow
Middlesex HA1 2AX
(0181 423 1066)

Architectural and building matters

The Architect's Journal and *Architectural Review*
151 Rosebery Avenue
London EC1R 4QX
(0181 956 3140)

Art and Architecture; Journal of the Art and Architecture Society and Public Art Forum
This is the quarterly journal of the Art and Architecture Society which was founded by Theo Crosby in the 1980s to encourage artists and architects to work together on building projects.

Art and Architecture Society
77 Cowercross Street
London EC1M 6B
(0171 373 0667)

Building Design
A weekly newspaper for architects.
City Reach
5 Greenwich View Place
Millharbour
London E14 9NN
(0171 861 6467)

RIBA Journal
Published monthly by the Royal Institute for British Architects
(see above).

TEXT AND ILLUSTRATIONS

Crown copyright material quoted in this chapter is reproduced with permission of the Controller of Her Majesty's Stationery Office.
Figs. 1.1 and 1.13: Photographs and © SH
Fig. 1.3: Photograph and © Sino Rista
Fig. 1.4: 'Healing Arts' Isle of Wight HA ©
Figs. 1.5, 1.8, 1.9 Guy's and St Thomas's Hospital Trust ©

Figs. 1.10 and 1.11 Crown copyright/MOD, reproduced with permission of HMSO
Fig. 1.12: Photograph and © John Miller 'Chair to Air'
Fig. 1.15: Photograph and © Bruce Robertson

Landscape, gardens and the space between the buildings

CHAPTER

2

Anyone who has needed to visit one of the older London hospitals will realise the chaotic situation which now exists within these sites. The heart of the hospital is normally occupied by the Victorian institutional building, around and among which have been deposited an array of later building additions. The site has been developed on a purely 'ad hoc' basis with a total lack of long term policy. The end result is a series of unplanned residual external spaces, through which is threaded the circulation system. Every foot of available space is adopted as a parking area, often as overspill to the designated parking areas, which are woefully inadequate.

(Chris Churchman, Chairman of HLM Landscapes, *Landscape Design, Journal of the Landscape Institute*, no. 189, April 1990)

These comments could be made about hospitals all over the country. How this situation arose and what can reasonably be done about it is what we discuss next.

Traditional hospital landscape

HOW IT HAS EVOLVED

Landscape is what you can see from one vantage point, whether stationary or moving along, and implies both size and scale. It may not have mountains, waterfalls and canyons but it ought to have some element of maturity and a horizon to qualify; otherwise, it is a mere 'outlook'. In our hospital context of 'landscape', there will nearly always be urban features but when the buildings dominate the scene visually, then it becomes the 'space between the buildings'. Gardens are a defined area which has received at some time systematic and intensive planting for the purposes of pleasure and delight.

The nature and extent of a hospital's land will depend on its past history and current situation, as do its buildings, and similarly the quality and

imagination of its care will depend upon the management in charge.

'Funny Farm'

The Victorian lunatic asylums were what the locals called 'Funny Farm' and a farm they usually were besides being a gentleman's estate with its complement of tennis courts, bowling greens, shrubberies, lakes and 'fine prospects'. This is why some of those splendid buildings set in mature parkland outside the towns are now a developer's dream with the estate agents hard on their heels; they aim to make an exclusive residential area out of the despised asylum where once the demented, the 'silly', the deformed and the simply unlucky fed the hens and grew their vegetables (Fig. 2.1).

These traditional hospital gardens and estates were often planted with imagination and skill. In a survey done of one psychiatric hospital's grounds, the variety of trees and shrubs, the walks and tennis courts, and all the paraphernalia were superb even as recently as 1990. Nowadays, the traditional means to maintain these grounds in the same manner is simply not available, but during the remainder of this chapter we shall be suggesting that this heritage of land can be handled well but in different ways. But it requires management to demonstrate skills necessary to manage the land with vision and discipline.

Fig. 2.1 Woman patient tending chicks. Leicester Mental Asylum, 1942, RCHME

The modern 'hotch-potch' of land

During the twentieth century, some of these large hospital parks were used as the site for a new hospital, as at Basingstoke, and it is now that 'end' of the park that is retained while the old asylum and its land are sold off (we refer again to Figures 1.10, 1.11 and 1.12). So, some hospital sites have contracted and others expanded while most of them have grown up in the hotch-potch way we described earlier.

Old hospitals will probably have retained at least some of their historic land and probably also the domiciled town will have spread around on every side to make it deeply urban so that this land becomes a 'green lung' in the conurbation. Look at any town map and odd-shaped spaces are usually scattered around that capitalised HOSPITAL. Like churches and the remains of stately homes, these green spaces can be of community significance and even ecological interest if they have been treated carefully or, better still, preserved as undeveloped green spaces. So, how do hospitals generally handle their land?

HOW DOES YOUR GARDEN GROW?

Small pleasures must correct great tragedies,
　　Therefore of gardens in the midst of war
I boldly tell.

(Vita Sackville-West, *The Garden*,
Michael Joseph, 1946)

While Mrs Sackville-West was talking of national war, the 'great tragedy' of severe personal illness equally deserves to be soothed by 'small pleasures', such as gardens. They can therefore be highly important in any hospital's life.

Our gardening heritage

England has a famous historic and current tradition of garden design and gardening which is probably attributable to the climate, the rapid changes of soil and landscape within this small country, the Protestant work ethic, literary and pantheistic romanticism, plant-gathering opportunities arising from imperialist adventure, social and agrarian circumstances and the peculiarity of national genius. The result is that we have thousands of lovely gardens that set a precedent of 'the aesthetic'. We also experience much contemporary environmental concern about land-use generally.

The tradition of small, public gardens

Our England is a garden, and such gardens are
　　not made
By singing – 'Oh how beautiful!' and sitting in the
　　shade.
While better men than we go out and start their
　　working lives
At grubbing weeds from gravel-paths with broken
　　dinner knives.

(Rudyard Kipling, 'The Glory of the Garden')

Many public institutions have a tradition of formal gardens: railway stations used to have 'a good display', town halls sported 'flower clocks' each summer and hospitals used to welcome all comers with banks of carefully tiered geraniums and an almost heraldic concern with formal, coloured shapes of flower-planting within a border boundary. All around there would have been raked gravel, the tubs and urns sitting like exclamation marks in the expanse, beyond which was probably the clipped hedge. Everything suggested the labour of many gardeners, at first for the glory of the gentry, then the pleasure of the public and perhaps eventually the hospital management committee.

Such traditional gardens take many hours of greenhouse and site work and this expenditure is not the sort that many modern institutions, including hospitals, can now expect to make. However, the average public expectation of a garden is generally stuck in this time warp whereby fine gardens imply labour and, to an extent, this expectation is true. Nowadays, many of the experienced, traditional gardeners have gone, retired and taken their dibbers and twine with them. Their replacement is probably contract labour that gives a basic service of mowing and chopping, strimming and spraying. This is bad for many plants, not good for wildlife and death to 'the aesthetic'. We believe there are viable, modern alternatives but first we need to look more specifically at the average hospital and its land.

Environmental issues

Land has become a precious commodity. Urban sprawl and our road network have grossly reduced its acreage, while intensive farming and the toll of herbicides and pesticides have diminished much of its quality.

Open land in towns and cities has always been valued by urban inhabitants, which is why squares, parks and gardens, playing fields and cemeteries are so precious; nowadays, some new areas such as community gardens and green-lines (created simply by leaving old railway lines alone) are developing. There is an accelerating demand for allotments and city-farms, and organic farmers and environmentalists urge a restricted use of herbicides and pesticides, strimming and chopping. These voices should be heeded and the handling of hospital land has a part to play in this.

CURRENT NHS LAND USAGE

There are four main reasons why so many modern hospitals do not use their land better:

1. land care is often the responsibility of estates staff for whom it is a less urgent priority than the maintenance of buildings and technical resources.
2. the old traditions of formal gardens and estate management have been largely lost, and have not been replaced with any new forms of garden creation and land management.
3. money is genuinely constrained.
4. low value is placed on the aesthetic benefits for patients and staff of quality land usage.

Inappropriate staff in charge

The handling of hospital land was, and still is, traditionally the responsibility of the estates department. However, although estates staff are often highly technically educated,

> With a few notable exceptions, most estate officers lack any awareness or knowledge of what landscape is. They are trained to maintain buildings and machinery, and to undertake cost benefit analysis of readily quantifiable factors, not to deal with the seasonal sea-saw of landscape management and maintenance.
> (Mary Brookes, 'Pressures on the hospital landscape', *Landscape Design, Journal of the Landscape Institute*, April 1990)

In their drive to manage their inadequate money, estates departments will wish to specify one type of light-fitting throughout the premises so that only one replacement fitting need be kept (see 'Lighting'), paint all walls magnolia so that only one paint need be kept (see 'Colour') and, regarding landscape, they will wish to specify that all land is grass and mown frequently; similarly, all paths are asphalt and regular herbicide spraying puts paid to anything else, creepers on buildings are banned because they deteriorate the fabric and clog the gutters and trees are tolerated only well away from buildings; all work is to be done by the lowest-charging contract workers who work mainly with machines.

Of course there are exceptions and this is painting the very worst scenario, and estates staff must be given their due regarding the technical aspect of their work which they usually do well; but they are not trained to deal with aesthetic matters. This is one reason why so many hospitals and their land look profoundly uninteresting.

There have been sincere efforts made regarding the quality handling of hospital gardens. In 1952 the King's Fund decided to appoint and pay for a team of garden advisers who would be available to help hospitals in London and the home counties on the design and layout of their gardens and grounds. Data from this scheme, which lasted for eleven years, is available from the London Metropolitan Archives but, unfortunately, no visual records are included amongst them.

Lack of specialist staff

Hospital managements believe that the main problem regarding land is the cost of labour, that well-handled land is necessarily expensive. Is this a realistic fear or could they use existing short resources better? We believe so.

Below we describe the appointment by the railway authorities of a vegetation management consultant. Dramatic changes were made to the management of railside land by appointing a single extra staff member with specialist knowledge.

We make this point many times in this book regarding specialist appointments, whether an 'in-house' architect, an interior designer, an arts co-ordinator, a landscape and vegetation management consultant and/or landscape designer. Salary money has to be initially allocated but the gains are great. Appointments can be funded from outside sources as we describe in the final chapter of this book.

The extensive hospital estate has largely gone and been sold off for development. What is left is the land between the buildings which may still be generous but will be made up of many patches between and around buildings. Difficult situations like this require capable staff experienced in

Fig. 2.2 This herb garden was planned and planted during the late 1980s in an area almost enclosed by buildings, attached to Park Prewett psychiatric hospital at Basingstoke. The top right photograph shows it before planting, but with the building complete, including the raised borders of different heights and using half bull-nosed bricks edging them. The other three show it mature, with wall planters commissioned from Steve Dixon (bottom left) and a 'celebratory' seat by Guy Martin (bottom right). Costs were met entirely by fundraising. Now demolished.

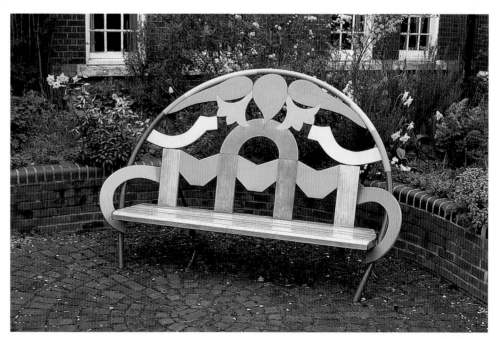

botany and design to offer solutions other than basic paving or mown grass (Fig. 2.2).

Anyone going around most hospitals will probably see that the desire for a formal border is still strong. However, these geometric borders depend upon being beautifully planted and then vigilantly maintained and it is this second stage that is nowadays neglected. The result is that you see a geometric border that is no longer smart, perhaps sited in a shabby lawn and with a 'Walls Ice Cream' sign plonked in it. This is again a sign that imaginative staff have not been appointed to find a 'new' way.

Since most hospital land including these borders fails to delight, would it not be better to use the equivalent time and money in a different way? This chapter will examine how this may be done.

Aesthetic benefits of landscape – the 'Urlich' study

There is about as little hard evidence for the therapeutic benefits of landscape and growth as there is for the effect of colour on mood or animals on well-being. It does appear that, once cultural, genetic, age and gender factors are discounted, there is not much factual evidence of the beneficial effect of any of these, but there is some, certainly enough to encourage those who love colour, animals, landscape and gardens to urge their incorporation into our surroundings.

However, a famous American study by Roger Urlich is constantly quoted. Two groups of postoperative patients were given either a bedroom with a bleak outlook onto a brick wall or a room from which 'a small stand of deciduous trees could be seen'. The twenty-three patients in each group were then assessed according to the length of hospitalisation, mood, attitude and use of pain killers.

The group that could see the trees were discharged earlier, were happier and had need of fewer drugs than the 'control' group. This was sufficiently clear for it to be assumed that an outlook has an effect upon a patient's well-being, as one would expect, but perhaps the experiment could be conducted again with more variants. The 'negative' view was very negative indeed and one wonders if the view of, for example, a children's playground or even a busy street might have a similarly good effect; was it the trees or the factor of interest that was significant? Either way, it is more clear than it was before that a dismal outlook slows recovery.

'English Nature' survey of reactions to landscape

Anyone seriously involved with society and the natural landscape should read this excellent unpublished paper (see 'Chapter information'). It is long, scientific and detailed and we shall merely cite some of its findings. Some of the experiments included were conducted by Roger Urlich, whose study quoted above is only one of many.

It does appear that, in general, exposure to nature can have a significantly beneficial effect on people's emotional state (Fig. 2.3). It also appears that children favour natural scenes but the preference fades during development, although this may be due to the modification of all emotional responses during growth. Women have a slightly higher appreciation of plant life, and men of space and scale in a landscape; water seems to be an advantageous feature, while there are some apparent differences of preference due to culture and background.

A surprising finding was that natural spaces in urban areas were not heavily used, even by those for whom they had been identified as a 'pleasure'. It may be that just the sight of an open habitat or wildlife site is a comfort, or even passing it and knowing it is there. The survey reinforces the importance for a hospital to use its land for the pleasure, and recovery, of even those who see it only through the ward windows.

New situations prompt new policies

LAND DESIGN AND LAYOUT

The current situation

A large hospital may have up to one thousand patient beds, and the necessary road system for this and all the support services besides the several thousand outpatients, staff and visitors has to be efficient and functional. This need not preclude visual quality but sadly often does.

We would refer the reader to the quotation we included at the start of this chapter regarding the disarray of London hospital sites, but the observation could apply anywhere. Look at hospitals in any group of major towns and the verity of this situation is clear; as more patients are treated, so more demands are made on land and so the muddle deepens, worsened by the need to contract out the landscape work so it is done at speed and usually without care or knowledge.

Fig. 2.3 'Earl's Court House, Old Brompton, near London. Mrs Bradbury's establishment for the reception of ladies nervously affected . . . sectional view showing the ladies at their calisthenic exercises.' Lithograph by G.E. Madeley; early nineteenth century. Wellcome Institute Library, London

Car parks

There is a constantly expanding need for car parking space and this is a problem for the Western world, not just for the local hospital. Where car numbers can be foreseen, as for staff in an organisation that has few visitors, car parking spaces can be designed, planted, screened with trellises and climbers and some of the new town development corporations in the 1970 and 1980s set a good standard for this.

But the constant onslaught of cars on a hospital site appears to preclude such planning, or does it? Until public transport becomes transformed from what we have at present, most people will arrive by car and that car must be accommodated. There are precedents and a good landscape designer will introduce a suitable version. The way cars are handled at big edge-of-town stores or shopping developments is a good example, using numbered bays divided by trees and clearly signposted. Payment for parking is unpopular but often pays directly for security in carpark surveillance and is found to be generally successful.

In a hospital site, security generally is an important issue and this should affect the handling of car parks regarding lighting, surveillance, planting and so on.

Feasible solutions

There are solutions to cars and the handling of land generally, but they cannot be achieved without expertise. Employing an experienced and imaginative landscape architect who could be involved at the planning stage of any building or site work to ensure developments relate well to buildings and human activity is essential but sadly seldom done. Hospital land has the potential for:

- 'soft landscapes': areas of lawns, meadows, water, trees, shrubs, hedges and other plants
- 'hard landscapes': of tarmac and asphalt, paving and gravel, walls, curbs, steps
- landscape furniture: seats amd shelters, bollards, signs and notices, lamp-posts,

trellises, railings, fences, arches, gates, bunkers, waste bins fixed and temporary
- landscape buildings: pergolas, pavilions, summer houses, sheds, bandstands, aviaries
- landscape embellishment and use: sculptures, fountains, sundials, 'swings and roundabouts'.

SOFT LANDSCAPE

British Rail Hampshire Lineside Vegetation Project

In 1990 British Rail collaborated with other bodies to appoint its first Vegetation Management Consultant in the southern region. The lineside vegetation had been unattended since the 1950s and thousands of trees had grown to possibly dangerous proportions. There was also concern that the chemicals sprayed onto the vegetation between the tracks was filtering into drinking water. It was also realised that an amenity for passengers was being neglected because rough growth, such as nettles and brambles, on the neglected railway embankments was displacing gentler native growth such as wildflowers, heathers and seedling oaks, maple, hawthorn and dog roses.

Under the sensitive and informed management of an experienced botanist, proper tree care was introduced so that trees were managed on a seasonal basis rather than an 'emergency' basis by felling only when they became an imminent danger. The new regime introduced coppicing, selective felling and pruning besides the transplanting of seedlings encouraging a better mix of tree and shrub growth. Greenhouses were set up to propagate wild flowers from gathered seeds and saplings were able to mature under shelter before being planted out. Spraying was continued between the tracks with herbicides approved by the Nature Conservancy Council and the flailing limited to within five metres of the rail track to allow varied growth to take place higher on the bank.

While the work may have started out as being mainly safety based, it became a significant amenity and conservation effort. No more staff were required than the original 'spray and fell' gangs except for the chief appointment; the greenhouses were manned by those on Employment Training. This type of appointment is being repeated elsewhere in the country on railside land and it could stand as a model for hospitals in the handling of their land.

Use of local, indigenous plants

This scheme shows that the use of existing plants can, if managed as a partnership with their indigenous vigour, clothe the land delightfully. During the blitz, bombed sites were in summer ablaze with fox-gloves and willowherb, buddleia and elder. It seemed strange that beautiful plants should grow in such dangerous places, but they flourished because they were self-sown, undisturbed and free from herbicides, while the soil was newly turned so it didn't matter that its quality was poor and that it was full of debris.

All parts of the country have certain plants which flourish vigorously because they like the soil and conditions. If they are left alone, as were these, they form dense natural ground cover. To find out what they are, look at any unsprayed roadside (if you can find one) or at some area that has been undisturbed. In Cornwall, *Allium triquetrum* grows in abundance; in Northamptonshire it is soft comfrey; and in Hampshire, the lesser celandine. There are many others.

These vigorous, local plants could be used to offer free ground cover for some of those bleak hospital grounds. Select what is native to the ground, weed out everything else, cease spraying and mowing and, eventually, sheets, drifts, even displays of native blossom will cover the worn corners of grass lawns, conceal the litter and offer 'delight'. All such a scheme requires is the patient application of a professional botanist and one or two years' establishment and maintenance; then it runs itself and this scheme can be multiplied for as many species that grow easily in the soil.

'Rationing' formal planting

We are not advocating that a hospital has no colourful, formal planting but the means of adequate maintenance is not usually available these days; garden formality has to be manicured. But since such borders have such a strong tradition, perhaps one good one outside the main entrance could be justified and it can serve as a splendid 'identifier' of place if it is impeccably maintained.

Alternative use of colour planting

That love of organised colour, besides the available budget, could be 'channelled' instead into hanging baskets. In spring, dozens of such baskets could be prepared, fully planted, padded with moss and be ready for a summer's display and then hung outside every window and door where patients have sight of them.

They would require regular watering and care and this is best done at night (when flowers react best to watering). In many cities there are firms who provide maintenance and watering services.

This may represent a major budget allocation but to try such a colourful and attractive scheme, run it professionally so that it is a success, and combine it with a new, natural vegetation approach to the land may make a significant difference to the site's appearance and health.

Grass and mowing

'A child said, What is the grass? . . .
    I guess it is the handkerchief of the Lord
A scented gift and remembrancer designedly dropped,
Bearing the owner's name someway in the corners'
(Walt Whitman, 'Song of Myself', Penguin 60s Classics)

Grass is usually the one commodity hospitals maintain but areas of lawn can be handled in a more aesthetically interesting way than simply overall short mowing.

In one large hospital with extensive lawns and many mature trees, a designer 'drew' with the lawn mower on the first cutting of spring several large abstract 'shapes' around the trees and elsewhere. Thereafter, some of the grass near the buildings was mown short every week as usual, but those other delineated areas were mown only twice a year and others still were never cut at all but narrow 'paths' only mown through them. The result was a visual, botanical contrast between the mown parts, the longer, flowered patches and the 'wild' areas; this took a couple of years to establish and staff had to be encouraged to accept what they saw as 'untidiness'. But it was apparent that patients, children and even staff in their lunch hours all gravitated to the longest grass, driven, apparently, by some anthropological desire to 'hide' or, as a psychiatrist sagely observed from an upstairs window, 'the aspect of escape'.

Trees, shrubs, hedges, creepers

These are usually inherited from thoughtful gardeners who planted them decades ago and, as such, they are often taken for granted. Great trees and large shrubs might be the remains of the asylum parks, hedges may mark the edges of land ownership or have been planted simply for their 'aesthetic', and creepers were a Victorian taste which modern building maintenance now prefer to remove.

To neglect their replacement is to imperil our reputation with future generations; these established plants, especially trees, need a steady regeneration to maintain the population. The great storms of 1987 and 1990, which felled millions of trees besides the ravages of Dutch Elm disease, may have awoken us to the need for energetic planting.

'The crying need is for miniature nature reserves of a completely unpretentious and un-publicised sort. They only need rabbit fences and immunity from tipping; nature will do the work' (Gerald Wilkinson, *Epitaph for the Elm*, Arrow Books, 1978). Although written twenty years ago, that cry still echoes and where better than on hospital land? This also goes for shrubs and hedges and there could reasonably be a reconsideration of the proximity of trees to buildings and creepers climbing on them. Is the caution that guides these matters perhaps too concerned with possible inconvenience and too little concerned with 'the aesthetic'?

Safety aspect

Hospital land does present the usual possibility of attack and assault on the many people who use it. Psychiatric hospitals experience their fair share of attack both by and on patients, and hospitals generally attract voyeurs, the unstable and those with a grudge. Dense shrubberies of a height to offer concealment may be felt to present an avoidable hazard so lower growth and trees above the head are alternatives, besides the usual precautions of lit pathways and camera surveillance. Shrubberies also tend to attract and accumulate rubbish underneath that trunked trees do not and the provision of rubbish bins (that are emptied) is another feature of environmental care.

The inexpediency of a water feature and a camomile lawn

There are four features for which hospital designers are always being asked: curtain poles (see 'Chapter three/four/five information', 'Pelmets and rails'), a fireplace (see 'Fireplaces' in Chapter Five), a camomile lawn and a water feature. They all have connotations of elegance and all are inappropriate for hospitals, but let us first consider that camomile lawn.

> 'Common chamomile is not common at all; in fact it is a rather rare plant . . . but its most conspicuous characteristic is its sweet apple scent, for which it was once much valued and even planted on lawns instead of grass.'
>
> (Richard Mabey, *Food for Free*, HarperCollins, 1972)

The work in establishing a camomile lawn is considerable; you weed, plant and encourage for a year and even then it all too easily resembles only green alopecia; it is moreover far too delicate for many people ever to walk upon, so plant some similar mayweed in a rockery instead.

'Water features' are always being requested but we firmly advise never to install a pond, fountain or anything to do with water for two reasons: one is that they are never, ever maintained (well, hardy ever!) and the other is that they arouse frantic fears of 'danger' amongst nurses. 'You can drown in an inch of water', we are lugubriously warned, again and again. There is a case of a pond carefully sited by a well-known architect in front of a new hospital being filled in during one weekend on the orders of nursing staff. Perhaps they had simply seen too many drowned victims in the Accident and Emergency Department (see 'Balance of Safety', 'Chapters three/four/five information').

This poor capacity to actually accept and care for water features is a great pity because water does prompt soothing reactions almost universally. There are good instances, award winning water gardens and so on but visualise them in ten years' time after yet more reorganisation to the NHS and consider what their condition might be like them.

HARD LANDSCAPE

The course of paths

We described earlier the need for a road system that works and has visual quality, but the best way to designate paths for walking is to let people's feet describe their course. If people are determined to take a short-cut, that is where the path will appear, and for the estates department vainly to place 'no parking' traffic cones on that path merely makes everyone step around them. Then the worn earth has a bulge in it like a snake that has swallowed a goat.

When people have voted with their feet, it is better to accept these determined footpaths and upgrade and pave them in some way. Stepping-stone slabs in the mown grass are a neglected variant and white flowers planted along the path edges give night guidance. Native, self-perpetuating or (once) cheap, flowers like snowdrops, alliums, alyssum, ramsons and so on traditionally lined the path to the outdoor privy to guide you in the dark and the same principle could be used to guide people to the car park, in spite of or in addition to lights.

Hard-surfacing qualities

Asphalt and concrete are unavoidable but they do not have to present unbroken sweeps; there is a great deal of landscape design expertise on the planning of minor road systems and car parking; the NHS has only to consult wisely and in time.

We limit ourselves here to looking at paving possibilities where people walk and sit and the message is that variation is not expensive.

Suppose you wish to create a courtyard for the elderly; you will think in terms of paving to allow wheelchairs, zimmer frames, unsteady walking and an easy passage, and it is usual to have one type of reconstituted stone slab, probably light in tone and laid absolutely everywhere, as many slabs as possible controlling as much earth as possible. On a sunny day, the unrelieved slabbing will reflect light and heat directly up into old eyes; on a dim day, there will be no variation in its appearance.

There is no reason why two or three colours of the same composite slab cannot be used, for variety. Gaps for low flowers do not impede wheelchairs if well placed, nor do small areas of gravel, which is cheapest to lay, and intersections in the ground of cobbles and brick make all the difference.

Also, to take paving right up to a wall loses opportunity for planting climbers and softening the engineering harshness of the building materials. Many courtyards have no relief in the form of large trees to interrupt visually the straight, hard engineering line of the surrounding roofs, but the planting of large trees, even up to twenty feet high, while a specialist job, is not difficult or even

Fig. 2.4 An internal paved courtyard, lacking both design interest and planting quality. 1997

Fig. 2.5 A similar internal courtyard for which a fundraising scheme allowed a professional garden designer to develop and plant. The problem of maintenance was met in this case by one of the hospital chaplains who had, before ordination, been a professional gardener. He quietly maintained this for years, giving it the care that the usual 'mow and spray' treatment would have denied. Chapel Courtyard, Basingstoke District Hospital. 1988

prohibitively expensive and it makes a dramatic difference (Figs 2.4 and 2.5)

Walls, curbs and steps

Walls to sit on, curbs and steps to step off should have two features, softness and variety. The use of half-nosed bull bricks is a much softer 'edge' than an ordinary square brick. If you have raised borders with walls for people to sit on, vary them from six inches high to two feet high. Any physiotherapist will advise that variety is what humanity needs.

LANDSCAPE BUILDINGS/ FURNITURE/EMBELLISHMENT

The well-dressed landscape

A classically well-dressed person will have achieved that state by careful planning; even if they have not bought their whole outfit at the same time, there will be a thoughtful co-ordination about it from the whole image down to the details of handkerchief and shoes.

An alternative is gipsy variety where assorted items are thrown together and given a sort of unity by the glamorous if eccentric style of their combination. If we transfer this metaphor of

classical and gipsy dressing to the appointment of landscape, we shall understand the alternatives.

A classically 'well-dressed landscape', such as the London Thames Embankment, has installed all its furnishings to present a unified scheme; it is the 'white tie' outfit of the landscape world. Hospital landscapes have usually grown up in the hotch-potch way we have described earlier so unity of style is unlikely. The best thing to do is accept the varied and various existing items and combine them in a powerful design scheme, your 'gipsy' solution. This should involve a fresh approach to planting and paving (as above) and painting but, above all, organising. These are a few suggestions of what can be done.

Organising and painting

Temporary rubbish skips are difficult to hide but they can be placed sensitively. Semi-permanent wheeled bins can be parked behind trellis screens, in the way caravans are hidden in a garden, and the screens stained green and covered with creepers. Several Russian vines and multiple other creepers can make a huge difference to a hospital site.

There are likely to be different designs of railings, bollards, seats, lampposts in a typically muddled site and some unity can be achieved by painting them in relating colours but in different ways to emphasise their design, whatever it may be; the traditional items can be painted traditionally, the modern ones in a hi-tech way and the trashy ones in a gaudy manner.

Colour washes on disparate buildings can unify them, doors can be painted to a scheme and nothing softens unsympathetic architecture like creepers. The linings of window curtains can be used as a colour opportunity since they are what outsiders see. In a 'Modern Movement' block (see Chapter One) all the outside-facing curtain colours can be handled like a huge abstract painting of coloured squares; it takes dedicated organisation but this could transform a bleak building.

Pavilions, sheds and huts are often interesting and reflect the hospital's history. One hospital had rough wood shelters built by Canadian servicemen in the 1940s and they all looked like log cabins; the history of such items can be highlighted and the fabric maintained. Seats are often 'donated' by well-wishers and there is a development whereby seats are 'heated' by solar panels. Other 'furniture' all has its place but everything needs maintaining in a heavily used site.

These are but some of the schemes that an experienced landscape designer, perhaps with an architect and a botanist, could contribute to a muddled site without any radical and expensive rebuilding.

Community and specialist use of land

We have emphasised that a typical hospital's land could be and often is a precious resource within a town. Psychiatric hospitals have been working to take patients out into the community, but the community can also be encouraged to come into the psychiatric or any other hospital site and use its land. This has to an extent happened for decades as large hospitals have traditionally had good games courts that have been rented out besides farming land, but nowadays wildlife trusts are also likely to set up schemes for nature preservation and land use (Fig. 2.6).

It can be reasonably feared that thicker and less obviously manicured vegetation may increase vandalism and likelihood of attack on the vulnerable. However, these things are controlled

Fig. 2.6 A children's rough-wood slide in a nature conservation area of hospital land. 1997

when there are a lot of people around; it is the desolate car park with a few unsupervised cars that spells trouble, but a well-used open track, for dog walkers, horse riders, cyclists, and other land uses, brings in people and they can be regarded as unpaid supervision.

But people are still in mourning, it seems, for the gentrified park. 'It used to be so lovely', they say, 'with all the herbaceous borders, and the summer fêtes with the Mayoress in white gloves, Matron in a white cap and the Administrator in a white Panama.' In the face of this nostalgia for the 'upstairs, downstairs' world, ecological and community values represent a very different, though valuable, philosophy.

WE ADMIT OUR OMISSIONS

Below we discuss several sorts of land use but we admit that the list is not complete; we do not discuss, specifically, landscape or garden provision for wheelchairs, for the mentally or physically disabled, for dementia sufferers, for those with head injuries, for the blind, for the orthopaedic patient, or for babies and young children; nor

Fig. 2.7 Male patients working on their allotments. Leicester Mental Asylum, 1942. Long-term psychiatric patients traditionally worked on the land and, during the 1940s, this was necessary to produce food. The scheme was generally discontinued because of fears of exploitation. RCHME

do we mention playing fields because they are not likely to have serious design implications – of course they are important but they are purely useful. In our 'Preface' we list the full range of subjects omitted from this book and briefly explain why, which is, in this case, as follows.

There are two reasons for these particular exclusions: one is that, when attention is given to these particular issues, the quality of 'the overall aesthetic' is somehow often left out; there can be created 'islands of excellence' in a drab setting when better planning might have achieved universal improvement. Therefore, our discussion tries to highlight overall site issues rather than too many specifics. Also, we are trying to offer some land use suggestions that are perhaps not usually associated with hospitals, but which we believe may contribute 'comfort' and 'delight' and not be too difficult to achieve.

ALLOTMENTS

Allotments and small-holdings with pigeon sheds and chicken runs imply the labouring classes

whose forebears were firmly excluded by the eighteenth- and nineteenth-century gentry who enclosed the land for their own aesthetic landscape enjoyment. Since hospital parks emulated this gentrification, of course there is nostalgia for elegance and resistance to renewed use of land for, perhaps, allotments (Fig. 2.7).

Nowadays self-sufficiency and land value are ideas that cut across class.

With the spread of ideas implying that we ourselves, rather than the medical services, are responsible for our own health, the allotment has increasingly become associated with healthy living.

(David Crouch and Colin Ward,
The Allotment: Its Landscape and Culture,
Five Leaves Publications, 1997)

Allotments are becoming popular with young people and many local authorities have waiting lists for available plots; hospital land could accommodate this requirement. (See 'Author's Anecdote', Chapter Eight.)

ORCHARDS

What can your eye desire to see, your ears to hear, your mouth to take, your nose to smell, that is not to be had in an orchard with abundance of variety?

(William Lawson, *A New Orchard and Garden*, 1618, quoted in *Orchards, a Guide to Local Conservation*, Common Ground, 1989)

Orchards need consist not only of fruit trees but also fruit bushes and climbers, canes and 'pleached' trees on walls. These require some care but the objections also raised are that 'people might eat the fruit', which seems an odd objection since that is what fruit is for, and that fruit attracts wasps and these are, of course, 'very dangerous'.

It was a wasp that in a glass of wine
Once killed a Pope.

(Vita Sackville-West, *The Garden*, Michael Joseph, 1946)

Orchards take some years to establish. You can get everyone's agreement, prepare planting plans, raise the money from suitable sources so you are not accused of wasting hospital resources, ascertain the type and condition of the soil, finalise tree choices, liaise with suppliers, hire a van and collect saplings, plant what look like muddy sticks and then wait twenty years. Within that time, the hospital may be closed and demolished.

Fig. 2.8 Courtyard view of the New Hospital and grounds at Bedworth, Warwickshire, showing the planting of a large tree to create 'instant' garden maturity. This is an option nowadays much easier to achieve with modern digging and lifting equipment. Lithograph by G. Hawkins the younger, 1839. The Wellcome Institute Library, London

It is advisable to plant an orchard only where the hospital and therefore the site are stable and where development is so unlikely as to be impossible. Even legal protection for it may be advisable, and this can be achieved if you plant an orchard adjacent to something that is listed and so protected by law; a barn, a listed tree and so on can extend that protection, somehow, to the new orchard.

The houses of the Bournville estate built for the factory workers in the early 1900s each have a garden in which was planted a fruit tree; alternating between four houses there was an apple, pear, plum and cherry tree so the house owners could interchange the fruit. This was done simply because it was believed to be desirable (trust the Quakers) and has largely endured.

The planting of fairly large trees, fruit or otherwise, is a reasonable option and it gives an immediate sense of maturity (see 'Chapter information' for commercial suppliers). The several garden festivals held during the 1980s planted thousands of such trees (not all survived) to achieve a mature parkland look, and there is a long history of semi-mature trees being transplanted (Fig. 2.8).

HERB AND HEALING GARDENS

These are attractive for a hospital but their success depends on professional planning and planting besides appropriate and sensitive maintenance. The suggestions we made in 'Hard-surfacing qualities' and 'Walls, curbs and steps' above are especially relevant, also the stability of the site mentioned in 'Orchards'.

A herb or healing garden has its origin in the 'gardens of physick' of which the Chelsea Physic Garden is the most famous. Our definition of a 'herb' is any plant that has an actual (in the sense of proven) or legendary quality beneficial to mankind. Also, some are simply interesting in historical and literary terms; witness the mandrake root, woad, the elder tree, the mistletoe and so on and on. There are fine studies of the inter-relation of plants and human society, most especially *The Englishman's Flora* by Geoffrey Grison (Paladin, 1975) and, more recently, Richard Mabey's magnificent study *Flora Britannica* (Sinclair Stevenson, 1997).

The extent to which we have relied, and may again need to rely, upon lowly plants of an edible, herbal or otherwise useful nature is spelt out in

'In a sense, the planting of fruit trees is a pledge of faith in the future, and even, perhaps especially, when the future is uncertain, it is important to make this gesture.'
(Francesca Greenoak, *Forgotten Fruit – the English Orchard and Fruit Garden*, André Deutsch, 1983)

the Introduction to the same author's youthful best-seller *Food for Free* (HarperCollins, 1972):

> Before the war something like 90 per cent of all the herbs that were used in the commercial drug industry were imported to this country. By 1940 almost the whole . . . of this trade was cut off . . . So, the Ministry of Health set up a structure of voluntary pickers under the County Herb Committees . . . During the five years of the war over 750 tons of dried herbs (something like 4,000 tons of fresh) were gathered. The Committees were also responsible for gathering rose-hips, nettles for camouflage dyes and, perhaps most importantly, the gelatine-yielding seaweeds . . . Without the large quantities of agar jelly derived from these seaweeds, the development of penicillin might have been seriously delayed.

If ever there was an advocacy for respect and care to be accorded to plants, this must surely be it.

WILDLIFE GARDENS

This is more of an element than a specific place. Its features are to encourage self-seeding, non-cultivated plants and so attract insects, birds and wild mammals. Large areas are needed, not tiny courtyards, as it is no use encouraging insects in one small patch when they are blitzed by pesticides throughout the surrounding acres. There will also need to be agreement that estates or contract staff will not suddenly mow all the seeding flower heads and remove them to a rubbish tip a mile away on the orders of someone who thinks anything wildlife is 'untidy'; of course it is, that is why we call it 'wild', otherwise we would have a tame garden and there are already plenty of those.

Wild animals

Do not assemble a pile of logs and leaf mould for insects, nor encourage hedgehogs by laying trails of cat food across the site (never physically relocate a hedgehog, for they simply waddle home again as soon as night falls). The logs will be removed by estates staff and you will be reprimanded regarding the cat food because both encourage rats, and rats do indeed represent a health hazard in that their urine causes Weill's Disease; not even David Attenborough allegedly

likes rats. Bags of rubbish piled high outside entrances are a more likely culprit but your 'wildlife' log pile will be banned as the cause of all vermin.

Bats, like 'water features', are best avoided. However, they are a strictly protected species, so if you have them and want to get rid of them you have to consult the county bat adviser, who will probably suggest leaving a loud radio on continuously because bats hate noise and will depart of their own volition. If you want to attract them, you can put up specified 'bat-boxes' but it is likely to be a waste of effort. Bats are rum creatures, difficult to attract, and they depend on insects, which in turn, depend on the state of the land, not your wildlife intentions.

If water is introduced as a pond or lake, ducks will inevitably arrive (see Chapter Four, 'Waiting rooms') and they are impossible to deter short of 'netting' the whole water area. A patient created a small garden in a long-term secure psychiatric hospital that included a pond, and ducks were the immediate, and popular, result (Fig. 2.9).

One large hospital site has the headquarters of the county wildlife trust on its premises, renting a house, and they are now handling half the site and have introduced interesting features such as a 'stone circle' of all the county's geological stone samples. This is the degree of political commitment and land allocation that is necessary to make any sense of a 'wildlife' policy. Otherwise, introduce a wildlife element into the allotments, the herb garden, the cemetery and the site generally.

Poisonous plants

Hospitals will have experienced pharmacists available and the extent to which you will need their advice on what you wish to plant will depend upon the degree of safety demanded. Management will have to decide this (see 'Children's play grounds' below) because the safety of plants, like water, dogs, plastic bags, rocking horses etc. is all a matter of degree.

'All parts of all poppies are dangerous' says a nurse, conditioned to fear the worst. 'Rubbish, even opium poppies don't make opium in our climate' says the local forensic botanist, until one hot summer a bed of opium poppy heads suddenly became very popular with patients in the nearby detoxification unit and the opinion had to be reviewed.

Fig. 2.9 Patients in this special hospital often serve long sentences and have time and opportunity, besides encouragement, to create a personal garden; the ducks introduced themselves. 1994

The best course of action is as follows: check on autumn berries, avoid the obviously poisonous plants such as monkshood (*Aconitum angelicum* and the similar *Aconitum napellus*) but do not worry about those of which you would have to eat a lot like foxgloves (*Digitalis*) or those it is impossible to eradicate, like common ivy.

However, in a special unit or hospital, where deliberate poisoning and suicide are likely, the extent to which forensic botany has to be taken into account is extreme: even apple-pips can be gathered for poison and cherry stones used for suicide. But these are exceptional circumstances for which exceptional advice needs to be taken.

CEMETERIES

These are a sad necessity of hospitals. Most people are usually removed by relatives to be buried in the place of their associations, but premature babies and young children often have a small cemetery to themselves, often tucked away and hard to find. But, once there, the evidence of grieving care is clear; flowers and toys are stacked around and the childish graves often resemble a cot or little bed with a counterpane of flowers (Fig. 2.10)

Cemeteries for adults are usually attached to long-term, in point of fact 'permanent', hospitals; the 'special hospitals' (Broadmoor, Ashworth and Rampton) have discreet and anonymous graveyards where, quietly, the hope of redemption is finally allowed to outpace societies' vindication. Here, one carved angel presides over a what looks like a rough field but is the cemetery (Fig. 2.11).

The imagery of flowers is close to the heart of Christian liturgy. The burial service contains the idea that the life of a man or woman 'cometh up and is cut down like a flower'. Inherent in this is the idea of resurrection. The dead will rise again as the wild flowers on the grave reappear in springtime. Perhaps this is why flowers are so important in graveyard ritual, and why so many of us feel that the churchyard is a place for grasses and flowers.

(Francesca Greenoak, *Wildlife in the Churchyard: The Plants and Animals of God's Acre*, Little Brown & Co., 1993)

Fig. 2.10 Cemeteries are a sadly necessary use of hospital land. This cemetery for premature babies and handicapped children is attached to a southern hospital. 1988

Fig. 2.11 In contrast to the highly personalised, tiny crib-like graves of young children (Fig. 2.10), the cemetery at a special hospital for the mentally disordered offender has no memorial headstones to commemorate who is buried there (although a record is kept elsewhere). Only this stone angel indicates the nature of the place. 1998

PROVISION FOR CHILDREN

There is plenty of material available regarding playing-fields for adolescents and adults, and playgrounds for children. The problem always arises whether such facilities should be available to the community generally or just the hospitalised and the staff. This will depend upon space and expediency.

The successful creation of children's playgrounds is always dogged by the 'balance of risk' factor. Plans for a play area can be prepared, the paediatric consultants, nurses and play therapists all invited to contribute, their suggestions incorporated, the money raised, the playground built and then no one is allowed to play in it because of the 'safety' factor. This scenario really does occur (Figs 2.12, 2.13 and 2.14).

These 'safety' objections arise for several reasons. One is change of staff: the new staff may have different anxieties from the previous ones. Another is the level of perceived danger. For example, a child eats grass, is sick, so grass is poisonous and 'astro-turf' is the alternative but that gives rise to 'skid-burns' when children run on it so perhaps rubber tiles would be best, or would they? Sometimes objections arise simply because of annoyance at one area being treated well and having money spent on it rather than another.

A wasted investment

The introduction of any new feature should be accompanied by careful management assessment of risks and benefits, care and maintenance and so on but also staffing and staff attitudes. A facility that remains unused because of staff resentment which management is unwilling or unable to resolve – whether it is a 'relaxation' room for expectant mothers, a garden for the elderly or a playground for children (and all of these situations have occurred) – is a wasted investment and a continuing reminder of failure.

ACCOMMODATION FOR ANIMALS

The problem with animals is that they defecate in a disorganised manner. Owners of dogs are prepared to 'clean up' if there are plenty of bins available and if everyone is seen to be doing it; few dog owners will clear up if the place is covered in dog mess but they will if their dog's contribution is the only embarrassing example in sight. A polite request, the threat of a fine and refuse bins solve the problem.

Horses passing through are a problem and a benefit; the problem is again defecation, and in a psychiatric hospital wandering patients may eat what they shouldn't. The benefit is that horses are beautiful and they bring an exciting element of outside life into the hospital. People, especially patients and most of all elderly patients who may have been brought up with horses, love to watch them; look at the viewing numbers for the 'Horse of the Year' show.

Corralled animals like donkeys, goats, sheep, chickens and geese need daily care but cheap grazing in a situation where there are lots of people around is attractive to those who seek to establish the city-farm life. The key is organisation, the disadvantages are less than is commonly imagined and the benefits incalculable.

Fig. 2.12 Children's Play Courtyard; Noah's Ark by George Carter 1988
   The scheme won a Wapping Arts Trust 'Art and Work Award' in November 1989

Fig. 2.13 'In the Garden of Eden, Adam Names the Animals'; mural by Sarah Hosking, 1988

Fig. 2.14 Notice on the access door.

A Children's Play Courtyard was planned in a large internal courtyard of a southern hospital. A fundraising scheme achieved nearly £40,000 to build it and, in discussion with the paediatric staff, a Noah's Ark was commissioned and built as a climbing frame for children. The whole courtyard was paved in rubber tiles for safety and the surrounding windows made shatterproof so games could be played. An Elephant Fountain by Sioban Coppinger was also installed.

   Once completed, nursing staff decided the ark was dangerous, although they had approved all working drawings and scale models. The chief executive who had commissioned it left, the courtyard remained closed and the fountain never operated.

'SECRET GARDENS'

This is an emotional desire, as much as a secret location. Like 'Never-never Land' it is not mapped, nor will it be found on any 'Hospital Site Plan' but any one of the land uses described above can become or contain a secret garden. Frances Hodgson Burnett's 1909 masterpiece *The Secret Garden* is a mythology about an embittered family who bring a neglected garden to life and discover happiness themselves in the process.

Hospices are good at herbal, wildlife and secret gardens because they value their intrinsic qualities. Privacy is the essence, a place where anyone can go to sulk, to grieve or smoke, to feed a baby, to shout or cry, to masturbate or drink gin, or to knit, eat chocolate and muse away from the hurly burly of hospital life. One feature of hospital life and illness is that you are observed, assessed and measured in intrusive ways; briefly to run away and sit underneath a lilac tree, concealed behind the waving mallow and on a pavement of old bricks and thyme should be an opportunity available in any hospital that cares for its people.

CHAPTER TWO INFORMATION

Landscape, gardens and the space between the buildings

This list of organisations and a few suppliers, sites and brief bibliography may seem to be an unrelated and an unlikely assembly. However, in our experience, it is the lack of co-operative sympathy between the horticulturalists, those who represent special patient needs, the design professions and those who bring a more naturalistic awareness that leads to poor garden and land development.

RELEVANT ORGANISATIONS

Centre for the Accessible Environment
Nutmeg House
60 Gainsford Street
London SE1 2NY
(0171 357 8182)

This is an information and training resource for the construction and design industry. It was founded in 1969 and is committed to assist in the provision of environments which cater for all users, including the disabled (whether by accident, handicap or any other misfortune) and the elderly. There are firms that specialise in 'safe' children's playgrounds and items such as 'bouncy' castles, and this is where information will most likely be available.

It provides a helpful centre for all possible aspects of impaired living but also includes consideration of aesthetic aspects. Their magazine *Access by Design* is available three times a year by subscription and should be a priority for anyone in this field. They also have an excellent publications list.

Centre for Alternative Technology,
Machynlleth
Powys
Mid Wales SY20 9AZ
(01654 702400)

This is a working community which has been promoting and displaying sustainable technologies for twenty years. It runs courses and offers practical ideas and information on environmentally sound technologies, such as gardening. Mail order catalogue and a good shop are available.

Common Ground
Seven Dials Warehouse
44 Earlham Street
London WC2H 9LA
(0171 379 3109)

Common Ground is a small charity, formed in 1983. They offer ideas, information and inspiration to help people learn about, enjoy and take more responsibility for their locality.

For exhibitions for hire, day events, seasonal projects and publications, write to the above address.

In the spectrum of environmental organisations, Common Ground pioneers imaginative work on nature, culture and place. In encouraging community involvement in local conservation, they link people, landscape, wildlife, buildings, history and customs as well as bridge philosophy and practice, environment and the arts.

They should be the first port of call on any quality land development, for something like a herb garden, orchard, public walk.

English Nature
Head Office
Northminster House
Peterborough PE1 1UA
(01733 455000)

English Nature advises the British government on nature conservancy matters in England (other agencies advise for Scotland and Wales). They also have established and manage the National Nature Reserves and encourage the creation of local nature reserves; they are responsible for the Sites of Special

Scientific Interest; they give grants and support and initiate research.

It was in collaboration with Reading University Department of Horticulture and Landscape and in association with the Research Institute for Care of the Elderly that the report to which we have referred was produced (*Human Well-being, Natural Landscapes and Wildlife in Urban Areas* – see Bibliography).

The English Sports Council
16 Upper Woburn Place
London WC1H OQP
(0171 273 1500)

Apart from their obvious involvement in playing-fields and other facilities, they can give help and even funding for play areas, including for disabled children. A local representative of the Sports Council will have good knowledge of playing surfaces and equipment.

Horticultural Therapy
The Geoffrey Udall Building
Trunkwell Park
Beech Hill
Reading RG7 2AT
(0118 988 5688)

Since 1978 HT has worked to promote and support the use of gardening to improve the quality of life for people with all kinds of need. HT has worked in hospitals, residential homes, centres for adults with learning disabilities, hospices and other care settings and also provides information for individual gardeners.

HT's information is based on this accumulated knowledge and on the work carried out at its five demonstration gardens, used by over 5,000 people every year. Some support comes from government sources, but the majority of funds are raised from donations.

The Landscape Institute
6–7 Barnard Mews
London SW11 1QU
(0171 738 9166)

Their magazine is *Landscape Design: Journal of the Landscape Institute*, from which we have quoted in the preceding Chapter. It is available from:

Landscape Design Trust
13a West Street
Reigate
Sussex RH2 9BL
(01737 223294)

Royal Horticultural Society (RHS)
RHS Gardens
Wisley
Woking
Surrey GU23 6QB
(01483 224234)

The RHS has a helpful information service for the general public on practical matters, such as contacts for local and national specialist nurseries for large trees and shrubs, or herb or fruit tree suppliers and so on. Members are able to receive more detailed advice.

The Tree Council
St Catherine's Place
London SW1E 6DY
(0171 828 9928)

This is an 'umbrella' charity for other organisations that deal with tree replacement, identification and preservation. It is associated with two major campaigns a year for the promotion of trees, it promotes a 'tree warden' scheme and produces a magazine twice a year. The Tree Council, with the environment department of the local authority, would be the first places to approach when any hospital seeks to provide care for its trees and increase them.

COMMERCIAL SUPPLIERS

Pantiles Nurseries Ltd
Almners Road
Lyne
Chertsey
Surrey KT16 OBJ
(01932 872195/873313)

This plant and garden centre specialises in semi-mature and unusual trees and a wide range of large plants, purpose-grown for transplanting. They also supply a planting service and advice for care.

We give this one nursery as an example but there are other such suppliers whose whereabouts can be found from the RHS. If you want to make a garden of 'instant maturity', to plant large creepers, roses and trees is one way to do it, and the price, while higher than for normal stock, is not prohibitive.

The several garden festivals held throughout the 1980s and early 1990s depended on the massive planting of huge trees and, properly treated, they survive.

SITES AND PLACES

Chelsea Physic Garden
(founded 1673)
66 Royal Hospital Road
London SW3 4HS
(0171 352 5646)

There are other specialist physic gardens but this is the best known. The annual yellow guide to houses and gardens open to the public, or local tourist board material, gives relevant information about others.

GENERAL BIBLIOGRAPHY

The Furnished Landscape: Applied Art in Public Places, ed. Jane Heath, Bellew Publishing – Arts Council and Crafts Council, 1992.

Hampshire Lineside Vegetation Project Report 1991; an unpublished report, commissioned and sponsored by British Rail Community Unit, Hampshire County Council (Planning Department), Countryside Commission, Nature Conservancy Council.

How to Make a Wildlife Garden, Chris Baines, Elm Tree Books 1984. This book has an especially good list of addresses and contacts.

Human Well-being, Natural Landscapes and Wildlife in Urban Areas: A Review, C.L.E Rohde and A.D. Kendal, English Nature 1994 (available from Telelink, PO Box 100, Fareham, Hants PO14 2SX – 01329 668600).

The Oxford Companion to Gardens, Geoffrey and Susan Jellicoe, OUP, 1986.

Risk and Safety in Play, 'Playlink' UK, Spon (imprint of the Taylor & Francis Group) 1997.

Spon's Landscape Handbook, ed. Derek Lovejoy Partnership, Spon (imprint of the Taylor & Francis Group), 1997.

ILLUSTRATIONS

Figs 2.2, 2.4, 2.6, 2.9, 2.10 and 2.11: Photographs and © SH

Figs 2.5, 2.12 and 2.13: Photographs Mike Englefield, SH ©

Fig. 2.14: Photograph and © LH

Principles of interior renovation
The role of the interior designer

CHAPTER

3

The chief requirement of a hospital is that it should do its patients no harm.

(Florence Nightingale, *Notes on Nursing*, 1859)

INTRODUCTION

Hospitals are peculiar places in which, for most people, many of life's most important physical events take place. Apart from conception, the major happenings of birth and death and the extreme events of diagnosis, illness, recovery or deterioration often take place within these complicated and strange buildings.

Having looked at how hospitals, throughout the last four hundred years, have been gradually assembled, and having considered the land and gardens that may or may not surround them, we now prepare to travel through our typical hospital visiting all its components in turn.

But before we examine the separate components closely, the part that can be played by a sympathetic and experienced designer should be considered. How would such a person set about making a typical hospital as delightful and comfortable as possible? We have already suggested the importance of the role played by architects and specialists for land and plant usage, so what does an interior designer contribute?

Inappropriate elements

Designing for a public place is not the same as designing for a private home. The fire and safety factors that govern public places are one issue; also, it is not one person, or even family, but a complex client who has to be satisfied. Healthcare premises have requirements even more stringent than those that cover, for example, shops and offices, and a hospital designer has to be aware of these.

A psychiatric hospital makes particular demands upon a designer; reflections in mirrors should generally be avoided, or certainly unexpected

reflections, although mirrors in expected places such as the bedroom are acceptable. Qualities of glitter and dazzle, of odd and unusual angles in walls, doors and placement of furniture, as well as any arrangements of lighting and furnishings that introduce qualities of mystery and shadow can all seem threatening to those who are in a state of mental distress. Theatrical qualities which are a perfectly permissible part of an exciting visual vocabulary are not really usable in these hospital circumstances.

Feng Shui

Pronounced 'phong sway' the words mean wind and water. The term refers to a set of principles laid down 3,000 years ago by Taoist thinkers who maintained that there is a relationship between humans and their environment that can affect people's health, wealth and happiness. It is an understanding and appreciation of this subtle relationship that constitutes its philosophy and way of life.

Feng Shui is becoming highly popular and there are several books on its use in the home; some superstores are even employing experts to advise on store arrangements and layout according to its principles. Some of its precepts are pure common sense, like not having a mirror opposite an entrance door or having sharp pointy objects over a bed, and generally it seems largely to depend upon sensible human sensitivity. We are not suggesting that a busy hospital should take account of this philosophy any more than of the influence of 'ley lines' but it stands as a reminder that interiors matter and their neglect does no one any good.

Basic principles

Renovation of any part of a hospital's premises varies from a 'lick and a promise' by repainting someone's office to major structural alterations and extensions. In either case, an experienced designer will be guided by eight basic principles:

1. The period, date and condition of the building
2. The client's requirements; clients are those who commission the upgrading and they may or may not own the building
3. The requirements of patients and staff; the client may be relying on the designer to ascertain and take into account staff and patient views
4. Elements which are to be retained and incorporated into the scheme, i.e. the flooring, lighting, furnishings may be kept.
5. Some period items may need to be kept, such as fireplaces and bannisters
6. The available budget and whether there are opportunities to supplement it from other sources
7. The planned life of the scheme
8. The budget available for maintenance (often omitted, but very important).

THE DESIGNER'S ROLE

Former regional design teams

There is some precedent for interior designers in the NHS. Before the reforms of the 1980s, the country was divided into regional health authorities and each presided over several district health authorities. Each region was able to offer specialised services and one of these was an architecture and interior design team that was available as a free service to the hospitals, departments and services within the region.

These design teams were small, specialised groups and the different regional teams were in contact with each other so that experience and information were easily disseminated; collectively, they were active participants in the adjudication of tenders for national NHS contracts for furniture, flooring, fabrics and so on.

They operated from studios and offices at each regional headquarters but visited clients in the districts and supplied designs for buildings, landscaping and interiors as requested. These teams are now discontinued which is a pity because, while service varied, the best of them were very good and the NHS has lost a source of knowledge, expertise and continuity.

Major upgrading – 'one of a team'

A designer would be one of a large team for a major upgrading which would typically include an architect, a structural engineer, a quantity surveyor, a building contractor and specialists for lighting, heating, security and alarms as required; if it is an outdoor site, there will be land surveyors, landscape architects and plant specialists too. These may or may not be health service employees but one of them would be the project manager who keeps the balance between all these professions and liaises directly with the client.

This project manager may be the head of the architectural practice or, increasingly in the case of major work, from a specialist firm of project managers. If the building is owned by someone other than the client, if it has a complex management structure, if it or parts of it are listed, if there are special security needs, all these will be sorted out by the project manager.

Within such teams, designers will have the key role in highlighting awareness of patient and staff delight. To do this, they will rely upon knowledge of relevant, published information and work elsewhere as well as regular contact with everyone concerned, from the ward manager to the cleaners. For all the importance of the fundamental work done by the rest of the team – for example, solving the concavity of the floors, the convexity of the ceilings, the spillage of the drains, the imminent explosion of the boiler – the work of the designer in dealing with those myriad details which contribute to the look of the place is what will be most noticeable to all users (Fig. 3.1).

Minor upgrading – 'sole involvement'

In contrast, a small clinic or office may require improvements that can be supplied without any structural alterations but just by redecoration and rearrangement of furniture and equipment. Whatever the scale of the project, the most demanding aspect will be staff consultation.

Staff consultation

The requirement for any interior designer to talk to relevant staff is both necessary and obvious. However, there can be many difficulties.

Staff reactions

Staff will probably either have little idea of what they want or else very strong ideas that may not be practical. Sometimes they want colour combinations that are currently fashionable but which would soon 'date'. Further reactions are likely to be:

- They may not see 'their premises' as a part of a whole scheme whereby one department, corridor, room leads to another and for which the designer's careful plan is to make a varied unity of 'different but linked' schemes.
- They may ask for schemes that are very specific to their personal tastes and then leave shortly after, with their successor demanding alterations (see Chapter Five, 'Personal offices').
- They are unlikely to link visually the interior premises with whatever may be outside the window.
- They often find it difficult to visualise what the designer's sheets of wallpaper, fabric and paint samples will actually look like 'in situ'.

It is the job of designers to listen carefully and uncover the meaning of the messages they hear. Staff may ask for a jungle mural in the Chiropody Clinic when the underlying message is that they are bored with the room and want something done about its smell and size.

It is the job of the designer to present options from which staff can choose, not to impose a single solution. Alternative schemes should therefore be presented, with a full explanation of the thinking behind each alternative, so that the degree of professional design experience, commitment and understanding of staff wishes is apparent.

Staff working on a rota basis are never there together; an experienced designer will know how to arrange several meetings with different groups and use a range of ways to involve everyone, so that all members of staff feel they have contributed to the end result.

Resultant problems

Because there is often little tradition of interior design being professionally led in hospitals, there is often resentment at 'outsiders' imposing their taste. This is especially so for staff who feel they have little control anyway and one of the few perks has been to choose curtains and colours.

If this becomes someone else's prerogative, there can be resentment.

Designers are often stereotyped and viewed as, frankly, frivolous. Modern art has a bad public image, with cows sawn in half and suchlike, and a designer is first cousin to all that nonsense. Most people who work in the health service come from an education with a scientific base rather than an arts base. The theatre sister who was an art school 'drop-out' and understands the values under discussion does occur but such breaks are rare. Many staff will be keenly aware of a number of areas where more money is urgently needed and these financial constraints can mean resentment at expenditure on 'frills'.

Designers can find themselves trying to seek approval for a scheme seen as unnecessary by many staff, and those whose involvement is necessary may not readily make themselves available for consultation. If there is also little support for good design from senior management, the results are unlikely to be successful, and design issues can become a scapegoat for other problems which staff feel powerless to solve.

Solution

You can always tell how important an issue is to an organisation by looking at the management level, wage and office of the member of staff responsible for it. An issue which is important beyond the 'lip-service' level will be managed by a member of staff who has status and 'clout' to introduce equal opportunities sincerely, disabled access effectively, or design excellence consistently. Without this status and the accompanying 'clout', little is achieved if the aim is to make a major change in culture, attitudes and behaviour.

If, therefore, the first designer appointed is expected to report to someone low in the organisational hierarchy, the implication will be that the organisation is not seriously committed to change; the result will be a frustrating and ineffective working life for that new appointee.

A design appointment should be of an experienced, well-trained and well-paid person who reports to someone of seniority. We discuss this matter fully in Chapter Nine.

WHAT CAN STILL GO WRONG?

Four errors are most usually made in the upgrading of hospital premises:

Fig. 3.1 Maudsley Hospital, Denmark Hill, London. Women's day-room and ward, interior designer, Paul Gell. 1967
   Paul Gell was a well-known interior designer active from the 1950s to the 1970s. He was design consultant for the Maudsley Hospital during the 1960s and refurbished the wards which had not been redecorated for several decades.

- designer ignorance of the client
- the necessity of constant maintenance is neglected
- refurbished areas are isolated and become islands of excellence in a sea of shabbiness
- cultural elements, such as art and decoration, windows and views, are ignored.

Designer ignorance of the client

Health services are complex. An inexperienced designer can simply have little understanding of what staff need and how patients react, and of hospital life in general. For example, they may well not realise the need for notice-boards and not supply them adequately, or be unaware how and where damage occurs. This is inexperience and is all too apparent in even some of the most carefully appointed interiors. Careful listening to staff, observation of hospital life, study of the published literature and a wide knowledge of good and bad design in other health service premises are essential attributes in a hospital designer. Experience of successful design of hotels

or offices is not necessarily a qualification for success in designing for health service buildings. It is for these reasons we advocate a designer to be a permanent staff member and not an outside consultant brought in for specific projects before moving on. Aquaintance with hospital life and familiarity with staff are essential.

In many areas of hospital service, sections of the workforce are now not employees but members of firms that have been contracted to provide the meals, do the laundry, care for the grounds or redecorate hospital premises. Whatever the advantages or disadvantages of this way of running services, it makes the task of consulting staff more complex and it makes it harder to achieve shared commitment.

Maintenance: necessity and neglect

A beautifully appointed interior can be completed, everyone is delighted and the staff and patients move in. From that day, deterioration starts. Design and implementation are only part of the challenge; the real challenge is to manage the

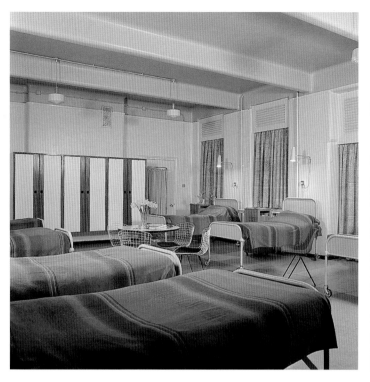

These photographs show the then contemporary use of colour, light-fittings and fabrics and the 'wire' chair designed by Harry Bertoia (1950–2). Privacy in each bed area was gradually being introduced but separate rooms and furnishing individuality for long-stay patients was not then an option. They are typical of pictures taken once the refurbishment is complete but before the ward inhabitants have returned.

system so that maintenance and repair are carried out, effectively and as they are needed. Our experience is that this is one of the 'challenges' the NHS most often fails and much good design initiative is wasted in this way.

If there is a good system for small repairs to be done easily every month, then the duration of the whole scheme will be significantly extended. The 'running repair' system should include:

- touch up paint
- repair wallpaper rips
- repair surfaces damaged by notices fixed with sellotape
- rub out scuffs
- tackle stubborn stains
- replace light bulbs
- rejuvenate or remove dying pot-plants
- replace tap washers
- fix ceiling tiles
- report more major needs.

A system for small repairs is another name for a reliable human being with 'handyperson' skills. Previous time and motion/efficiency/value for money studies and the like seemed to prove that reliable human beings with these multiple skills were not the best way of maintaining our buildings; it was in much the same way that park-keepers were shown to be replaceable by visiting security firms and contract gardeners. However, park authorities are now excited to rediscover that park-keepers seem to be the answer to maintaining parks, giving a greater sense of safety and taking action before major damage occurs. The general 'handyperson' in hospitals may be due for a similar renaissance.

Refurbished areas isolated

However beautifully appointed a particular ward or clinic may suddenly be made, if you approach it through corridors of squalor, the impact seems insincere. A building is a whole unit and its parts need to be considered in relationship to each other to achieve any decent standard.

Cultural elements excluded

'Cultural elements' refer here to art and decoration, windows and views. Visualise a beautifully decorated clinic with nothing whatever to look at apart from notices on the walls, and every window blocked off with frosted glass; the effect is bleak and soulless.

Boredom and claustrophobia are sadly seldom considered by those with the power to induce or banish them. This is partly because staff do not have to spend long hours waiting and resting as do patients, and also because staff leave at the end of their shift and go home. Claustrophobia tends to occur, even mildly, when there is no visual access to the open air, such as in rooms where there are no windows or they are visually blocked off, for example, with frosted glass. Of course, there are many occasions where this is imperative but there are several ways of treating blank windows and creating interiors which alleviate claustrophobia and counter boredom; an experienced designer can always make inventive use of opportunity.

The next chapter will explain the many ways this can be done.

Departmental components of the average hospital

From reception to chapels

CHAPTER

4

In this chapter we shall discuss all the functional components in terms not only of efficiency but also their aesthetic qualities, including comfort and delight. How can the car parks, entrance halls, canteens, mortuaries, corridors and all the other necessary functional components of any hospital be designed and maintained not only to work well but also to give pleasure? We shall discover.

'THE NAMING OF PARTS'

The average hospital will have the following areas:

1. Main roadway entrance
2. Car park and route to the main door
3. Large communal areas: reception foyers and waiting rooms
4. Circulation areas: corridors and staircases
5. Specialist examination and treatment areas: body scanner and x-rays units, anaesthetic and recovery rooms, operating theatres
6. Interview and counselling rooms
7. Traditional rooms: orthodox halls, management boardrooms, committee and meeting rooms
8. Kitchens and serving hatches
9. General eating areas: dining rooms
10. Patient wards, rooms for birth, rooms for death
11. Living and activity areas: day-rooms
12. Washing areas: 'lavatory' versus 'toilet', bathrooms
13. Public areas for private use: chapels and mortuary viewing rooms
14. Staff areas: changing rooms, rest rooms, bedrooms
15. Administration areas: general and personal offices
16. Storage

Components described and discussed

MAIN ROADWAY ENTRANCE

General layout

Hospitals with buildings dating from before about 1940 may still have the gates, or at least the gate posts, which suggest the approach to a building of substance. But the metal conscription of the 1940s, the subsequent hospital philosophy of un-impeded access and discharge besides the cost of personal attendance which all gates require have dealt them their deathblow. If a hospital gate survives, it is unlikely to be in use. What is left is the roadway which in older towns will describe the curve demanded by a horse-drawn vehicle, being characteristically a tight curve, while all subsequent roadways will describe the curve required by a vehicle at speed, which is an open or wide curve.

So, whether driving fast in a strange town and possibly peering through a fuzz of rain and windscreen wipers, or limping slowly with your overnight bag and an appointment card, what does the visitor see? What are the essential features to give the visitor a sense of human comfort, of being cared for and understood?

Checklist

Positive reassurers

- A large notice of the hospital's name, nature and town, placed first at some distance from the main entrance with an indication for drivers that the main entrance is one hundred/fifty/twenty yards further on, and then repeated at the entrance, well lit at night.
- For people arriving on foot or by bus, small direction signs at bus stops and street intersections.
- Clear directions as to what the visitor does next: main reception/information point,

direct route to emergencies, dropping-off point for patients, disabled parking, visitor's car parks.
- A well-maintained entrance, neat verges, shrubs, flowers, litter-free, with a well-lit, safe route such as a footpath beside a road clearly leading to the main reception/information point.

Positive unreassurers

- small notices and small print
- information about name and nature of hospital not given
- poorly lit at night
- signs hidden by trees
- no notices for pedestrians in the streets near the hospital
- litter at the hospital entrance
- a 'forest' of signs at the hospital entrance (if a large number of signs are needed they should be placed within the site, where it is safe to stop and read them)
- notice too near the entrance to enable a driver to indicate and make a safe turning
- a large number of signs with negative messages

Notices and directions – main content

Some hospitals declare they are an NHS trust but many, even when they are, do not although since 1997 all NHS premises have been required to display the NHS logo. Hospital renaming has often meant that the town name has been abandoned and a new, more obscure name imposed so we suggest that, like road signs, renamed hospitals could carry also the words 'formerly the Such-and-such Hospital' with the town name used as a subheading. This can result in a confusing and forbidding entrance.

The reforms of the 1990s coupled with political correctitude mean that few hospitals now declare what sort of hospital they are; certainly, the reaction of many people to encountering 'lunatic asylum' hugely carved in stone meant they indeed abandoned hope but there must surely be a middle way.

Wherever feasible, the purpose of the hospital or unit – whether 'general' or 'maternity', 'renal', 'rehabilitation', 'orthopaedic' and so on – should be declared and also whether it is NHS or not. If a hospital entrance sports a charity number and is

accompanied by a neat tiered border of banked geraniums, it will probably be a private hospital.

However, sometimes the search for a positive term, though laudable, can defeat the purpose of signs which is clarity. Hospitals which signpost patients to 'Venepuncture' or 'Podiatry' will have to invest significant time to guiding patients who are looking for 'Bloods' and 'Chiropody'.

Subsidiary signs

We recently counted forty-seven notices within one hundred feet of the (vandalised) main sign at one Midlands hospital. Many were duplications but they included:

- prohibitions on parking, dogs and trespassers
- cautions against theft and speed
- exonerations of blame should the worst occur
- information about closures, resiting
- multiple and contradictory general directions.

Each notice was separate and included lettering, mounting and fixing. The cost must have been enormous and the effect on visitors, many of whom will be in an anxious state, is that they will be mentally mugged, run over and ravaged by dogs and have no recourse in law before they even reach reception (Fig. 4.1).

Solution

Treat main entrance signs like an army; organise them according to rank, select wisely, demonstrate authority over underlings and don't keep changing your mind. The enemy is muddle so make sure everyone understands what muddle looks like and can recognise it; then, when they can see the whites of its eyes, shoot to kill.

Information about good signposting is available and an important part of the management of health service buildings is constantly checking that every effort is being made to guide people appropriately. Half an hour spent observing people as they come on to a site or enter the main reception area will give a good picture of whether people hesitate, look anxiously around and appear uncertain, or whether they move confidently and approach the destination or information desks readily. Staff who work in reception can tell you which questions people ask most often and you can then get expert advice on how to signpost

Fig. 4.1 Disorganised signposting that could confuse rather than guide visitors

them in those directions, which avoids the situation whereby staff put up a handwritten notice. However, handwritten notices at least indicate a well-meaning attempt to make directions clearer.

Signposting systems are available to enable you to alter and add information easily and quickly. They are worth the investment. It is very easy to make people feel hesitant and uncomfortable from the first moment they enter a building: signposting gives you an opportunity to achieve comfort and confidence.

CAR PARK AND ROUTE TO THE MAIN DOOR

Vehicular access

Most people arrive by private car and the sheer numbers that have to be accommodated have led to vast car parks, confusing directions and sometimes unpopular parking fees. The possible landscaping of car parks to make them as attractive and welcoming as possible is discussed in Chapter Two. If you do charge parking fees it is worth thinking about how you explain them to the public. A notice on the fee-system saying that by

charging fees to cover the cost of car parking more money is available for patient care, or for site surveillance, is helpful.

Pedestrian access

There has been such determination to accommodate the disabled in hospitals that this is now less of a problem than formerly. Most hospitals now realise that it is essential to involve disabled people in planning access and adapting facilities, and local disability groups will test possibilities and offer a critique of existing provision. Trying out your own facilities in a wheelchair, wearing ear plugs and fogged glasses, can give the able-bodied useful insights.

Some of the horror stories we have seen too often at entrances include:

- *Rubbish.* Impermanent skips or permanently parked wheeled rubbish bins situated beside the main entrance are not inviting. If there are litter bins they must be emptied before they reach overflow point.

HORROR STORY

A psychiatric hospital had a dispute between the porters who collected the rubbish and the estates department who removed it. Subsequently, when rubbish began to collect in a small garden space beside the Main Entrance, it was outside anyone's direct responsibility.

A used incontinence pad was then dropped in the small garden space but no one believed it was their job to pick it up; so it continued to lie prominently amongst the display of alyssum and marigolds which, some drought-prone months before, had been painstakingly pricked out to spell 'WELCOME'. It lay there while the sun shone and the rain fell; the soluble detritus gradually drained into the soil but the pad structure was designed not to disintegrate when wet so it remained to greet all comers to the hospital. Perhaps it is still there.

Doors. Expensive, highly manufactured automatic glass doors often have shabby notices stuck all over them.

Smoking. Hospitals which have non-smoking policies often have carpets of cigarette butts outside the main entrance, and frequently a group of furtive smokers too, sometimes in dressing gowns and nighties, attached to drips and equipment.

There is a good pictorial survey of hospital entrances which constitutes about a third of the book. *The Whole Question of Health* (The Prince of Wales' Institute of Architecture, 1995). This looks at the way architecture has been used for modern purposes and all the same issues of signposting, doorways and rubbish bins. We would refer readers to it also for its observant commentary (Fig. 4.2).

LARGE COMMUNAL AREAS

Reception foyer

The checklist of essential furnishings could continue with these items:

1. *Clarity.* Is it absolutely clear where you go for information?
2. *Signposts.* Are they clear, logical and organised?
3. *Written instructions.* Maps/leaflets etc., are they unambiguous in telling people what to do next?
4. *Cleanliness.* Are the premises clean?
5. *Furniture.* Is it clean, comfortable, well arranged?
6. *Lavatories.* Are they well signposted, accessible and maintained?
7. *Telephones.* Are they working and well sited?

8. *Drinks/food dispensers.* Do these offer a variety of goods, are they clean or surrounded by rubbish?
9. *Refuse sacks and laundry bags.* Are piles of these in view?
10. *Items for repair.* Are old chairs and broken telephone hoods left near the door for eventual collection?

Decorative appointment and general amenities could be listed as follows:

1. *Decor.* Is the place well decorated and maintained?
2. *Art and decoration.* Is there anything pleasing or interesting to look at?
3. *Diversions.* Are there varied and updated magazines available?
4. *Children.* Is there any provision for them?
5. *Shop.* If there is a shop, does it sell a good range (i.e. of papers and magazines) and is it well or even imaginatively stocked?
6. *Exterior views.* Has what you can see through the windows received attention?

An aura of helpfulness

This is the most important requirement. On arrival, is there someone there who would notice people in distress and help them appropriately?

Are reception staff easy to identify and available? In a number of reception arrangements staff are given other tasks to do, such as switchboard duties or typing, and it is easy for visitors to feel they are an interruption. In one hospital the most obvious information point is staffed by people in charge of security and keys: it is hard to combine these 'policing' tasks with being available for ordinary questions. Do porters, passing management staff and visiting peripatetic staff look approachable and pleasant?

Fig. 4.2 Two hospital entrances with rubbish skips and grit bunkers

Who is in charge?

Is it apparent that someone is in overall charge who is able to welcome and direct everyone on arrival? A well-managed and organised interior can imply that authority is in command and suggest that if a problem occurs during hospital treatment, it will be sensibly handled.

Client requirements

An example from Marks & Spencer shows how far client reaction is influenced by environmental circumstances. They upgraded one selected department of menswear; they redecorated, lit, labelled, signposted it and generally redid all aspects but kept the same merchandise on sale. Takings increased significantly and they were congratulated on a new range of menswear. The public's favourable perception of the service was manipulated by good surroundings and this led to economic success. Findings such as these are relevant to the health service's aim to provide quality care for patients and public.

Waiting rooms

As for airline pilots and surgeons, ennui is the enemy with a background of anxiety lest things go wrong. The best way of reducing anxiety is to provide something of interest to compete with the anxiety. Most hospitals will have lots of different areas where people wait. Sometimes they wait and wait, apparently unnecessarily, as in a five-hour wait to have a limb plaster removed in ten minutes; on other occasions their long wait is essential while life-saving procedures are performed on their relative. People may be accompanied by small children, or someone old, sick and incontinent, so what sort of diversions can be introduced?

CIRCULATION AREAS

Corridors

The design treatment of corridors is a major challenge. They are the main roads which have to carry the traffic of many people and heavy goods. Long, bleak, featureless corridors are the enemies of comfort and reassurance. So what can be done?

The problem of perspective

There are many architectural precedents of interior and garden perspective vistas handled with visual eloquence which rely on three basic things:

- vista-end attraction
- intersection and interval interest
- high-quality decor.

Vista-end attraction

The aim of a corridor is to encourage people to progress along it; you want them to reach their destination in good shape, avoiding exhaustion or despair. Something in the visible distance that attracts the attention is an age-old ruse for achieving this.

SUCCESS STORY

A typical but dreary waiting room in a southern hospital had a pond built outside its main windows. It was inaccessible to the public because safety regulations required this, ('you can drown in an inch of water', see 'The inexpediency of a water feature' in Chapter Two), and with its rigid, concrete sides there was no possibility of bulrushes or frogs or anything that could rot or defecate and make what the estates department called 'a mess'.

However, the 'no animal' policy of the hospital was defied by a pair of wild ducks who arrived, appreciated that they had the place to themselves and hatched a cheerful brood of ducklings. Animal lovers amongst the staff fired bread at them with catapults from the nearest window and the next year the ducks brought relatives who all bred. They became a major attraction to everyone in the waiting area.

Local children came in especially 'to see the ducks' and management was helpless in the face of 'A Problem' that could take to its wings and temporarily remove itself whenever interference occurred. They are still there (see Fig. 2.9).

Fig. 4.3 Corridor design utilising its perspective by combining the colour scheme with the signage and a specifically commissioned painting by Daphne Gradidge 1988. The interior design team worked closely with the arts co-ordinator. Winchester Royal Infirmary. 1988

Fig. 4.4 Hospital architecture varies from the featureless to the grand; this lofty central corridor of a Victorian hospital had its door-carving restored and a suitable interior scheme installed to enhance and echo it. 1990

Fig. 4.5 A 'period' corridor has had its dado rail not only restored during redecoration but extended to form a rectangular display area for historic photographs of the adjacent town. Graylingwell Hospital, Chichester 1987

Fig. 4.6 These rubbish bags waiting collection in a busy hospital corridor would never be tolerated in a high-street store

Fig. 4.7 Builder's rubbish left in the thoroughfare

It could be a manned, lit and well-appointed reception desk, a bank of plants or an artwork of some sort; we illustrate a commissioned painting using the corridor's perspective (Fig. 4.3). The use of lights, mobiles, free-standing works of art are all further possibilities. The best solution is a window showing daylight and, if you have the architectural luck to have this, make sure it is not frosted glass but a clear and well-dressed window.

Much depends on the quality and nature of the architecture. Some period buildings have restored and redecorated their corridors well (Fig. 4.4); others have cleverly reintroduced elements of period interest (Fig. 4.5); while a modern anonymous corridor end can be attractive simply by being well appointed and maintained.

If your corridor is characterised by a pile of laundry bags (Fig. 4.6), or rubbish awaiting collection (Fig. 4.7) or a vandalised lift bay, you have not achieved vista attraction!

Intersection and interval interest

Most corridors will have intersecting features, whether doors, lift bays, other corridors and so on. These can be used to differentiate visually the long expanse and so help people find their way.

This need not be structural but can depend on decor: for example, intersections could be differentiated by colour or flooring variation.

High-quality decoration

There is no disguising these integral features familiar in every hospital in the land, so the only solution is to accept them and give them strong treatment.

The problem was once discussed in the press of disguising a proposed nuclear power station on Anglesey. It was deemed absurd even to contemplate concealment so it was suggested instead that the unavoidable bulk of the thing should be openly declared; that it should have black and white squares or red dragons painted over it so that it could scream its huge existence within its gentle, mossy and sea-girt setting.

The interior design of hospital corridors is similarly 'challenging' and one such 'challenge' is that many departments and therefore many department heads and numerous staff will hourly disgorge into the corridor, taking territorial impulses with them. Hospitals are in use twenty-

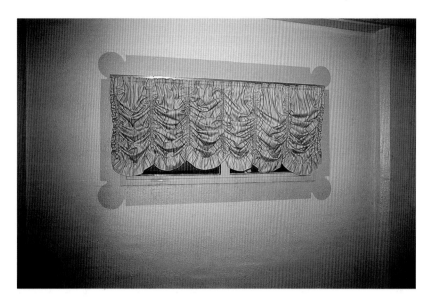

Fig. 4.8 An internal corridor window and door have been painted with architectonic shapes around them as part of a scheme devised by the interior designer to give variety in a long corridor; the window is given a ruched curtain which transforms its ordinariness. 1987

Fig. 4.9 'Sheep' mural painted onto the lower doors and walls of a corridor at Ashworth Special Hospital, Liverpool.

This ward was for seriously ill women patients; sheep were chosen because many of the women were Welsh and from sheep farming areas, and the animal shapes 'fitted' the available spaces.

The upper half of this corridor's walls and doors had so many viewing windows, handles, locks, alarms, notices, switches and cables that there was little space for decoration. But the empty lower half of the wall and fourteen doors gave the opportunity to paint this simple mural of sheep extending unbroken over the walls and fourteen doors, using four colours and black while the lambs were sprayed by stencil with aerosol car paint. The effect intended was that when all the doors were open, the corridor looked full of sheep and when they were closed, it appeared to be empty. The green carpet was intended to complete the illusion of a meadow.

Mural by Sarah Hosking. 1994

four hours a day and all users have to be accommodated. For example, people die in hospital and their bodies have to be brought down to the mortuary, usually at night. Similarly, bodies are delivered by ambulances at any hour and whatever corridor it is that leads to the mortuary and viewing room has to be lit constantly, allow discreet and quiet passage but be cleanable and, of course, the same route may be used by the public all day. This is a genuine instance of multiple use and a corridor's decoration taxes the invention of the most experienced designer; there is no easy solution and, sadly, good corridor design is rare.

One approach is to unify the ceiling, walls, floor and doors with colour and make one's journey along the corridor 'progress' visually, perhaps through the colours of the spectrum, or through variants of one colour, or by identifying departments by colour. Another is to paint architectonic shapes on the walls (Fig. 4.8), perhaps surrounding doors, windows and noticeboards with a wide band of colour or using a linked scheme of interchanging colours.

Tiling, works of art (and if anywhere demands a series of pictures in a sequence, it is here – see Fig. 4.9, 'Sheep mural'), mirror tiles, any of the suggestions we describe in Chapter Five and especially series of picture panels that are sequential or 'tell a story' alleviate the boredom of corridors (Fig. 4.10). There will be many mandatory notices in a corridor, such as those indicating Fire Escape Routes; they need to be installed in conjunction with the designer.

Fig. 4.10 Mural by David Gomman in St Crispin's Psychiatric Hospital, Northampton; 1976. This corridor mural is of the Creation, from light brought out of darkness, the emergence of dry land and creation of life to the Seventh Day when God rested.

David Gomman was commissioned to paint this mural because, as an older artist (he died in 1987), he was easily accepted by the mainly elderly patients; he took a year to paint this, working almost daily with a trolley-load

of paints. His work reflected his older generation to whom narrative, decorative and accessible mural painting was a worthy end in itself. He did not seek to 'emotionally challenge' or 'energetically engage' his audience, as contemporary 'art in hospitals' schemes sometimes claim to do, but to amuse, enchant and befriend his audience. The hospital is now closed and, had this mural been painted on removable panels, it could have been preserved.

Staircases

Corridors and staircases are like the outside street in that they are public pathways and can suggest menace. They can also look as though their main function is as an escape in the event of fire and have notices telling you so, but even the most utilitarian of fire-escape staircases have opportunities of design 'delight', as the three budget options to a specific example of a staircase on pp. 66–7 show.

The situation

We envisage an older hospital with a shabby staircase landing which has a window. We assume this is a staircase that the public use, which is not supervised closely and which takes hard wear. The walls are battered magnolia paint, the old curtains at the window are falling off their rail, the glass is cracked, the stairs themselves are aged grey vinyl. The ceiling has one fluorescent strip light studded with dead flies and there are some peeling 'No Smoking' notices.

'And afterwards'

Whether adopting Solution one, two or three on pp. 66–7, this upgrading will need to be maintained. Plan to make checks for damage, unsolicited notices and so on as often as staffing allows, and initiate immediate action. If this is done conscientiously, it maintains standards and the hospital could look to a seven-year re-decoration rota instead of a five-year one.

SPECIALIST EXAMINATION AND TREATMENT AREAS

In any hospital there will be several areas where the demands of clinical technology will dominate design unless these areas are given special attention. Here are some examples.

Anaesthetic and recovery rooms

There is a difference in design requirement between these two; the anaesthetic room is where conscious patients are wheeled for their operation pre-medication and then full anaesthetic. There is no need for bacterial sterility while an anaesthetic is administered, so one such room was wallpapered on the ceiling and upper walls (which patients see most) with a William Morris

paper; what better way than to float off looking at his magical forest full of birds?

The recovery room is where patients 'come round' from the anaesthetic and the need for sterility is absolute. Post-operative bleeding and projectile vomiting mean the room has to be washed down with hoses; floor joints must be sealed and the curved, pre-moulded skirting board is usually used for cleaning ease. No one, least of all the post-operative patient, cares what it looks like.

Operating theatres

It is surprising to those of us who regard surgeons and airline pilots as professionals who are 'ipso facto' swathed in glamour that boredom is a hazard of their professions. Therefore, although operating theatres are seen only by staff, some Dutch hospitals have still regarded them as sufficiently important to decorate and appoint carefully.

Operating theatres are traditionally green because in the colour spectrum green is the opposite of red and blood is red. Blood and other fluids are 'shiny' so surfaces should be matt and never glossy.

SUCCESS STORY

Body scanner suite

During the late 1980s, a southern hospital embarked upon the purchase and installation of a diagnostic CT body scanner. As everyone at that time was becoming aware, this is not just another machine but a whole new technology requiring a suite of rooms to accommodate it, a team to run it and a budget to maintain it.

A fundraising professional was employed to raise the required millions for capital outlay and, over three years, this was achieved. The number of professional people engaged in building the suite (within the structure of a hospital that had been designed in the 1950s) and in the organisational, financial and technological control was considerable, but everyone performed well. After all this, it was discovered that no thought had been given to the interior decoration apart from sending down a painter with a pot of magnolia. Therefore, at the eleventh hour, reparation was made as follows:

- *A scheme of decor* – including curtains, colours, furniture, even the overalls of the staff, the towelling dressing gowns, the large, silent trolley wheels and signs on the drinks dispenser – was agreed with staff.
- *A ceiling mural* situated directly above the scanner couch was carefully commissioned from an artist known to have completed suitable work elsewhere; it was a comparatively cheap commission because all the tiles used for the mural were delivered to the artist's studio where they were painted ('work on site' costs considerably more). They were inserted in the ceiling grid later (Fig. 4.11 on p. 68).
- *Decoration and pictures* – including vases of silk flowers, mobiles and a variety of pictures and prints – were installed, carefully sited with the mandatory notices and signs. These included a large print of a commissioned photograph of a well-known, local landmark.

Green therefore offers eye relief but there are many sorts of green (see Chapter Six, 'Colour') and other subtle variants on design expectation can also be offered. Viewing windows can be circular, not square, and floors can be varied. Visual interest and appropriate organisation are likely to reduce stress and promote mental harmony and there is no conflict with rigorous infection control.

The operating room is lovely . . . because the nature of surgery is such that it has to be extremely calm, quiet and well-ordered. It's like an extremely posh restaurant . . . a well-organised place; the waiters are in the right places, the tables are laid nicely, you just feel that it is all going to work properly. A well-run operating theatre is like that. You walk in, you immediately feel at ease, the team, the nurses, the anaesthetist, the porters, all the registrars, just have a calmness about them. Wonderful.
(Danny Danziger, *The Noble Tradition: Interviews with the Medical Profession* – The Surgeon – Viking 1990)

INTERVIEW AND COUNSELLING ROOMS

In the past, hospitals generally did not have rooms designated for these purposes; someone's office or consultancy room had 'to double' up when needed and this is not ideal. Sometimes patients need to talk to their families or hospital staff need to tell people bad news, and for this to take place while perched on a clinic's examination couch or in an office while the phone rings and people pop in for a file and their cardigan, only adds insult to distress.

By far the most important and widespread criticism of the admission ward was the lack of privacy. Seldom was it possible for an individual to spend time in a quiet sitting room and almost never was it possible for a patient to talk to family out of earshot or sight of others.
(*Mental Welfare Commission for Scotland 1990*, HMSO Scotland)

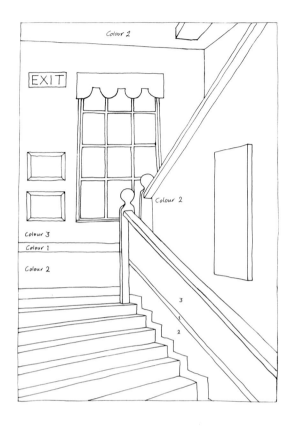

SOLUTION ONE – THE CHEAPEST POSSIBLE

Preparation. Repair the plaster adequately.

Paint and wall protection. Chose three tones of one colour type (e.g. browns or greens). Colour-1 (darkest tone): in gloss, paint a broad stripe about four feet from the ground wherever walls receive the most wear.

Colour 2 (middle tone): vinyl silk to be used below the stripe on the lower wall and on the ceiling.

Colour 3 (lightest tone): vinyl matt to be used above the stripe on the upper wall and up to the ceiling.

Stairs. Clean the stairs with wire wool and an abrasive; chewing gum is removed with petrol. Select a very dark floor paint (such as is used on garage floors) and paint the stairs and the edge down the wall, either straight or in 'steps'; finish with a non-slip sealant.

Lighting. Clean the light-fitting and repair as necessary.

Window and curtains. Simply clean the window structure and glass, whatever the condition. Find some old curtains (hospitals always have piles of them) and make a pelmet that is scalloped or otherwise decoratively shaped; fix securely.

Pictures. Select some posters or cut up a paperback book of anything that does not demand close attention (puppies, roses, sea-side views) because this can cause people to stumble; mount the pictures on hardboard covered in felt, fix perspex over them and screw them to the walls. Make use of the tall, upright shapes any staircase offers with several small pictures arranged vertically.

Other. Simplify the mandatory notices making them few but clear; remove all others.

SOLUTION TWO – MIDDLE COST

Preparation. Repair the plaster as well as funds permit.

Wall protection. At the height of greatest wear, install a deep strip of cushioned material (see 'Chapter information') to absorb knocks.

Paint and wallpaper. Select a suitable wallpaper border and use it around the ceiling edge (it can also be used for picture mountings). Chose three tones of a colour which relate to this. Use as in 'Solution one'.

Stairs. Re-lay them with new linoleum and nosings. Paint the wall where it meets the stairs as a skirting board.

Lighting. Replace the light with a short cable and round shade (if paper, treat for flammability – see 'Chapter information').

Window. Clean the window structure and repair the glass. If the view is pleasant, install clear glass; if it is awful and needs to be concealed, design a pattern that is cut out of frosted adhesive and stuck onto the glass.

Curtains. Choose some discarded, old ones and select a coloured lining that relates to them. Clean them and remake with the coloured lining and give them a wide border each side. Loop them back with tie-backs made of the same fabric (in order to deter theft, close the hooks that hold them with pliers). Also make a decorative pelmet (as above in 'Solution one').

Other. Pictures and notices as above.

SOLUTION THREE – COMPLETE REFURBISHMENT

Preparation. Repair the plaster immaculately.

Wall protection. Install a wooden banister and/or a dado rail, and a 'stepped' skirting board. Stain these.

Paint, wallpaper and fabric. Select new co-ordinated curtain fabric, wallpaper and a border. Paper the ceiling, possibly with borders, as appropriate. Select two colours related to these; use them on the ceiling and upper and lower walls as specified in Solutions one and two. Select a third colour in gloss for all woodwork.

Stairs. Carpet the stairs with a co-ordinating, short-loop stain-resistant hessian-backed carpet.

Lighting. Replace ceiling light with one central pendant fitting, and add several small spots on a separate circuit for emergency or night lighting.

Window and view. Make new decorative pelmet and curtains. Consider whether it is possible to make any improvements in the view, i.e. might the planting of some Russian vines conceal those bleak sheds?

On the window ledge, put a vase (screwed down) full of dried or silk flowers. Fill the vase with sand or sawdust (this deters the casual thief). Alternatively, have some wooden ornament that can be screwed down.

Other items. Notices as above. Install planters with shade-resistant plants; hang pictures with security frames.

A small but pretty room with easy chairs where there will be no interruptions, the means to make tea and coffee, a private lavatory with tissues and mirror, and a telephone (pay-phone if necessary) are all that is required.

TRADITIONAL ROOMS

Orthodox halls

We envisage here a typical school-type 'hall' which any hospital with pre-war buildings will have. It may have a stage with proscenium arch, even 'flies' and 'wings' and red velvet 'drapes'; the body of the hall will probably have a timber-supported ceiling with clusters of lights, serried windows and a good floor for dancing.

In the days when a large hospital engendered an extensive and varied community, award ceremonies and Christmas dances took place here; often, they still do and such halls are nowadays 'hired out' for events and theatricals.

The restoration of these halls is an opportunity for flamboyance, such as the Roman blinds and the gilded pediments that are not feasible elsewhere. But the different events which such a hall may nowadays host are not easy to reconcile; the technology for modern music and for cinema projection may be difficult to install while preserving acoustics for the human voice, and honouring possible listed-status requirements may present serious problems.

However, such halls have ever been a 'showpiece' of older hospitals and they require good designers who will be able to reconcile technology with restored Edwardian glamour.

Management boardrooms, committee and meeting rooms

It is not unknown for a hospital to remove all original features, fireplaces, skirting boards, flooring and so on and lower the ceilings before inviting an interior designer to give it 'character'; by this time the original period 'character' is lying in the rubbish skip.

We are not suggesting that everything old is beautiful and everything modern is not, for this is

Fig. 4.11 Ceiling mural by Daphne Gradidge in the Body Scanner Suite at Basingstoke District Hospital; 1988. We describe the circumstances of this commission in Chapter Nine.

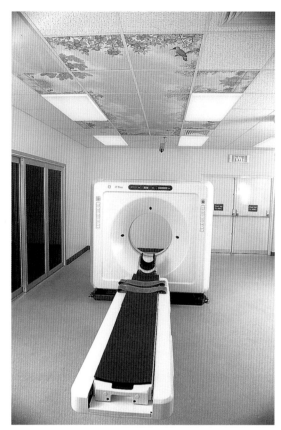

not the case, but older things are more difficult to replace once lost and it takes professionalism to make the two blend together. They are like the oldest child and the youngest, both valuable but different.

However, it is these traditional senior-staff meeting rooms that tend to be the only interiors to have been allowed to retain the quality and dignity of their period, because their 'function' has not changed; well-behaved people still meet, sit down and talk for hours while someone writes it all down, a tea trolley is wheeled in and out again and they all go to the lavatory before departing, much as people have done since the Agora in ancient Greece was popular.

The bane of these 'traditional' rooms is complacency; photographs of past hospital chiefs and mayors usually hang around the walls with an aerial photograph of the hospital years ago. This quality of gravitas can be retained in some innovative way; one hospital asked their arts co-ordinator to compile a series of photograph portraits of philanthropists who had worked for healthcare and asylum reform. It was appropriate, cheap to produce and diverting but not distracting.

KITCHENS

Size and complexity

However large or small the kitchen, there will be problems of noise, condensation, heat and smell; these are endemic in domestic kitchens and similarly, to a greater degree, in mass-catering kitchens. Whether it is a 'raw to ready' conventional kitchen that undertakes the whole cycle of meal preparation, cooking and serving, or a simplified 'cook-freeze' or 'cook-chill' kitchen that only has to heat and serve, or a 'finishing kitchen' that uses only frozen, chilled, canned or dehydrated foods, or a 'call-order' small kitchen such as a snack bar with kitchenette that cooks by request simple foods such as sausage, fish and chips, whatever the size and complexity, these disadvantages prevail.

Invariable problems

Condensation occurs when hot air, or steam, meets a cold surface such as a window pane; only ventilation can ease it and the low ceilings and fixed windows of many hospital kitchens do not help. The days of high-ceilinged kitchens which Mrs Beeton recommended should be pale-coloured distempered every summer are no more.

Most kitchens in the public sector have stainless-steel work surfaces and most also use large, stainless-steel implements so the resultant noise is considerable. The surfaces can be muffled against noise and vibration, to an extent, by strong underpinnings and a coating of bituminous material underneath. Also rubber and plastic mats, trolley wheels and cooking implements can be used, but kitchens remain generally noisy, stressful places.

The floor has to be as clean as a hospital can manage. Ceramic tiles, glazed or not, are traditional but noisy and the grouting can shrink so insect life invades the cracks. Terrazzo tiles are precision-cut and so can have a tight and sterile join but they are expensive and again noisy. Thermoplastic tiles and sheeting are quieter but anything that is studded or ridged to prevent slipping is difficult to clean. Linoleum and vinyl sheets or tiles are the quietest and the best-looking, and there are some attractive, flat slip-resistant versions, but skirting boards, or moulded units, have to be continuous and welded.

Decor opportunities

The only realistic decor opportunities in kitchens are for a coloured ceiling, interesting flooring and good use of 'featured' tiling. The outlook from kitchen windows is usually bleak because of delivery lorries and rubbish bins and, because of the need for cool stores, they usually have little sun. A retreat away from noise, heat and smell for staff to relax should be arranged somewhere, somehow.

Serving hatches

These are common where the kitchen is adjacent to the dining room but the problem is that as food is passed over the counter, the kitchen noise goes with it. Both kitchen and dining room can have ceilings of acoustic tiles which absorb noise considerably (Fig. 4.12).

GENERAL EATING AREAS

Most hospitals in the past would have had at least a staff dining room and also another separate one for consultants. Cost pressures and the pursuit of egalitarianism mean that most hospitals now have one staff dining room/self-service cafeteria, often with automatic vending machines for evening and night meals.

Dining rooms, their 'image'

These are also noisy because people raise their voices to be heard over the clatter. This can be decreased by acoustic screens (commonly used in offices), by having window curtains and carpeting. Although some of the acrylic carpets can be scrubbed, modern linoleum, with its textures and opportunity for pattern, may be the best option.

Hospital dining rooms look their best when they are empty, as when they are busy there is the inevitable sense of bustle and untidiness. Many hospitals have upgraded their dining rooms successfully, using good lighting, well-designed furniture, plants, mirrors and pictures. An experienced designer will analyse people's patterns of use to ensure that the dining room works well when it is occupied but that lighting is used to make it attractive throughout the fluctuations of use during twenty-four hours. Any hospital's dining room has to appeal to all who use it, and one which looks like a top management haven will not necessarily appeal to busy ward staff.

The best solution is usually to let the period architecture be the guide for the decorative style; if there isn't any, invent some stylish feature that is strong and memorable because people are not there for long (unlike in a ward), they come and go and so need not feel overwhelmed by some strong visual statement.

Regarding the organisation of feeding many people continuously, this can be copied from some of the large stores for whom style is compulsory, like IKEA. They are used to large numbers of people arriving and eating in a hurry, but also manage to make each person feel well treated and therefore presumably more likely to return.

Dining 'al fresco'

The opportunity to eat outside is always popular and, from April to October, people will do so if given any opportunity; it may be the only time many have for genuine relaxation and good

Fig. 4.12 'Before' and 'after' photographs.

This secure male ward in a northern special hospital shows the patients' dining room. The floor is laid with linoleum tiles in a chequer-board pattern, tables, chairs and clock are from IKEA, and the locker doors have a retained small semi-circle of unpainted wood so that keys do not chip the paint. The planters give a sense of 'division' from the adjacent day-room but allow staff surveillance. The 'patchwork' on the wall is made from all the curtain materials used throughout the ward. 1993

facilities in a pleasant garden should be possible as we suggested in Chapter Two.

PATIENT WARDS

'More but different' patients

Wards are still as full of patients as they have ever been but they now cater for more and different patients (Fig. 4.13). The recovery stages that once took place in hospitals now take place at home or elsewhere, so the length of hospitalisation per patient is reduced, and more individuals are treated. There are now few elderly patients hospitalised for longer-term care, although terms like 'slow stream rehabilitation' are an acknowledgement that some patients will have to spend many weeks and even months in hospital.

'In-patient' care is also being reduced by the new trend for day surgery and small operations, the 'lumps and bumps' service, being performed by GPs in their local surgeries. The days when an appendectomy required hospital care for three weeks is past, and new keyhole-type surgery, development of local anaesthetics and improved diagnosis means that conditions once requiring hospitalisation no longer do so.

Because 'in-care' patients stay for a shorter time, there is a far greater 'turnover' and intensified coming and going as more is done for more people, so wards are less peaceful places; patients have less time to get to know each other and develop friendships, and they are more likely to be next to other patients who are acutely ill.

A typical Nightingale ward

The 'Nightingale ward' is the traditional version dating from the 1860s whereby forty or more beds were ranged down each side of a long, narrow ward with the nursing station at one end and a convalescent bay at the other. Before the availability of central heating, there would have been a stove in the middle, stoked with coke by a gnarled retainer and the beds furthest from it were given the extra blankets; there were usually windows down each side which were opened every morning (read any wartime novel set in a hospital). When you were really ill, your bed was up by the nursing station (see 'The origins of this book' in Chapter Eight); as you recovered, you were moved down the ward until you could sit in the convalescent bay and take yourself to the green-tiled, unheated lavatories; further recovery meant you had to help serve the dinners, whereupon you hung your walking stick on the horizontal funnel-chimney of the huge stove where it scorched and became charcoal before pudding was eaten.

The two lines of beds converged in a neat perspective on the desk at the end. The crude design on the cotton counterpanes were shrill and unfaded, hard reds and blues on a buff background. The deal lockers, the low beds, even the prefabricated walls were new. New things were everywhere; it was only the men in the beds who looked shabby and worn.

(Mary Renault, *The Charioteer*, Longmans Green & Co., 1953)

Nightingale wards are sometimes still in use (Fig. 4.14) but now more often seen as of historic interest; they became unpopular because they failed to meet developing expectations of privacy and many older hospitals will have tried to disguise their Nightingale wards by subdividing them into bays; new hospitals will have built wards to a four-, six- or eight-bed design.

Advantages of bay wards

Wards divided into bays should have many advantages, and they certainly offer more flexibility:

twenty beds in one open ward can be used differently if they are divided into four- or five-bed bays. If more women need to be admitted than men, the balance can be achieved in a bay ward; if there are several patients needing special attention they can be grouped in one bay and progress towards discharge can mean progress away from the bay nearest the nursing station.

In theory, bay design should have overwhelming advantages for patients: there is greater privacy and the intimacy of a smaller 'unit' means they only need to get to know a few other people and they are likely to be grouped with others at a similar stage of ailment and recovery.

However, bay-design wards have disadvantages, many of which were not foreseen. Some of these are linked to changes in the pattern of hospital care. Shorter stays mean there are fewer patients who are up and about. Often patients who had recovered from the acute stage used to play a social role on the ward and had time and inclination to help new patients. This is now seldom the case.

Fig. 4.13 Bright Ward, Guy's Hospital, London. Postcard postmarked 1902.
  Many of the items in this ward would today be considered unsanitary (lace cloths and cushions) or dangerous (loose floor rugs) but the impression is that of homely comfort and good housekeeping. Wellcome Institute Library, London

Fig. 4.14 'The busy ward and being a parent' from the series 'Living with Leukaemia' by Susan Macfarlane 1995.
This series of paintings and drawings of childhood leukaemia follows the long and arduous treatment and staff work involved to combat this disease.
This painting shows the hustle of visitors arriving in a large ward; the small, monochrome pictures down each side of the main panel illustrate the quiet of evening and eventual sleep as parents and children take what rest they can.

Nurses' roles have also changed because patients are only in hospital for the acute phase; although nurses may wish to spend time with patients, it is in practice often difficult for them to do so because of the demands on their time for acute nursing. Other disadvantages are linked to bay design itself.

Disadvantages of bay wards

In a Nightingale ward, the open vista meant that everyone was aware of what was happening and could see where staff were. Patients could spot a nurse coming down the ward towards them and could, if they wished, attract her attention. In a bay ward patients can only see people as they flash past the entrance and it is difficult to catch them.

In an open ward patients can also see that nurses are busy and what they are doing; in a bay ward if there is no one in view you do not know what is happening and there may be a greater level of anxiety. The anxiety may be about noises which cannot be identified or some apparent emergency to which nurses are rushing. The anxiety is also related to the difficulty of knowing when you press the call button whether your request for help has been registered; a nurse used to be able to turn around and wave an 'I'll be with you in a minute' type of acknowledgement, but in bay design there is no easy way for your request to be noted and for you to see what other priorities are being dealt with before yours. People are more tolerant if they can see that there are problems taking nurses' attention.

Companionship

The bay design tends to limit the number of fellow patients felt to be approachable. Patients in a four-bed bay have a more restricted set of potential 'buddies'; with bay design there is an unwritten assumption that you belong in your own bay, and it can feel quite difficult to visit another one. Patients can feel more exposed to any irritations, such as a portable television, mobile phone, radio playing, groups of relatives and friends, snoring, groaning, coughing, and also more isolated.

Individuals are also cut off from the pool of knowledge, the invariable 'gossip' about hospital life which is available in a Nightingale ward. For some patients, of course, the smaller number of people in the bay may be welcome, and with very short stays interaction with other patients is not likely at other than a polite level.

This is not a hymn to the open ward, but it is a reminder that managing patients well in a bay ward needs care and thought. Although bay wards will look more modern because they are newer than Nightingale wards, they certainly offer less visual and social stimulation and patients experience less contact with staff.

Noise levels

Bay design may also give staff the feeling that bays offer protection from sounds in the corridor and elsewhere, making it harder for staff to maintain vigilance about noise. There are new sources of noise as more equipment is used to care for more seriously ill patients; if you are unlucky enough to be beside a patient on a mattress with a motor to vary pressure you will understand this point. There are many more bleeps, blips and thrumming noises than there used to be in hospitals.

Open and longer visiting hours are another new source of noise. One patient's welcome visiting family is a potential source of exhaustion for the neighbouring patient, and bay design may encourage visitors to feel more private and less likely to lower voices.

We discuss noise further in Chapter Eight.

Mixed-sex wards

The Patients' Charter of 1996 stated that, except in emergencies, you have the right to single-sex washing and toilet facilities and to be given single-sex ward accommodation if at all possible.

Mixed-sex wards and even clinics cause distress mainly to women since men can and do, unreasonably or not, represent a threat.

> One problem with mixed-sex wards is that staff do not see it as a problem . . . Nursing staff say that no-one complains . . . but it is a well-known fact that people undergoing treatment are loath to complain because they fear they may be subject to some action if they do.
> ('The perception of safety', *Nursing Times*, 19 July 1995)

Perhaps the most important requirement in a hospital is feeling safe; a number of studies have shown that patients in mixed-sex bay wards do not feel safe, in part because the bays are not under the direct eye of a member of staff. There is a trade-off between the wish for privacy and the need to feel safely supervised.

Patient 'hotels'

Based on a Scandinavian model, some hospitals have built a 'hotel' unit where patients can go to recover in surroundings more like a hotel than a ward. Medical care is available if required but they are assumed to need only 'room service', food and a quiet private room for a short, convalescent spell before going home. Similarly, patients such as those who have had eye surgery and are therefore mobile, or orthopaedic cases who may not be mobile but who are not ill, are being discharged into a nearby hotel. Here they can recuperate in comfortable surroundings and the arrangement with the hospital ensures that nurses are always on the premises in case of medical difficulty.

Patient food

The characteristically brief modern hospitalisation means that many patients will only be there long enough to have three or four breakfasts, lunches and teas, long enough perhaps to be given nutrition advice but not long enough for their diet to make a significant difference to them.

However, for many people the enjoyment of food is an important sign of well-being, and the taking and enjoyment of food are socially important as markers of stages in our lives; the baby's first solid food, the person near to death taking a little soup, the first meal after a period of sickness, these are all awaited, commented upon and celebrated.

Nutrition and nursing

'Nutrition' and 'nurse' share the same Latin root, '*nutrire*' (to nourish), and for most of our history this has been seen as women's business, linked to motherhood and motherly caring. Traditional nursing in the Florence Nightingale tradition gave nurses a clear role in ensuring that patients' diets aided recovery. Regarding this, Florence Nightingale wrote: 'The nurses' observations will materially assist the doctor . . . the patient's "fancies" will materially affect the nurse' (*Notes on Nursing; What it is and what it is not*).

Nursing has now redefined its roles as part of its wish to be treated as a 'profession' rather than a 'handmaiden service' to doctors, and feeding patients and taking part in serving meals is now seen as a non-nursing duty. Although nurses still know that the food patients eat is a valuable indicator of their well-being, they now rely on patients' reports of the amounts eaten rather than personal observation as they serve and feed patients. Patients' reports are not necessarily reliable.

'Markers' in the day

Even during short stays, meals are important markers in a patient's day. For many in the past the first such morning 'marker' was a cup of tea at 6 a.m. so that patients could be washed and ready for the nursing shift handover inspection. This should now be a thing of the past, but the timing of meals still remains linked to working shifts of catering and ward staff, resulting in regular reports that the last meal of the day is unacceptably early. It is often hard for patients to get a light snack of something which they fancy at the hour when

SUCCESS STORY – BUT ONLY JUST

In a long-term ward for mentally handicapped women, large dormitories were being replaced with single bedrooms during a major upgrading. Staff asked for an incinerator to be conveniently placed as they had for years dealt with soiled sanitary napkins by putting them into plastic bags and carrying them to a central collection point some way away for disposal. Since women living together in close quarters tend to menstruate all at the same time, this was a significant undertaking every month.

Staff had also asked that patient beds and bedding could be improved by providing ten- (rather than five-) centimetre-thick mattresses, which, in the case of women who tended to be overweight because of medication and lack of exercise, was of personal importance. Two pillows instead of one, their own duvet covers, a rug, a cushion and small quilted headboard covers to soften the institutionally hard, plywood bed-heads were also specified to make daily life more comfortable for the patients in their new and private small bedrooms.

However, the inevitable budget cuts occurred and these comfortable, personal items were omitted by the project manager at the request of the commissioning client who was the hospital management, even though the cost was a tiny proportion of several tens of thousands of pounds being spent.

The objections raised were cost and also that such items were unnecessary; staff suggested that many things in a home are not strictly necessary but that personal comfort emanates from their availability.

The real problem was one of lack of sympathy towards the women patients and the female staff who cared for them by the project team and the commissioning client.

Eventually, the requested facilities were supplied but only after intervention on a high level due to an impending inspection of a team concerned with the welfare of women in confinement. Left to the natural course of events their intimate needs would have been sacrificed to a better sort of drain lining.

they fancy it. Some wards have installed automatic vending machines for drinks, but it is hard to believe that tea or coffee in a plastic cup from such a machine is what health service managers or non-executives would like to drink if they were sufficiently unwell to be hospitalised.

The rituals of eating

Most meals will have been prepared in a distant kitchen and delivered to the ward in individual portions, and efforts have been made to give patients much more choice. However, choice in the hospital setting is usually defined as choosing meals a day ahead from a printed menu, which is not how choice is defined when we stay in hotels or go to a cafeteria. We are all aware of the 'choice' involved in a newly admitted patient receiving a meal ordered the day before by a patient well enough to leave hospital (see 'A patient's comment' in Chapter Eight). Most hospitals now make an effort to provide vegetarian options and cater for ethnic minorities.

A number of hospitals have rebelled against these traditions and have moved to a catering and ward waitress service offering patients a choice at meal times as the meals are served by staff who are trained to serve food pleasantly and helpfully. These hospitals have realised the emotional importance of food and the role of meals as indicators of time passing. They have also thought about the way food is presented and have invested in alternatives to thick white institutional crockery.

Where patients are in hospital for longer stays food is of more central importance. If the food provided is not planned to be nutritionally sound, patients can be malnourished, and have been found to be so. If the nutritionally sound food is cooked badly and served in an unappealing or hurried way the patients can still be malnourished. If, physically, patients find it difficult to eat and there is no time for anyone to help them, they will be malnourished. Patients who are elderly, confused or handicapped need support or encouragement to enjoy eating, besides intelligent meal planning and presentation which will make meals a more enjoyable marker in the day as well as contributing to well-being.

There is a very strong set of rituals linked to eating. Patients brought to a table laid for a meal –

with some thought to its appearance, including tablecloth or table mats, napkins, flowers, salt and pepper set, places laid with pleasant china, water jugs and glasses, gentle lighting and so on – are taking part in a comforting social ritual. Patients sitting at a formica table with thin paper serviettes, thick white crockery, and minimal thought to making the meal-time pleasing are not comforted and are not encouraged to be social.

Alternatively, eating on a bed table in a small bay ward, perhaps as the only person eating, and possibly watching someone nearby vomiting are not conditions conducive to appetite.

Involvement of the long-stay patient

Many patients would enjoy involvement in meal preparation, and after the trend towards centralised kitchens there is now a trend back to home-scale cooking where patient involvement is possible. There is of course a trade-off between the pleasure of involvement in preparing, feeling, smelling and anticipating a hot drink, snack or meal and the risk of burns, cuts and scalds but one hopes that the pleasure of involvement will prevail.

The actual taste of food is perhaps subjective, although judgements about cold, heat, lumps, grease and sogginess are more objective. It is the issue of taste in the sense of how food is presented, appropriate size of portion and attractiveness which will give as much delight as can be achieved in an institution where the budget for a whole day's meals is less than the average price of a cup of coffee and a sandwich.

Meal-times are also an important marker for staff during their working day. The staff canteen or dining room should offer some sense of haven and relief from the stress of work and many hospitals have revamped their dining areas and menus to good effect. Food for staff working night shifts and for doctors on call remains a problem; it is clearly uneconomic to provide full catering for the small numbers involved, but it is demotivating to work nights and also find vending-machine meals the only option.

Rooms for birth

After having a baby, you first went downstairs on the Friday afternoon of the third week.
(Kate Hosking, the author's granny, born 1878, had her twin children 1904)

'The taking of food has many psycho-social connotations . . . and appetite is helped by sitting at a table and watching others eat.'
(Mary Britta Taylor, *Improving the Nutritional Care of the Patient*), 1989 – unpublished paper in the King's Fund Library)

'Delivering babies makes every day like Christmas day.'
(Community midwife)

The National Childbirth Trust and women's groups have had a tremendous effect upon the nature and quality of childbirth; the realisation that peace and calm are important could be applied elsewhere in hospitals. Any hospital will have tried to make its birth suite more attractive. The universal design principles of colour, texture, lighting can be used to create delivery rooms which give pleasure, reassurance and a sense of intimacy. There is a need to combine a sense of quiet and separation from the activity and intensity of a hospital with the confidence that expertise would be available as soon as needed. To some extent scan systems and electronic monitoring can give this, but the most reassuring features remain human ones, such as someone arriving to give a medical check-up just before the patient's anxiety commences, and calculating the time they stay so that confidence is high.

Maternity wards are now nearly all laid out as bays. Happily for most parents, birth is a time for celebration but there is the risk that a large family group around one bed can become intrusive for another patient, and for some there will always be little cause for celebration or few people with whom to rejoice.

Longer visiting times mean more disturbance. Most mothers are up and about almost immediately after birth, and if it is possible to provide more attractive day spaces rather than have groups forming around beds, this is helpful.

Noise is a problem, from crying babies as well as from patients coming up from labour suites and leaving the ward; nowadays very short stays mean that a high level of activity is inevitable. Airlines offer earplugs and eye-shades so that people who want to cut out activity can do so, and this might be copied here.

Rooms for death

Like the arrival of babies, death can require a long wait, and in both cases it is the family or support group – not necessarily the central character – who are most vulnerable to psychological distress. Death is unpopular in hospitals because it implies, however unreasonably, a failure of medicine and also because it is not integrated into our irreligious and scientific age that has banished so many of its causes. It is the new 'unmentionable'.

> The ninth visitor is life,
> The tenth visitor is not usually named
> (Charles Causley, 'Ten Types of Hospital Visitor')

Solution

The hospital referred to in the 'Horror story' below had many side rooms, mostly half full of stores, and organisation could have allowed one room to be allocated for dying. Objections to this are that such a room will be stigmatised 'the death room' but this ignores the need of the family or those in attendance. Where hospitals have designated and designed private rooms for those who are near the end of their life there has not been a stigma issue; the dying and their relatives on the whole know that the end is near and it is hard to think of anything more humane than giving them an appropriate room which shows that their feelings have been understood.

> I was with a dying woman in a grim side room … it was large with peeling grey paint, a smeared window, a faulty bedside lamp, a dirty sink and a scuffed floor with torn tiles rising up through wear. I sat on a plastic chair, close to where the woman lay under a torn NHS

HORROR STORY

An old man was dying in a twenty-bed ward for the elderly. Throughout the day, all the other inhabitants were in the noisy day-room next door and his attendant family hoped he would die before they returned. He did not and, as the other patients came back to their beds for supper and television, the curtains around his bed were the only privacy. With 'Emmerdale Farm' within five feet on one side and boxing on the other, food trolleys being wheeled past and noisy conversation all around, this dignified old man died, fortunately unaware of the careless conditions in which he did so.

bedspread . . . For a while we spoke and wept together, and then I felt her die. I imagined her family on the way to that grim, shabby room . . . and I wanted them to picture her death in dignity and peace, not the pain and loneliness made sickening by the squalid room.

(Bob Mills (formerly an NHS nurse), 'Degree of sacrifice', the *Guardian*, 21 January 1998)

Surely most hospitals could provide a comfortable room, well decorated, with comfortable chairs and a side room for relatives to rest. Add a washbasin and, in the ideal world, a private bathroom, also the means to make drinks, access to the open air, even a little garden and something diverting such as pictures inside or a bird-table outside; like most cultural improvements the cost is minimal and the effect incalculable. In many towns the presence of a hospice shows what a difference this facility makes.

LIVING AND ACTIVITY AREAS

Day-rooms

Perhaps because life, death or recovery do not depend on day-rooms, the latter are often bleak and unattractive. Their use is often dominated by the 'smoking and non-smoking' issue; if the only day-room is also the only place in which smokers are permitted, the non-smokers have nowhere to go. If the day-room has a television, there are the problems of who controls it and selects programmes.

Day-room use has changed as the length of hospital stay has shortened and nowadays more people leave hospital before they are well enough to be walking about, but for some patients the opportunity to spend time away from the ward is important. If the only day-room is bleak, ugly, smoke-filled and dominated by television, many patients will avoid it, and so it becomes less important because it is little used.

Rooms for longer-term care

Day-rooms are obviously even more important for patients in longer-term care, the elderly in 'slow stream' rehabilitation, the mentally ill, people with severe learning difficulties and those needing long and complex treatment (Fig. 4.15).

Experiments have shown that elderly rats which are given a stimulating environment with 'toys' have a thicker brain cortex than those given a depleted environment. It seems a pity to have to rely on such experiments, on people or rats, to prove the beneficial nature of environmental stimulus, but such experiments command more respect than mere belief and common sense ('Rooms of the past strike a chord in the mentally infirm; design experiments at Powick Hospital, near Worcester'), article from *Geriatric Medicine*, July 1979).

WASHING AREAS

Apart from laundries that tend to be steamy, companionable places, all these ablutionary rooms tend to be small and should be pristine rather than tatty. The lobby for better toilet facilities for mothers and babies and the disabled has led to some improvement but pristine levels are not often allowed.

'Lavatory' versus 'toilet'

Few words are confused more often than 'lavatory' and 'toilet'; here we refer to a 'toilet' as the whole area with washbasins, nappy-changing area and so on besides the ceramic 'lavatory' itself. Some major stores have introduced 'Family Toilets' so that fathers with small daughters and mothers with small sons can accompany them.

Building and planning

1. Ascertain that this facility is permanently allocated to that place and not likely to be moved; then it is worth spending some money on good appointment and finish.

2. *The approach*. Apart from being clearly signposted using symbols as well as words – give the entrance some privacy, i.e. do not site the public telephone directly outside the women's toilets where men can loiter. If it can be within sight of staff, this helps, because voyeurism and attacks on women are not unknown in the 'Ladies' even if the fear is stronger than the likelihood.

3. *The entrance*. Avoid corners where voyeurs could loiter; a well-lit double door, easy to open to help those who have their hands full, with an inside arrangement of corners and angles so no one outside can see in.

Checklist

Fig. 4.15 'Before' and 'after' photographs of a day-room for elderly patients in a southern hospital. This room had its period elegance restored by utilising its fine architecture and restoring its dado rail and fireplace and giving it quality refurbishment. The Lloyd loom chairs were found in storage and were sprayed with fire-resistant paint. This excellent scheme was achieved by experienced interior designers working with a similarly experienced architect. Graylingwell Hospital, Chichester 1987

An experiment

A large day-room for the elderly infirm was subdivided into four smaller rooms and each was decorated and furnished with fabrics, colours and furniture as a small sitting room of a different period:

1. in the Victorian/Edwardian style
2. in the 1920–1930s' style
3. in the 1950s' style
4. as a usual hospital day-room.

Rooms 1 and 2 were least popular because they were both furthest from the lavatories and also because they were perhaps too 'posh'. Nevertheless, the very old patients became less passive, more active physically, and went around polishing the furniture surfaces, but their social behaviour remained withdrawn except for one factor: a chenille table-cloth had been spread on the table in the Victorian 'parlour' and this with the lace mats and some velvet cushions stimulated touch, thereby interest, therefore patient and visitor enthusiasm.

Room 3 was the most popular because the furniture, all bought second-hand from house clearance depots, was heavy, solid and the sort the patients knew. By hospital standards, the room was overfurnished and cluttered but there was a significant reduction in falls and accidents – despite there being hearth rugs and carpets with edges – because there was so much furniture to hang onto and dressers and trolleys with handles; familiar possible hazards were expected so avoided.

Room 4 remained unpopular with its fierce 'anti-hazard' blandness but an unexpected result of the whole scheme was the level of staff interest. As one nurse commented: 'Rather than just taking their temperature and feeding them, this experiment taught me to observe them with interest.'

4. Women will need to perform many small actions once inside for which space should be allowed. Imagine a near-term pregnant woman accompanied by a toddler and a collapsible push-chair and a bulging bag; she will need to:

- fold the push-chair
- get herself and child and luggage into cubicle
- use it as necessary and come out
- wash her hands and those of child
- dry them under hot-air machine (that hopefully has an 'OFF' mechanism) or on paper or fabric towels
- use a vending machine for towels or tissues
- change child's nappy
- dispose of items
- look in mirror/comb hair/powder nose etc.
- sit down to attend to child
- reassemble the push-chair.

If such a customer is not comfortable, the toilet is too small.

Incidents do happen in toilets; people miscarry, hang themselves, break down in tears, slip on the floor or lock themselves in. An obvious alarm whereby staff can be summoned is a comfort but an alarm system which looks like a light pull cord or is not clearly labelled is not only far from being a comfort but causes embarrassment and wasting of staff time.

Design and appointment

All these washing facilities do not usually have access to daylight; if they do have windows, these are likely to be frosted for privacy. To counter this, install bright (but not dazzling) lighting and 'decor charm'.

Decor charm can best be introduced with tiling: ceramic tile borders, patterns and pictures, mirror tiles and hologram tiles. These need not be expensive; some of the most sophisticated tiles rely on two-thirds plain and one-third decorative for their effect (see 'Tiling' in Chapter Seven and 'Chapter information' for suppliers). Such tiling needs to be well done, with fitting and grouting to a high order but, once done, it is highly durable.

Daily management

Some shopping superstores declare that 'These premises are checked every hour'. Whether or not this is the case, the statement evokes surveillance and provokes good behaviour. This with the alarm mentioned above are advisable.

One would assume that cleanliness is next not only to Godliness but to health, but too many hospitals leave waste bins overflowing, soap dispensers empty and floor corners dirty. A pity.

Bathrooms

All the points listed above pertain to bathrooms except that bathrooms are usually only available for 'in-care' patients so more nurses and fewer outsiders notice and use them. Privacy is an added element and this requirement is discussed in Chapter Seven, but shower curtains, folding screens and partition walls all help to provide this.

Baths

Of all places, for bathrooms the opinions and requirements of the nurses who use them should be heeded regarding arrangements and equipment. However, the belief that 'modernising' means throwing everything away needs to be questioned.

Many hospitals still have their original baths and we do not mean tin bath-tubs, hip-baths and baths that held the coal, but ordinary old-metal white-enamelled baths. These get stained over the years but they can be re-enamelled, given new taps, possibly have the old surround removed to disclose cast-iron decorative 'feet' underneath, and all at half the price of most new fibre-glass baths. Cheap versions such as fibre-glass baths give the sensation of bathing in a cardboard box, so steel baths still have the advantage. To retain the old baths and possibly basins in this way and give a new setting around them makes dramatic improvement at lowest cost. The greatest decor opportunity is usually tiling, well and decoratively done, but a mural can also fulfil a decorative need.

One 'has' a bath but 'takes' a shower

Showers were originally used in prisons and armies; then they were introduced in Europe at

SUCCESS STORY THAT TURNED TO HORROR

A designer was touring a ward for elderly women prior to redecoration. 'What', she asked the nursing sister, 'is your ladies' greatest problem?' 'Their bowels' was the reply and she was taken to the toilets, put inside and told to sit on the lavatory seat. 'Imagine you are there every day for an hour', the nurse called through the door, 'dreading an enema while looking at that tatty door. I would like proper provision of pictures on the inside of every lavatory door for my ladies' mental diversion.'

So, a framed section of coloured bulletin board, as large as possible, was fixed on the inside of each lavatory door and a varied pile of poster/pictures assembled with a bucket of coloured drawing pins to display them. By far the most popular picture was one from the SPCK of a kitten saying 'Jesus and I make a good team' but others had their devotees.

The horror was that a new nursing sister was appointed who hated the scheme, preferred to rely on enemas and had the bulletin boards torn off the doors so they reverted to their former state.

This suggests a failure of management in not insisting that a sensible scheme, once complete, should remain, but it also shows a lack of sympathy. Most of us can remember, perhaps in childhood or on foreign holidays, being nervous about going to a strange toilet or having an illness in which severe constipation or its opposite temporarily dominated our lives. Many patients have clinical reasons for feeling anxious about their trip to the toilet; making the area attractive and secure is important, not a design extra.

hydropathic establishments but, even until after the last war, showers and bidets tended to imply foreign practices to the cautious English.

It was the clean Americans who perfected the plumbing for the necessary water pressure and marketed showers.

> Showers have until very recently been a mainly male choice, tough and swift, forceful and athletic; women have tended to engage in longer, gentler grooming routines, which typically included 'bath-tub soaking' until, of course, the advent of the modern competitive, 'get up and go' woman whose image is used to sell shower fittings.
>
> (Margaret Visser, 'Taking a shower', *The Way We Are*, Viking, 1994)

In a hospital, showers are used to wash many people quickly, and to wash the elderly or disabled who cannot be lifted, but baths are for those who need or like peace and pleasure as well. Many people feel less concerned about infection when they use a shower, so both baths and showers should be provided.

PUBLIC AREAS FOR PRIVATE USE

Chapels

Many hospitals have lost their chapels which were often elaborate and demonstrated long and continuous use. The sectarianism of our age, the demands of other faiths and the loss and 'rationalisation' of premises have led to their closure. Accommodation for Sunday worship nowadays often has to double up with a space used for weekday lectures and evening aerobics.

The chaplaincy

Most hospitals will have a chaplain; in the care of several huge and scattered sites, ministering to members of an ever-shifting cross-section of a multifaith and atheist society in which people often have to face personal devastation with little spiritual preparation, such chaplaincy teams have often developed adaptability without compromising faith. The same could be done in those 'rooms reserved for worship' that have managed to survive.

Design and embellishment

Churches and chapels have for centuries accumulated a complex and unmistakable design language that for some represents essential comfort but for others is either irrelevant or alienating.

If your hospital has the luck to retain a good chapel, get it listed if possible; then no one can mess it about.

However, if you are given a bare room to share with other functions, consider creating a 'room within a room' which is a useful principle. Operating theatres have been developed and manufactured for battlefield surgery whereby a new, plasticised 'tent' can be installed within a barn or building of any sort, giving a sterile temporary interior. The principle of a new construction created within a large, older building has been used most famously by the Royal Exchange Theatre in Manchester where the huge Victorian bank is host to the hi-tech, modular theatre construction comfortably sited within.

In a similar way, a church environment can be created by putting screens around the walls, either solid and permanent or movable. This principle could be done with fabrics on screens and this would be the lightest and most impermanent scheme of all, but the richest and most dramatic version of the idea is to commission stained glass. Its success, as usual, would depend on the calibre of artist commissioned to undertake it and the sense of those commissioning it.

Mortuary viewing rooms

The principles that we have suggested in 'Interview and counselling rooms' and 'Rooms for death' also apply here.

People need the brief opportunity for privacy in which to meet their grief before going out to face the remainder of their daily lives once more.

STAFF AREAS

Changing rooms, rest rooms, bedrooms

Staff changing rooms are often bleak. Rows of metal lockers in industrial colours, depressing lighting and no view of the outside world because of the need for obscured glass are all the usually dominant features. If we care about staff morale, we want to make arrival at and departure from work a positive time. A visit to the nearest hotel leisure-centre changing rooms will give you ideas about how to create attractive rooms and necessary locker space.

ADMINISTRATION AREAS

General and personal offices

Checklist of requirements:

Checklist

1. A pleasant place to be: good decor and housekeeping
2. Opportunity to control heating, fresh air, lighting, noise, interruption
3. Personal convenience: clean and secure toilets, cloakrooms and kitchen
4. Professional convenience: good office facilities with both personal and general noticeboards and storage
5. Flexibility of premises: facilities for blackout, presentations, viewing videos, etc.
6. Items of visual interest and relaxation: works of art, use of views, etc.

STORAGE

One of the things which you notice about the NHS is the lack of storage. A walk from the entrance of any hospital down the corridor and past some wards and offices and you will see piles of empty containers, boxes of incontinence pads,

Multifaith provision

At Heathrow Airport there is a large 'Quiet Room' that provides for four faiths; one wall is dedicated to Christianity, one to Judaism, one for the Muslim faith and one for Hindus. It is a favourite room for many people and such a room treatment could be copied elsewhere.

stacks of equipment, papers piled on office floors and an assortment of items waiting to be put somewhere. Better use of flexible shelving systems using wall space, a maintenance system which can put up shelving without an interminable delay between request and result, and a helpful portering service could largely solve the problem.

IN CONCLUSION . . . HOW IT CAN BE DONE

We hope that this chapter, with its 'Horror' and 'Success' stories, will convince readers that the reasons why most hospitals are not as comfortable or as delightful as they reasonably could be is not necessarily because of lack of money but because of poor professional input and inadequate management response.

But within average, existing circumstances achieving comfort and excellence can be done and we suggest interior schemes are tackled in the following way:

- Convene a committee to meet each month from the inception of the proposal to its completion. Include the most senior manager responsible for the building, senior finance personnel and estates staff, also the architect and other technical staff. Invite to specific meetings those staff whose premises will be affected or who will be involved, such as cleaning and maintenance staff.
- Appoint an experienced designer.
- Offer designs suggestions, accompanied by architect's drawings and 'projections', full sets of samples, costings and other suggestions for incorporation of signposting, alarm boards, fire notices, etc., also pictures, displays, works of art, planters etc. to be presented to staff.
- Once accepted, the work is undertaken, completed and a scheme of frequent maintenance is initiated.
- Once complete, no alteration is permitted, such as Coca-Cola machines suddenly being installed, new notices put up, etc. Assessment from staff should be sought one year after completion when inevitable and initial resentment at the expenditure 'of all that money' has died away and outsider compliments may have encouraged acceptance and even pride in the scheme.

We discuss in more detail the appointment of professional design staff in Chapter Nine but we will leave the final word with that Lady of the Lamp: 'Oh, leave these jargons, and go straight to God's work, in simplicity and singleness of heart' (Florence Nightingale, *Notes on Nursing)*.

HORROR STORY: 'AN OFFICE SHOULD NOT BE TOO PERSONAL'

A hospital Ward Manager in a large psychiatric hospital had an office that was to be redecorated and he admitted that he wanted to keep several large photographs of tigers displayed on his walls. He and the interior designer had developed a rapport and she wished to please him. Rather than allow these pictures to continue to fall out of their tacky frames, they were reframed. The designer wrote to 'Esso' to ask for any further free tiger photographs, and they sent a generous bundle. The overall colour scheme was tawny, brown and brass and the noticeboards were covered with a cotton 'tiger' textured fabric. A tiger rug was bought and a tiger's eye was smartly painted to conceal the spyhole used to observe the adjacent ward.

Within two months of his office completion, this manager was unexpectedly transferred elsewhere. His successor hated tigers and the room was wrecked by semi-alteration. The designer had erred in that she had listened too closely to personal preferences, rather than appointing the office well but impersonally.

Interior features
From floors to furniture

CHAPTER
5

DOES INTERIOR DESIGN AFFECT SUCCESS?

Standards and 'statements'

Successful interiors are not accidental. Both in the world of the affluent where wealthy individuals live and the world of commerce where firms work, the design and quality of the surroundings display values which are felt, in each case, to be central to existence. The interiors of these public buildings are given careful attention and seen as an important means of promoting the substance, quality and aims of the organisation to which they belong.

Premises that are designed and restored, decorated, furnished and then maintained to a high standard declare that those in charge of them believe in certain values. Hotels, banks, good restaurants, stores, private hospitals, large corporations and galleries all seek to state their values and aims by the environment in which they greet and receive their public.

All these public premises represent a purpose – whether to make money or dispense it, attract audiences, clients or pupils – and aesthetic values are one of the ways in which those aims are stated and achieved. We wonder whether there is an example of success in whatever field that has ignored its premises? For well-appointed premises have to come first in order to attract success, not last when success might have earned the means to achieve it.

If we accept that a public building declares by the good quality of its premises that those in charge believe interior design is important and not simply an optional extra, then the reverse is also true: neglected premises imply a belief that such matters are not important. How does the NHS fare regarding this consideration?

The NHS and the 'plea of poverty'

The NHS appears to have a puritanical streak which suggests that money spent on environment is money wasted. This partly relates to the problems of stretching a finite budget to cover accelerating medical and social demands but there is perhaps something more. The NHS sometimes seems to imply that people should be grateful for what they are receiving and should not ask for more, which may be a legacy from its origins in post-war Britain. This attitude is almost a moral self-delusion akin to the wearing of a hair shirt.

The argument might go something along these lines: 'If we show that we are working in poor conditions, that we are concentrating all our resources on the care and treatment of patients, then the whole world can see that we are not wasting money on fripperies and that we still do not have enough resources to fulfil our role properly.'

In other words, there is almost a cult of shabbiness, of neglect of interiors and presentation, to reinforce the message that this is an over-stretched health service which cannot afford environmental quality.

We believe this 'cult' rests on an assumption that environment is not a part of direct care and that presentation and style are alien to the public sector. The plea of 'limited finance' is often an excuse rather than a reason; frequently we see substantial sums spent on interiors, furniture and equipment, but the design and co-ordination of these features fail to take into account aspects of suitability, endurance, surroundings, usage and so on.

Complex aims of the NHS

The aims of a bank, a theatre or even a palace are easy to define, but the aims of a health service are comparatively complex; hence its constant re-evaluation both politically, medically and socially.

We quote here the aim of the Health Service as it was described by our founding fathers who created it in post-war exuberance.

A comprehensive Health Service designed to secure improvement in the physical and mental health of the people of England and Wales and the prevention, diagnosis and treatment of illness and for that purpose to provide or secure the effective provision of services.

(From the 1946 National Health Service Act)

Exactly fifty years later, the assessment seems to be: 'The overall verdict in the NHS must be positive. It has achieved Aneurin Bevan's main aims, largely removing the fear that care during illness would be unavailable or unaffordable.'

(Geoffrey Rivett, *From Cradle to Grave: Fifty Years of the NHS*, King's Fund, 1998)

We suggest that to achieve the NHS's purpose fully, we need to look, not simply at the technology, not just at the training of staff, not only at the organisation of systems, but also at the presentation of the environment and its effect on those who encounter it.

This is not a simple study but a complex one; hence the length and detail of this book. But Chapters Three, Four and Five and the associated 'Information' section are those that deal most directly with the interior that surrounds us at each stage of a visit to an NHS building. Most of our examples refer to hospitals, but the points we make apply to all NHS buildings, such as health centres, clinics and surgeries.

Constructional components

The progression throughout this book reflects the diminishing scale of our subject. From looking at whole hospital sites, we travelled through the many departments from reception to the chapel and now we consider the floor upon which we walk, the ceilings that we may lie under and the walls we see.

In the subsequent chapters we shall consider the pictures we might examine, the door handles we turn, the bed into which we climb, the overhead lamp we turn on, the meal that we eat.

But these are all physical aspects of solid objects and our enquiry is how the average hospital handles them in order to present the ambience of delight that is conducive to recovery.

FLOORS

Construction

The floors in old buildings might be assumed to be extremely strong since they are often supported underneath by piers, usually of cast iron. In some ways this is true but it is an inflexible strength; any heavy weights put on them, such as a safe, have to be placed very exactly so the weight is concentrated and this can limit the use of the room.

Similarly, recent floors of the cheapest kind that consist of chipboard placed over underfloor supports can be so weak that even the pressure of high-heel shoes can damage them and vigorous physiotherapy or therapeutic dance is quite out of the question. Health authority rooms can experience frequent changes of use so you need to be aware of the weight-bearing capacity of a floor before deciding on its new purpose. The key message is that the floor is a critical factor which needs to be expertly assessed before plans are made to alter room use.

Floors can be found to conceal floors. For example, all Byron admirers know that Newstead Abbey, the poet's home and now a romantic Sunday outing destination, was once a monastic abbey.

The exact location and whereabouts of the abbey in relation to the eighteenth-century pile was a matter of uncertainty until one of the many rooms' floorboards were taken up for the repair of plumbing; directly underneath, the amazed plumbers looked down onto the tops of the medieval floriated pillar capitals still crowning their pillars, with the abbey floor itself far below. It appeared that the domestic home had been built on top of the old abbey.

Flooring materials

Many Victorian and Edwardian hospitals still have their original wood-plank floorboards, wood-block or terrazzo floors. Terrazzo floors may also still have a cast curve, a coved corner, joining the skirting board to the floor for ease of cleaning – old mops were large and inflexible compared to their modern plastic counterparts. Terrazzo floors are composed of subtly coloured marble and stone chips with a brass insert separating different areas of colour. Woodblock floors were frequently laid in a herringbone pattern and, if they have escaped damp, may be in good condition. Modern floors are usually chipboard or concrete, both of which are purely functional and require covering.

Upgrading period floors

It is an unfortunate aspect of much upgrading that overall carpeting is specified which involves the drilling and therefore destroying of these enduring floors. Before carpeting, which has a comparatively short life, and its cost are seriously considered, keep in mind that there is an alternative.

Old 'hard' floors can be cleaned with gentle soap and wire wool and this will often reveal the colour and burnish the inset brass while wood can be cleaned and then resealed. If this is still felt to be too harsh, carpets can be laid as if they were very large rugs with a double sided adhesive to hold them in place. This does not damage the floor and retains the sense of period and allows future flexibility.

FLOOR COVERINGS

Changing fashions

All floor coverings have evolved from the rushes and straw that were once the only barrier between unshod feet and a cold earthen or stone floor. Since then, various coverings have evolved and then experienced changes in fashion (like hairstyles and modes of transport) that depend not only on need and availability but also on perceived need and products looking for markets.

Original floors in hospitals were usually left alone until they started to get worn or people became tired of them. In the post-war 1950s and 1960s, the mood was to 'brighten up' hospitals and 'lino' (that was probably vinyl) was often installed. Carpet became popular in the 1970s and became almost universal in the 1980s, before the 1990s introduced a radical rethink. People discovered that carpet wore out and became smelly while financial constraints precluded easy replacement. In the meantime, the manufacturers

of floorcoverings other than carpet were working hard at manufacturing and marketing.

HARD FLOOR COVERINGS

These are all more hard-wearing than any carpet, are easier to clean thoroughly and last longer but they are also noisier, allowing clatter and echo, besides being colder and possibly harmful to anyone falling.

Terrazzo

Modern terrazzo floors have benefited from the new resins available in which the chips and chunks of marble and other coloured stones are set; this suspending agent is called the matrix and more usually it used to be cement. While the name 'terrazzo floor' evokes visions of fine Venetian floors that are a mosaic of alabaster and quartz gracing Italian palaces, modern floors can be made with a chemical matrix that is resistant to chemicals and abrasion. Floors with this resinous matrix are 'softer' than those that are cement-based.

People often ask for a 'tesserae' floor but what they mean is a 'terrazzo' floor; the little pieces of stone which compose it are the 'tesserae' although the word is more usually used in the context of a wall mosaic.

Ceramic tiles

These are simply clay tiles made of a thickness and fired to a hardness that makes them suitable for floors. They are virtually indestructible but are harsh. They need to be laid well with a suitably toned grouting cement.

Wooden floors

If you are lucky enough to have period floor-boards or woodblocks, cherish them and the worst thing that can be done (apart from drilling, gouging or scraping) is to put rubber-backed mats on them as the rubber 'attacks' the surface. Since wood is organic and continues to absorb oxygen and so darken, any mats or rugs will eventually show as pale squares on the floor; that is why dark timbering is associated with 'olde worlde' properties, and hence the range of wood stains (including 'Jacobean') developed to evoke such traditional qualities.

Modern woodblocks come in laminated sections, like large tiles, the individual pieces preassembled at the mill and with a variety of patterns and stains; they are a good option providing they are well laid and not subject to water or fluids as this makes the laminates split and pull away from the adhesives.

Cork tiles

Modern cork tiles are made from granulated cork and resin binders and, once laid, sealed either with wax or a synthetic 'skin'.

They present a sensible but unadventurous choice providing the cork is good quality (so it doesn't crumble), thick enough and beautifully laid; also, it should be treated well and not be subject to slops or damage.

Rubber tiles and sheeting

These can also simply be called 'resilient flooring' since they can be made of natural or synthetic rubber, the criteria is that they spring back to their original form when dented; in other words, they are soft to fall on and are used in areas where people are likely to fall, especially outside.

The disadvantages are that they are very restricted in colour (at the time of writing they are green or black) and are studded on the surface which makes them hard to clean. Hence, they are used outdoors. They are available in tiles or sheeting which is most usually seen in stations and public lavatories.

Linoleum: its origin, composition and qualities

'Linoleum' derives from the two Latin words for flax and oil and is made from natural ingredients which comprise linseed oil, pine resin, wood flour, cork, clay, chalk and natural pigments. These are then combined and pressed onto a canvass backing.

It was invented during the mid-nineteenth century by a Scottish paint manufacturer, Frederick Walton, who wrote in his autobiography:

There was a paint-pot in my room and, as is usual, a skin of dried oil had formed upon it. It occurred to me that I could use it as a water-proofing material . . . full of my imaginative impulse and really believing that I was in possession of something of importance, I said to

my Father, 'I intend to go to London and make my fortune'. He replied somewhat sarcastically, 'I suppose you think you may become Lord Mayor of London.'
(*The Infancy and Development of Linoleum Floorcloth by Its Inventor Frederick Walton*, published by Simpkin, Marshall, Hamilton, Kent and Co Ltd., date unknown but the Introduction was written in 1925 – Forbo-Nairn archives)

Fredrick Walton did not become Lord Mayor but he did make a modest fortune and his product is still manufactured .

During the last thirty years, linoleum has experienced a renaissance of design and marketing. To visit the main British factory which makes the stuff is to encounter huge vats of bubbling, coloured ingredients which gradually achieve the right degree of density before being decanted and rolled out, like pastry. Gradually hardening, these huge, continuous sheets are eventually cut into more handleable sections and are then 'cured' in drying ovens for a number of weeks before being chopped up into saleable rolls and tiles. They are then advertised, distributed and sold in order to render flat, beautiful and clean a hospital operating room or someone's kitchen floor. Like other organic materials, such as wood, it is not static but gradually hardens so, once laid, a floor become more durable with time.

Unfashionable 'lino' becomes fashionable 'linoleum'

Many people dislike what they call 'lino' because it is associated with unglamorous commerce and industry, with wartime canteens and cheap digs but they are probably remembering early brown vinyl that chipped and curled at the edges.

However, in the same way that wholemeal bread became popular in our health-conscious age after being for centuries the diet of peasants, so modern 'linoleum' is becoming fashionable and is now used by the National Trust and for the conservatories of the *nouveaux riches*. This may be due to its natural 'green' components, besides which it is durable and water-resistant, it does not melt and is resistant to cigarette burns, in a fire it does not give off hydrochloric gas and it is naturally bactericidal. Also, it is available in carefully researched and beautiful colours and colour combinations and it remains cheap.

Its historic uses are also intriguing and it has

Fig. 5.1 Two floors laid in linoleum to imitate a road. These floors, once laid, are extremely long-wearing. Material and design by Forbo-Nairn (see 'Chapter information').
The children's ward, St Mary's Hospital, Manchester, c.1990

had industrial besides domestic roles. Before the First World War, Admiral Jack Fisher of the Royal Navy (according to Jan Morris, his biographer) suggested covering the decks of warships with linoleum; while this was not done, there is some evidence that it was so used by some American warships. Nowadays, it is used in all manner of patterns, different colours interchanging, and it has been found to be suitable to be cut by laser and laid in designs that can make patterns as delicate as a drawn line (Fig. 5.1).

Vinyl: its properties and uses

Similarly vinyl is originally a viscous medium, this time a chemical man-made medium that is then set hard under pressure to form a washable and enduring floor cover. Its disadvantages are that it scuffs easily and melts with, for example, cigarette burns, and when it burns it emits toxic fumes.

It is appropriate to use vinyl for washing areas that need a non-slip surface and where small burns are less likely to happen, such as in bathrooms; and linoleum in larger living spaces. Both vinyl and linoleum are made in sheet form and tiles.

Sterile qualities

Both vinyl and linoleum can provide not only a clean but a sterile floor when the inevitable joins and edges have been bonded with welding cable

and sealant. In any area requiring constant dousing and bacterial control, such as operating theatres, recovery rooms, sterile units and so on, their use is invaluable. Both are also made in slip-resistant versions and both have a fine range of colours and textures. Once laid, they may need sealing, depending on expected wear.

Around the edges: skirting boards, sills and junctions

The quality of skirting boards and the way they meet the floor are also of importance, in terms of design, maintenance and cleanliness. There are products made of a cast-plasticised material that will allow linoleum or vinyl floor to blend into a curved, coved skirting board which permits ease of cleaning and such products are also extremely resistant to wear and tear from trolleys and feet.

Older hospitals often have plaster skirting boards painted in a dark colour or made of traditional hardwood or softwood. To insert hardwood skirting boards these days is prohibitively expensive but softwood skirting boards that are then varnished can be excellent.

Protection of lower walls from chairs, trolleys and so on can also be managed by introducing a wooden sill which many Edwardian hospitals used. This projected from the walls at skirting-board level and was rounded off so that it does not give a hard corner. It keeps all furniture away from the walls and is a good protection.

SOFT FLOOR COVERINGS

Uses of carpet

Carpets evolved for reasons of comfort and it is almost invariably believed that carpeting makes a place homely and welcoming. This is true when it is new and fresh and clean but it is not true when it is dirty and smelly which it can be even when comparatively new.

Since the floor covering of whatever sort in any hospital will be the most expensive part of an upgrading (apart from technical equipment), it is important to make the right decision in terms of practicality, looks and cost.

All carpets will eventually, some sooner than others, stain and wear and some will fade. It is simply the nature of the beast and there is no avoiding it. Some carpets incorporate a wire amongst the threads in order to encourage the mud to disattach itself from shoes and there are also various heavy-duty doormat-type products that can be used in entrance lobbies; these are 'the heavies' of the species and not for all-over use.

Other carpets are remarkably impervious to fading. One such product has been tested by leaving a sample in a bucket of pure bleach for a week and even then the colour was constant, although this particular product is likely to compact. Overall, there simply is no carpet that is impervious to cigarette burns and accelerated shabbiness from general wear. Certainly new carpets can make a hospital look homely, but a hospital is not a domestic environment; it is a public environment with particularly heavy and prolonged use and therefore needs to be treated differently from a private house.

For a description of the different sorts of carpet, see 'Chapter information', and before you decide to install carpet in your hospital, visit some similar premises that have had the product for a few years; note its condition and ask yourself if the equivalent is your aim.

Infestations and pollutants – 'Is it clean and does it smell?'

The dirtiest part of even a fastidious domestic room will probably be the carpet. Its pile, however made, will retain dust and a high proportion of domestic dust is composed of human skin scales. Microscopic wildlife lives in the dust comfortably lodged between the carpet fibres, partly because to them it is a tall forest of concealment; electromagnetic forces do the rest. Altogether, dust and what feeds on it are difficult to control, witness Mrs Ogmore-Pritchard in *Under Milk Wood*: 'And before you let the sun in, mind it wipes its shoes.'

Hospitals are supposed to be clean and this microscopic wildlife might well interfere with our expectation of cleanliness. So, of what does this microscopic wildlife consist? George Ordish in his book *The Living House* (Rupert Hart-Davies 1960) examines the entire population of a farmhouse from when it was built in 1556 to the present day and this includes the beetles, flies, moths, mites, lice, cockroaches, fleas, bugs, gnats, ants, wasps and mice that live as near-invisible partners to the humans. All these creatures have experienced changing fortune with modern heating and chemical defenestrations, but they all need privacy, which wall-to-wall carpeting provides, and water, which they can get from people. In the hot and crowded conditions of hospital environments, a human being gives off an amazing quantity of water per hour by quietly sweating; we are, after all, 75 per cent water.

All this is apart from excretory and other body fluids. Florence Nightingale writes: 'Of the fatal effects of the effluvia from the excreta it would seem unnecessary to speak, were they not so constantly neglected.' Then as now, it seems, so perhaps it might be better to have a floor that you can mop (see 'People as pollutants' in Chapter Eight).

WALLS

The 'packhorses of an interior'

Walls are the packhorses of any interior in that they carry everything; they bear the load of information and of services such as tannoy systems and loudspeakers, they carry the pipes for water, ducts for ventilation, wires for power and they shoulder the fluttering mass of notices, signs and exhortations with which hospital walls are inundated. Whether we lower our eyes in despair to the floor or raise them as we must when on a trolley or in a bed, the walls and ceilings are what most of us will usually see. Are they worth looking at?

Construction and durability

Walls are either constructional, weight-bearing and solid or merely a partition, usually of stud and

Fig. 5.2 Staircase in an Edwardian building, home for severely mentally handicapped men. Wallpapers and borders are used on the ceiling, the original plaster indent at dado height is dark-painted with one colour above and another below. Bannister rails are re-stained, linoleum stair treads treated with new nosings, a picture at the stair-head is in a secure frame, all combined by an interior designer who worked with staff to understand the clients' needs. 1993

plasterboard. Pre-war hospitals were plastered with hard and enduring plaster, moulded around junctions and corners and fashioned into cornices. Such walls often had an 'indent' in the plaster at about dado rail height and this can be used decoratively (Fig. 5.2). More recent buildings usually have a skim of more powdery, soft plaster, all junctions are simple right angles and resistance to wear is usually poor.

Modern stud walls of plasterboard cannot easily conceal the strips that blend the board junctions; modern plasterwork is thin and has to be dried quickly so shrinkage is considerable; gaps appear and tend to stay forever. Prefabricated walls of plastic-covered material do not even try to conceal their junctions.

Protection of walls

Traditionally, coloured and decorative tiling was used to protect the walls in many public buildings, such as swimming baths and hospitals. Today as before, the decor of any walls has to take into account the punishment the walls will receive.

One Dutch hospital made sure that all trolleys were of the same height and then they simply painted a long, dark-coloured, continuous stripe on the walls throughout the hospital that was of a height to receive the bumps. This stripe was all they needed to repaint or touch up so the walls remained smart.

Alternatively, there are excellent barriers either in hardwood or in coloured cast material over an aluminium base, and corner guards are available

as well. Guarding barriers do not have to be the usual dull aluminium strip. They have been researched and manufactured to take punishing treatment and are made in excellent colours. These can be co-ordinated with skirting boards and flooring to create a united interior. This, however, is seldom done. The ceilings, walls and floors are often treated with different materials by different people and at different times, giving the impression that those in charge care little about appearances (Fig. 5.3).

CEILINGS

Ceilings represent promising space which can be used imaginatively. They are also a large surface that is out of reach and can be painted or wallpapered with a good chance of remaining undamaged. However, many hospital staff think of a ceiling only as the top of a room and not as an indicator of style or as a space with design possibilities (Figs 5.4 and 5.5).

Lowering ceilings: aesthetic and practical considerations

The height of ceilings and their space and proportion in relationship to the room are indicative of the period of the building, whatever that might be.

During the 1980s there was a fashion to lower ceilings in older, pre-war buildings. There were two reasons for this, one being that services (wires, conduits and so on) could be concealed

Fig. 5.3 Two corridors in a modern hospital where the floors, colours, wall barriers and signage are thoughtfully combined. c.1990

Fig. 5.4 'Oak Ward' in an Edwardian building. The oak-patterned Sanderson wallpaper has been kept clear of the 'coved' ceiling (a curve joining the wall and ceiling) and an imitation stained-glass light shade and long-life bulb have replaced the former fluorescent strip light. 1992

Fig. 5.5 Ceiling in a secure male ward in a northern special hospital; the double lighting circuit allows for domestic and emergency lights, but even secure light-fittings can look like a hotel when combined with Designers' Guild wallpaper and curtain fabric. 1993

above it and were easily accessible, as in modern suspended ceilings that are built with this intention.

The second reason was to save heat because heat rises and is therefore wasted, although often you find these suspended ceilings are only eight or so inches below the original one. This short-sighted attempt at modernisation often cancels out architectural character. If there is a genuine problem with heat rising, single-shaft fans can direct it down again for the benefit of those who need it.

WALLPAPER

Its 'pros and cons'

Most basic wallpaper is vulnerable to damage and expensive to replace but the design input that the major firms have made with wallpaper and borders tempts designers to use it; it is also popular with many staff who feel it domesticises premises. Wallpaper can be used effectively, but care and knowledge are needed.

The best use is to apply wallpaper on ceilings and high walls where it is out of reach and this gives a room or area the sense of a rich 'lid'. Wallpaper borders can also be used inventively to give a hint of domestic richness. The observant Reverend Sidney Smith (1771–1845) wrote from his Scottish rectory, 'No cornices that gather dust, just a wallpaper strip and 'tis so cheap.'

Wallpaper in general should be used where the public are unlikely to have the inclination to damage it, such as in the mortuary, or in a super-vised area. Hospitals tend to be hot and dry and therefore wallpapers peel off the walls easily, so they should be used with a strong paste.

Wallpapers are now available that are not paper at all but a plastic compound that is virtually scratch-proof; these are used extensively in public buildings but so far the quality of design has not kept pace with the quality of technology.

PAINT

Coloured pigment has traditionally been sus-pended in either a water base (water-based paints) that dries quickly by evaporation or an oil base (oil-based paints) that dries slowly by oxygenation.

The cave paintings were basically made from the surrounding earth-pigments suspended in water in much the same way that simple paint washes using local soil were used for centuries on vernacular architecture; a little bit of animal grease may also have been used. Some pigments have become obsolete (such as lead white or a purple-brown that was made from decomposed animal brains) and pigments are no longer suspended in wax or egg yolks as they have been at different times. Paint has developed dramatically over the last forty years, experiencing transformation in its ingredients, manufacture, its marketing, usage, and its colour coding and identification.

Ingredients and manufacture

Modern acrylic water-based paints are not like traditional distempers, whitewashes and lime-washes where dry pigment and other basic (usually organic) ingredients were simply mixed with water; instead, a pigment fragment is wrapped in a synthetic, latex molecule that is then dispersed in water to form a water-based emul-sion. This means that once painted onto a wall, the emulsion forms an enduring, waterproof, synthetic 'skin' and this is the basis of 'acrylic' paint.

Paint application

Acrylic paint was first produced in the 1950s for external house painting in Alaska for navigational aid, useful because the bright colours were quick and easy to apply in the arctic atmosphere. It is bright, malleable and enduring and is suitable for outdoor use. Like many developments made for one specific use, the extent of its wide applic-ability only gradually became apparent.

While acrylic paint is hard-wearing it is also inflexible in that it does not 'breathe' like the old water-based distemper or whitewash-type paints; neither oxygen nor damp nor insects can penetrate it. If damp penetrates the wall from underneath one of these modern paints, it pushes the paint off the wall and you see big blister-type bubbles. Old house walls contained a high percentage of water and were customarily redistempered each year to get rid of damp patches. But house damp has been largely con-quered during the late twentieth century and paint has altered accordingly.

Paint varieties

Paint research and development has become a major industry and paint categories have been extended by these new acrylic paints which include undercoat, gloss, eggshell and all the primers but are water-based and dry by evaporation. Oil-based undercoat, gloss and satinwood are still widely available, as any DIY shop shows, but acrylic alternatives offer advantages which a professional estates department will understand.

Paint ranges now also include non-drip gel paints, exterior paints for masonry, anti-porosity and alkali-resisting primers, 'multicolour' paints, floor and radiator paints, primers and paints for metal and plastic and the 'fleck and tone' finishes used to disguise shabby walls. Fire-resistant paints are also available, even in aerosol form, and Dulux do a range of non-allergic paints for patients with a high allergic reaction.

Hospitals rely upon effective redecoration because they receive heavy wear daily. All these paints have their appropriate uses. Coloured wood stains can be used to perk up woodwork but they are prone to fade unless covered with a varnish, which is either oil- or polyurethane-based and blocks the light from the pigment. Aerosol 'spray-on' paints and enamels can be used on top of any paint once it is dry and form a thin, hard, shiny surface film (like car bodywork); they are usually used for decorative effects. Stencilling has become a popular decorative paint finish in recent years but is fairly expensive to have done well, and messy and unsatisfactory if done badly.

There is a constant stream of new paints and finishes, which are the outcome of intensive chemical development and industrial expansion. But however sophisticated the paint, however appropriate and lovely the colour, it will not look attractive when dirty or chipped; as much thought should go into planning the maintenance of a paint scheme as goes into the selection of paint.

FABRICS

Technical and design evolution

Fabrics have evolved from the prehistoric realisation that warp and weft weaving (fibres interwoven at right angles and copied from basket and hurdle weaving) could form material, to the iridescent, plastic fibres made by extrusion but still woven on the same 'warp and weft' principle for modern needs. Some fabrics are knitted or plaited but the only fabrics that depart from the principle of the basic, single thread are those developed for the space industry: they are not woven but are basically a man-made dollop of viscous material rolled out thin (like pastry) to form a 'fabric'. This 'rolling out' is done on the principle of centrifugal force so that even this minimal thickness is scrupulously even.

Furnishing fabrics are in a sense related to tapestries which evolved in medieval times as large pictures that also usefully kept out drafts. They were available only to the wealthiest but furnishing fabrics of quality should be affordable to the most constrained health authority.

Curtaining fabrics offer one of the greatest opportunities for decorative 'delight' in an interior since they often occupy many square metres of space and are therefore visually powerful. Their selection in 'design' terms is therefore especially important. The design of fabrics has in itself a long history and when the NHS was founded, the eminent designer Marianne Straub (who had designed Utility fabrics) was commissioned to produce woven fabrics for curtains and counterpanes (Fig. 5.6).

DOORS

Barbara Woodhouse's great maxim was that 'there are no bad dogs, only bad owners'. So we similarly suggest that there are no bad doors but only abused doors, elderly doors, inappropriately placed doors or neglected doors (Fig. 5.7). Whether a door is the highly technological access hatch to the latest space shuttle or a pair of swinging plastic sheets in the corridor leading to a hospital theatre, its job is obvious: let people through and then close nicely. Hospices demonstrate that doors need not be noisy and their quality of door-stops should be emulated everywhere.

The things that happen to doors

Specialist doors to, for example, a sterile area are maintained because this is mandatory. It is general, non-specific doors that are allowed to have things happen to them; they squeak, bang and get notices and pieces of chewing gum stuck onto them. The likely scenario is then as described in the 'Horror story'.

Fig. 5.6 There have been surprisingly few fabric design commissions made within the NHS; fabrics are bought from existing ranges but an exception is this cubicle fabric commissioned in three colourways by Sian Tucker after a competition in 1991 run by 'Healing Arts', Isle of Wight Healthcare Trust.

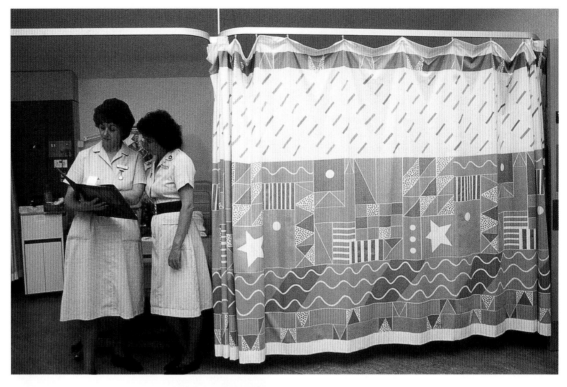

Fig. 5.7 Shabby doors covered in notices lead to a large hospital dining room.

WINDOWS

'The wind's eye'

> Windows are made to open; doors are made to shut – a truth which seems extremely difficult of apprehension.
>
> (Florence Nightingale)

Florence Nightingale wrote her inimitable *Notes on Nursing* before the introduction of air conditioning and well before this was found to be not the panacea once expected. But people, sick or well, still require that 'The air they breathe should be as pure as the external air without being chilling'.

Hospital windows have security implications (who can climb in?), safety implications (who can fall out?) and danger implications (who can decapitate themselves on this window edge if it is open?). They also have associations with human contentment since the 'Sick Building Syndrome' studies have shown that people, hardly surprisingly, like to be able to control air, temperature and light.

Windows also have organisational implications since one department is often responsible for cleaning the inside and another the outside. Window cleaning is one economy often made that is immediately depressing to everyone (Fig. 5.8).

Transparent glass windows are for unimpeded sight; translucent windows for light alone and darkened glass for obscurity. How these are used is the concern of staff but how to achieve them is described in 'Chapter information'.

Window dressing

The dressing of windows, introducing what our grandmothers called 'drapes', is one of the main decorative opportunities in any interior. The selection of design cannot be left just to individual preference but has to take other factors into account – will it work? will this design rather than that one combine visually the strawberry-coloured

Fig. 5.8 This broken window was adjacent to the hospital mortuary viewing room.

upholstered chairs with the terracotta-coloured ceramic wall panel? and so on. It is remarkably easy to get it 'wrong' when combining a colour, texture and pattern; a professional designer will get it 'right'.

FURNITURE

Furnishings of the 1940s

When the NHS was set up in 1948, it equipped its hospitals with basic furnishings such as bentwood and Lloyd Loom chairs and cast-iron bedsteads. The fabric designer Marianne Straub (who had earlier designed Utility fabrics) said in one of her lectures that she was commissioned to design woven fabrics for cubicle curtains, blankets and so on and, while there was little variety, everything was of solid, rather Puritanical but enduring design quality, similar to Utility products.

Then the Scandinavian influences of the 1950s, the psychedelic phase of the 1960s, the Habitat/Mellor creations of the 1970s, the hi-tech

adventurism of the 1980s and muddle of the 1990s all eroded this solid start; there were bonfires of those boring chairs just before they returned to fashion and arrived in auction rooms and antique shops bearing high price tickets. The iron bedsteads and quantities of enamel equipment were sent to war zones or sold to developing countries, departing in fleets of vast pantechnicon lorries from hospitals being closed or reconstituted. Disposable products became fashionable before they were found to be costly and environmentally unfriendly by which time the white-and-blue enamel buckets and vomit bowls had gone for ever.

The problem of cost

We suggest that, apart from the many specific needs for specialist furniture such as physiotherapy beds, beds for burn victims and birthing and so on, furniture can usually be retained and used creatively. The best-known example developed specifically for hospital use was the 'King's Fund bed' of the 1960s which replaced the simple iron bedsteads that had been the staple version since the nineteenth century. Obviously, items need to be increased for higher patient numbers and furniture wears out, but money is wasted frequently on replacing furniture when knowledgeable redecoration and reuse would be a better solution.

Furniture represents a major investment and hospitals of any size have quantities of the stuff. But it is often poorly organised so that chairs, tables and so on that have been bought in sets have been split up and distributed in a haphazard manner everywhere.

An 'audit'

It makes sound financial and design sense to commission an audit of all furniture throughout a hospital or clinic premises and ask for professional recommendations on its care, restoration,

HORROR STORY

Someone wedges a door open with a piece of old cardboard which holds it half open so that trolleys bang into it on every journey. Eventually, a new rubber door-stop is introduced by the people in the office opposite because they cannot stand the noise, but the door is then designated a fire door that has to remain shut so this is removed. Since its 'shut' state renders life intolerable for busy staff, it is soon propped half open again with another piece of old cardboard.

grouping and uses. However, this has to be a professionally planned total audit because one of a set of Thonet chairs could be lurking in the pharmacy and another in the finance department while the associated hat stand is a door prop for physiotherapy.

Such an audit needs photographs of the furniture to enable items to be identified and matched. Once such an audit is completed and its recommendations prepared from its findings, the next step is to implement it properly and maintain the result. Again, this calls for committed and intelligent management, prepared to show concern and to control the issue by initiating the employment of someone who is a design specialist.

FIXTURES AND FITTINGS

This is a wide term covering anything that is fixed to a surface:

- *mandatory items* such as fire extinguishers and hydrants, exit and fire signs, lights, door closers, switches, alarms
- *organisational items* such as signs and directions, noticeboards, doormats, leaflet racks
- *cultural items* such as fireplaces, mirrors, tiles, planters, pictures, fish-tanks, display cabinets, mobiles

Discussion of all these items can be found from the Index as they are scattered throughout this book but two of the above belong here, noticeboards and fireplaces.

NOTICEBOARDS

When you see a newly upgraded interior with small noticeboards, neatly framed and placed within an area of virgin wall, you can be sure that the specifier has no understanding of the

Fig. 5.9 A typical notice board in a public corridor.

whirly-gig freneticism of hospital activity. Staff are compelled by necessity and habit to put up notices about everything everywhere: instructions, exhortations, reminders, warnings, advertisements and all in different languages. Nothing is ever taken down, only more and more pieces of paper are added to the overflowing board, onto the walls and down the corridors like the flood that the sorcerer's apprentice was powerless to halt (Fig. 5.9).

Average humans can consciously absorb and retain about seven pieces of information, and this means seven notices. But we each need a different seven so seventy staff could need seventy times seven. But who stems the seventy times seventy times seven?

The solution

The first step is to ask staff their requirements and also observe them working to see exactly where they need noticeboards. The second is to supply larger boards than you think are possibly needed; introduce huge boards, from ceiling to three feet from the ground, corner to corner on specified walls, dividing them with clearly printed headings into the main areas needed. There must be a clear heading on each board requiring all notices to be dated and originator's name to be on each

---

An example of control

'This board is for all staff who work on G floor. Mrs Jenny Smith (internal phone 1234) checks the board weekly. Any notice which does not have the date, name and internal telephone number of the originator will be removed at the weekly checks. In general, notices will be taken down after one month; please contact Mrs Smith if your notice needs to remain up for longer than a month.'

Fig. 5.10 A poorly handwritten notice.

fluttering piece of paper, with the local policy on length of time displayed, and the name of the person who is in charge of 'policing' the scheme. Small boards near desks are also always needed as well as on those doors that clearly require them.

The third stage is to appoint someone to check each day that nothing whatever is stuck up anywhere else, not on windows, lift interiors, chair-backs, anywhere. Undisciplined notices that are handwritten and amateurish are one of the most disfiguring aspects of NHS premises (Fig. 5.10).

During the third stage it will be necessary regularly to patrol the walls and doors, to remove any unauthorised notices and make it clear to the originator that such 'wandering' notices are against the rules.

This degree of control is rarely found. Chaotic noticeboards and odd, hand-written notices contribute nothing to communication and give a poor image of the NHS.

FIREPLACES

Enduring popularity

It may seem that fireplaces are an issue only in old buildings that were built when fireplaces were still a necessity. However, a hospital interior designer is most frequently asked for four things: a camomile lawn and a water feature (see Chapter Two), curtain poles (see 'Windows' above) and fireplaces. These four features all suggest traditional values and the immutability of long-established houses and gardens (we would refer readers back to Chapter One in which we analysed the popular 'aesthetic' of historic houses, castles and gardens).

The hearth has traditionally been the centre of the family. Indeed:

> the Latin word for 'fireplace' is *focus* . . . A modern fireplace usually has a square opening but originally, and still important for its meaning, the hearth was circular. Round and quintessentially female, it contained fire, a masculine element.
>
> Olympic flames and the fire of the Unknown Soldier are other participants in hearth symbolism: continuity with the past and remembrance of the dead. We still put photographs of dead relatives on the mantelpiece. A Yule log that once burned in the hearth to mark the twelve days of Christmas was always lit with a brand saved from last year's log.
>
> (Margaret Visser, 'The fireplace', *The Way We Are*, Viking, 1994)

Fireplace simulations

We are not suggesting that anyone today would tolerate the inconvenience and uncertain safety of open fires or stoves in public buildings, but their mere visual suggestion may be all that is required.

'Flicker fires'

In any hospital where a domestic and homely environment is intended, the installation of a substantial fireplace with an electric 'flicker fire' and all the accoutrements of the fireside – armchairs and magazines, photographs on the mantelpiece – will prove calming and 'focus' the aimless wandering characteristics of many long-term, distressed or disturbed patients.

Fire videos

A continuous video of a fire can be popular, played on a television neatly set into the fireplace. It can show a fire being lit, burning with different sorts of fuel – brightly with twigs, smokily with wet leaves; also the process of burning logs crumbling away, then the fire damped down with coal dust, flaring with crumpled paper, being stirred and poked, before being allowed to die down and go out.

LIGHTING

Florence Nightingale and her symbolic lamp

In the Crimea War pre-electricity days, that lamp was symbolic of healing in a violent world. Even nowadays, during natural storms or civil conflict, power for hospitals is covered by emergency generators and is the priority for repair. It is not only necessary but an emblem of civilised care.

Lighting for public buildings has developed range and improved quality greatly during the 1980s and 1990s. It may therefore not be surprising that, of all the interior aspects we discuss, lighting is the most technical so that the means of achieving appropriate quality can only be achieved by a specialist, to whom staff should explain their requirements clearly and in detail.

Even more than most technical jargon, the terminology of lighting is not obvious to the lay person; 'decorative luminaries' are table lamps, 'compact source luminaries' are square fittings, and so on. Hospital lighting is not just a matter of ensuring that all those staff working in the various hospital components enjoy 'optimum seeing' conditions, but also important are the associations of light and mood, and the need for individuals to be able to control lighting levels.

Natural light

Most hospital designs utilise daylight with the use of large windows and skylights, clerestory windows and so on. Skylights should have clear glass whenever possible; the sudden sight of clouds floating by through an until then unnoticed small high window can banish claustrophobia and lighten mood in the way that contact with the natural world is believed to do (see Chapter Two). The effects of daylight on emotional well-being seem to be well enough documented to make it worthwhile installing full spectrum 'daylight' in a number of patient areas.

The interaction of natural and electric light is not a simple process of adding more, but of control and quality. People's eyes adapt differently on coming in from a dark night to a lit hospital foyer than on coming in during a sunny day, and lighting quality and intensity need to take account of this.

Domestic and personal light

Road lighting, heat-activated security lighting and bollard lighting outside, together with down-lighters and diffused lighters inside are all now an expected part of a hospital environment, and the situation when a hospital light had only two states, working or broken, really has been superseded by better standards.

But simple requirements remain important and are still not always met. For example, a bed-side reading light that can be controlled by a patient and which is angled so it does not shine in the eyes of the person opposite is imperative for comfort. There is some evidence to suggest that nightmares and phantasmagoria are more likely under a ceiling that is even slightly illuminated than one that is dark, so the opportunity to provide a fully darkened ceiling is advisable. The 'hum' that characterised fluorescent tube lights was perhaps not troublesome to busy staff but was so to bed-bound patients. Nowadays this can be muted.

There is little use yet in the NHS for energy-efficient, long-life bulbs or for 'dimmer switches' although there are strong pressures for energy conservation so this situation may be changing.

SUCCESS STORY

A ward for mentally disabled men was being upgraded. The lights on the high ceiling were fluorescent strips which, since many of the patients were so severely disabled that they spent much time lying on mattresses looking up, were not a 'comfortable' form of lighting for them.

The new scheme of decor included clear-patterned wallpapers on these high, Edwardian ceilings and the beams and cornices were repainted and repaired. The lights were replaced with ordinary cable and bulbs inside the largest size of simple round wire and paper lightshades. Since the ward was warm and hot air rises, these large white spheres gently swung against their coloured ceiling and the patients gave every indication of pleasure at their new 'view'.

It should be mentioned that these paper lampshades were treated with Environgraf 321 (see 'Fire' in 'Chapter Seven information') as they are not normally permitted in public buildings. This scheme was extremely cheap and only required nursing and technical staff to accept a novel way of handling the matter.

Emergency and clinical light

There is always separate tracking for emergency and 'stand-by' power sources (hence suspended ceilings) and clinical light is highly specialised; its quality is important for patient diagnosis regarding skin and tongue colour and the whites of the eyes. The light needed in the mortuary is different from that in the viewing room (where gentle, often rose-coloured light is used); the light needed for labour is nowadays muted as soon as the baby emerges so as not to dazzle or frighten it. All these issues are best dealt with by medical staff communicating with lighting staff.

SNOEZELEN ROOMS

This name is a composite of the two Dutch words for 'sniff' and 'doze' and is used as its trademark and also as its 'logo'. It was developed in Holland and consists of a system of lights that are programmed to gently move and change throughout a room's interior; it is intended to relax and calm those who are agitated, whether because of mental illness, learning disability or behavioural problems. Soft flooring, bean-bag chairs and music tapes are usually installed as well and patients can spend up to an hour in a 'Snoezelen'.

It originated with the realisation that, for some patients, their world depends on the primary sensations of sight, touch and smell and the environment we usually offer them does not particularly help them. In many wards the only visual stimulation is television and the content of most television programmes must be far beyond the comprehension of many patients and may add to their sense of confusion.

A Snoezelen can be installed in a small hospital room or community building and its effect is generally found to be helpful. They can be part of an overall 'sensory' development scheme which can include a jacuzzi, a sitting and quiet room, a 'touch' corridor and a white room, using paint and white light for deep relaxation. Like many imaginative developments, such a scheme is not as expensive as you might think, and it can be a good focus for fundraising or trust-fund expenditure.

SERVICES

These include all the wires, cables and conduits, trunking and boxed pipes, alarms, smoke detectors, loudspeakers for tannoy systems, display screens, key boxes, switches and activating buttons that characterise any public building but especially hospitals. They are installed according to necessary regulations but unless the manner of their installation, placing and grouping is carefully thought out, they can dominate appearances.

In new buildings architects usually design access systems for internal services, but in old buildings it is a challenge to make changes without creating a muddle of pipes, cables and gouged-out surfaces.

Camouflage and concealment

When it is necessary to put in a new lighting cable and switch, it costs far more to chisel out the plaster, sink the wire then repair the wall than it does to lay a surface conduit casing on the surface. It is the placing of this conduit that makes it apparent or not apparent, and subtly placed with the area painted appropriately, it can all but disappear. Placed insensitively, it can be a visual irritant in every way possible and imply that while the NHS is understandably not prepared to spend too much money on its interiors, it is not prepared to take the trouble either. Surface wiring can be encased in circular tubing that is painted in bright colours, so making a virtue of necessity, and this can look fine on a brick or breeze-block wall. This demonstrates the need for a clear understanding between the design team and maintenance staff.

A virtue of necessity

Clever concealment and camouflage are not the only option, and an alternative is to emulate architects such as Richard Rogers of the Pompidou Centre in Paris where all the services are used in a way that is overwhelmingly obvious; they are actually presented as part of the structure itself and all of the cabling, pipes and so on are defined in bright colours and aligned in joyous display on the surface; to an extent this approach has been used at the new St Mary's Hospital on the Isle of Wight. It is the completely opposite approach from camouflaging everything, but either way needs to be done consistently and well.

CONCLUSION

Paint, wallpaper, linoleum, noticeboards, curtains, lockers, these are such mundane things and yet this is the 'face' of the NHS which its public sees. Behind the too frequent façade of chipped paint, torn wallpaper, stained carpet, chaotic notice-boards, skimped curtaining and clumsy lockers, there may be clinical excellence that represents high-level strategic thinking, long-term planning, corporate governance, admirable control of finances and successful attainment of charter standards. But these are invisible: the public makes its initial judgement on what it sees.

But the public are generally tolerant and judgement is also made on the total hospital experience; and this is usually good and sometimes excellent. The NHS is not expected to offer aesthetic delight, and the public contribute excuses such as, 'The local hospital is very run down and the bathrooms were pretty awful but the staff were doing their best.' They also respond with delight when aesthetic delight is achieved, but all too often this is only thought possible when premises are newly built or expensively refurbished.

It is a paradox that many staff choose to live in older, period houses; they lavish care on them to make them pleasant to live in, preserve the features which give them their charm, and spend part of their leisure time visiting the nation's finest old buildings. And yet they accept that their NHS premises lack charm and appear neglected, because they leave their aesthetic senses at home.

This may be partly because the NHS system has defeated them. It is remarkably difficult to get small maintenance tasks done in many NHS organisations and perhaps people just give up the struggle; it may also be because there is a constant raid on those budgets which could contribute to delight so that trusts have millions of pounds' worth of backlog maintenance work, sacrificed annually to other more pressing demands.

Such neglect may be tacitly endorsed because no one in the hierarchy thinks these issues of 'comfort' and 'delight' are important; no one sufficiently senior recognises that 'the aesthetic' requires sustained top-management attention and support. No one with power apparently recognises that there are specialist skills which make delight possible and that well-intentioned amateurs asked to select any aspect of the environment are simply ill-equipped to even understand the issues, let alone solve them.

These people who work for the NHS claim to care about the general public besides patients and staff, but hospital premises often fail to show it. Central to the commitment to provide a quality health service should be an undertaking to manage health premises so that care is visible in our hospital buildings. Sustained, responsible management attention to bringing in the design expertise to co-ordinate the many small details which together achieve human comfort and delight is a central part of the responsibility of those who run the NHS's complex services. Where there is co-ordinated, top-management-supported care for comfort and delight the heart lifts, confidence grows and people feel cared for.

However, there are so many pressures nowadays in the health service that it requires real leadership to insist that high-quality design is an essential feature worth investment and experts. It also requires leadership to achieve the culture change necessary in many of our NHS organisations. We hope this book will help in a practical way to show that those management skills of clear purpose, seeking out expert advice, realistic planning with appropriate involvement of staff, rigorous implementation and disciplined maintenance and monitoring, work just as powerfully where your purpose is 'delight' as they do to achieve those many other objectives.

CHAPTERS THREE/FOUR/FIVE
INFORMATION
Products and materials
Information and availability

The three preceding chapters were about the closely related topics of interior features and components, what comprises them and makes them both comfortable and delightful.

This section could easily have become a complete 'manual' for any hospital's purchasing department, but that is not our purpose so we have limited this 'Information' section in the following way.

Items that are purely functional and have little inherent opportunity for design inventiveness have been omitted; an area of cork tiling or a metre of trunking cable offer little visual scope and items such as sanitary ware and light-fittings, while they have considerable design potential, are best selected from the plethora of catalogues available on site. Our aim is to give information on items with visual potential and technical data is only included when it relates to this.

LOCAL AND NATIONAL AVAILABILITY

It takes time to compile a reference library of samples designed for public use, so how is this done?

Some items for hospital redecoration are best bought from one of the national NHS contract suppliers and some from the local stores. Items of which you need a vast amount, like carpeting, or numerically many, like pillow cases, or where there are intrinsic safety regulations, like light-fittings, all these are best bought from national NHS contract suppliers. They will sell by trade prices, not retail, which makes high-quality goods affordable. Their goods will be of the required safety levels and should offer a warranty system. They will also

have area representatives who advise on installation, maintenance and contractors.

Local outlets vary enormously but small items of which you need a comparative few, like plant holders or picture frames, may be a significant order to a local supplier so always ask for a discount; 10 per cent is an absolute minimum. Even Christmas decorations can be bought cheap if the vendor had a granny well cared for in your hospital, so always take professional identification when shopping. Helpful vendors can benefit from any local publicity your upgrading efforts may attract so remember to include them and next time you might get a 20 per cent discount.

Paint is a material in constant demand and there are many paint retailers so it is usually bought locally; select a well-established firm which is used to selling to the public sector and will operate a discount scheme.

HOW TO FIND LOCAL AND NATIONAL SUPPLIERS OF PRODUCTS AND MATERIALS

Annually there are several large 'fairs' for the interior and hospital industries. These are held in Birmingham at the National Exhibition Centre and in London at Earls Court, Alexandra Palace and Syon Park. Important contacts with manufacturers, suppliers and their representatives can be made at these.

A full set of magazines relating to all aspects of hospital care will be in any good hospital management library. Library computer searches will find the most up-to-date information. The national library set of magazines is at King's Fund Library (see 'Chapter One information'). Manufacturers advertise in them and there are often related articles on the use of such goods in publications such as *Hospital Development*.

Another method of gathering such information is to ask the relevant staff at other hospitals.

Finally, scan the press and magazines and keep a scrapbook because the data you need will be there in 'short print-life' publications and not in any book.

CRITERIA FOR SELECTION

There are a great many manufacturers of specialist flooring, furniture, fabric, paint and wallpaper and we have not tried to list them comprehensively. Trade fairs, catalogues and computer searches will give the most up-to-date information. Where we mention a specific supplier it is because they fulfil three criteria:

- they present consistently high standards of design
- their price range falls within the expectation of most health authorities
- they have a long record of supplying public buildings and all standards of safety and quality are fully met.

We have not included suppliers of constructional goods or the necessary plethora of medical items because these have little aesthetic element and catalogues will be carried by most estates departments.

NHS CONTRACT LIST PRICES

Many of the manufacturers that we list operate a discount scheme of between 10 and 40 per cent (trade price) for local authority, charity or NHS purchasers because such large quantities are generally purchased by such bodies. Ascertain whether the retail or trade price is quoted on enquiry and whether VAT is included.

RELATIONSHIP WITH MANUFACTURERS

The large manufacturers have a network of representatives who cover sections of the country; a long working relationship with many of these has led to the sponsorship of colour printing in this book (see 'Acknowledgements').

The nature, purchase and care of products

FLOORING

Concealed costs

The main cost implication of any floor upgrading will be the state of the floor underneath; until that is assessed and costed, the price per square metre of the covering is irrelevant. All floor coverings have to be laid on a scrupulously prepared floor, screeded and level, and this can be a concealed cost which is often forgotten.

Principles of cleaning

Any flooring should require only a single process during daily cleaning, i.e. once over either with sweeper or hoover, not twice with a sweep and then a wash, or sweep and polish, as this is labour-intensive. Carpet is popular because hoovering is a 'once only' process and dust cannot be seen. Thorough cleaning every few months is another matter, but before flooring alterations are made, any new equipment needed to maintain the floor should be checked to see it will fit underneath furniture, flexes reach plugs etc.

Before deciding upon the type of floor covering, the cost of daily cleaning and annual maintenance should be costed, since a cheap floor usually requires high maintenance and is unlikely to be a good long-term bet.

HARD FLOORING

The costs involved in flooring are often related to the condition of the floor itself; the cost per square metre of terrazzo, lino or carpet may be the least consideration.

For any product, always ask the manufacturers' area representative for a recommended contractor as all products need to be well laid or they will curl up at the corners and 'lift' from the underfloor.

Ceramic and terrazzo are especially suitable for kitchens as they can be precision-cut for necessarily clean and hard-wearing areas. A recommended supplier of these is:

Quiligotti Contracts
PO Box 4
Clifton Junction
Manchester M27 8LP
(0161 483 1451)

Linoleum and vinyl

Main supplier of both products:

Forbo-Nairn Ltd
PO Box 1
Kirkcaldy
Fife KY1 2SB
(01592 269933)
This firm conducts particularly interesting factory tours.

Forbo-Nairn give clear instructions on cleaning their products but basically both products need only dry cleaning in a single daily process.

They produce other related products such as desk-top linoleum and Bulletin Board for noticeboards.

SOFT FLOORING

Carpets – construction and usage

Carpets evolved for reasons of domestic comfort from rag rugs and floor cloths via the importation of oriental carpets to their modern mass production. They were traditionally made by weaving, or by hand-tufting and then clipping. Eastern carpets and rugs are still made from thousands of tiny knotted tufts which the small hands of children make most readily, leading to recent accusations of enforced child labour.

Modern carpets can be woven, tufted, felted, looped, plaited or made on the principle of a sewing machine. Designs can be printed onto the finished product or dyed fibres used during its composition.

Materials

Most tough carpets are combinations of at least two man-made fibres; wool is seldom used for heavy-duty wear and pure wool carpets 'pill' and shed fluff even in domestic use. It is usually only mats that are woven or plaited today and then out of hard-wearing natural fibres (see below) because any softer material quickly shows wear.

Carpets are usually backed onto either a hessian-type fabric, which allows both air and liquids to penetrate it, or a rubber-based substance that is impervious.

In hospitals, it is usual to use the cheaper hessian-backed carpet where liquid spillage is unlikely (as in the Board Room) and the more expensive rubber-backed carpet where such events are likely (anywhere connected with the young, the old or the very ill). Modern carpets do not need underlay.

Pros and cons

Tufted carpets tend to compact under wear so the tuft length should be considered and, basically, the shorter the better; the number of tufts per square metre imply whether, for example, on a staircase the backing would show through but most public staircases are best treated with a hard 'stair nose' (see below). Tufting is done through a hessian background and then glued; an impervious rubber backing can also be added.

Looped carpets are often preferable because they do not compact but cheap ones can unravel. However, they have security implications in special hospitals and prisons because threads can be dragged out to make a strong cord then used as a weapon.

Carpet design

Only very expensive carpets or very cheap ones tend to incorporate significant pattern; as middle-class taste prefers magnolia walls, so any carpet salesroom or fair will show apricot-pink or muted stone-coloured carpet by the square mile. An adventurous example may incorporate a modest fleck but strongly patterned ones are nowadays largely out of fashion because carpet is intended to 'set everything off' in the same way as a discreet frame around a picture.

Inventive carpet design has tended to confine itself to huge rugs and while there have been some splendid designs for continuous carpet (see 'Mary Quant' of the 1960s) it has generally been based upon small, regular repeats. There have been very few carpet designs that present an irregular motif (Anker 'Continental' was one, now sadly discontinued). Currently, some of the best textural and small-repeat designs available are those in the NHS contract lists from

Anker Contract Carpets
Unit 6
The Horbury Business Complex
The Old Town Hall
Westfield Road
Horbury
West Yorkshire WF4 6HR
(01924 274004)

Gradus Carpets Ltd
3 First Avenue
Poynton Industrial Estate
Poynton
Cheshire SK12 1JY
(01625 859000)

Felted carpets

Felted carpets are cheap to buy and look even cheaper once worn.

They are a poor investment for any public area but can be used in a little-used area where quietness is essential. Recent developments of colour combination have transformed their appearance which is now often good. There are several suppliers.

'Designer' carpets

Some 'designer' carpets are made on the principle of a sewing machine but while these are visually exciting, they are not suitable for areas of heavy wear because they have heavy ridges that collect dirt between them. However, they could be used in areas where this is not an issue.

The Tsibel Range *Sans Frontières*
26 Danbury Street
Islington
London N1 8JU
(0171 454 1231)

Entrance area carpets

There are products that use rigid slats with carpet and rubber, and these (and other essential products) are made by:

Construction Specialities (UK) Ltd
Conspec House
Springfield Road
Chesham, Bucks HP5 1PW
(01494 784844)

Threshold carpets are manufactured specifically for the heavy wear of entrance areas and the pile incorporates wires to tease the mud from footwear. There are different grades and prices but the 'de luxe' product incorporates aluminium strips with tufted carpet to remove shoe dirt. All Threshold carpets have wire tufted in with the pile and there is a higher water-absorbency rate than in normal carpeting besides the 'shoe-scraping' action. They are best used as large areas and they can also be cut in a shape, such as a semi-circle.

PSA Threshold Ltd
Vorda Works
Highworth
Swindon
Wiltshire SN6 7AJ
(01793 764301).

Natural fibre carpeting/matting

This is made by plaiting and weaving tropical plant-leaf fibres such as sisal, seagrass and jute, and coir which is from cocoanuts; when sisal is combined with wool it is called 'sisool'. Like 'lino', natural fibre carpeting is associated with drab, pre-war school staircases that lasted for ever but the modern range has benefited from the same high standard of design manufacture and modern marketing.

The main advantage is that it is considerably cheaper than other carpets and it is not all in natural colours; colour combinations, using subtle dyes, and different weaves have been developed and the best product ranges are beautiful.

However, specifying it for public areas where heavy wear is expected is a false economy. It absorbs liquid immediately and stains irrecoverably, one spilt cup of coffee can ruin an expanse. It is expensive to lay because it is very coarse, the edges tend to look rough which is noticeable in a small room, and its weave is not regular like most carpeting but the pattern lines vary and 'wander' which is anathema to the tidy-minded.

This product's ideal use in a hospital would be in a large, traditional hall or meeting room; it offers variety of texture, it is beautiful and cheap. It is most usually seen as large woven mats in National Trust houses where period atmosphere is required (it is even called 'medieval matting'). Like all mats, it needs to be secured with industrial double-sided sellotape (supplied by carpet layers) or the public will sue you when they trip over the edges.

For natural-fibre carpeting contact:

Crucial Trading Ltd
The Market Hall
Craven Arms
Shropshire SY7 8ZZ
(0588 673666 Head Sales Office)

Crucial Trading Ltd
77 Westbourne Park Road
London W2
(0171 221 9000 Showrooms)

STAIRS

Traditional wooden stairs with stair-carpet and brass rods required constant cleaning; also, the 'waterfall' movement of stair-carpet whereby it quietly slid downstairs is no longer tolerated. Hospital stairs are usually only carpeted for vulnerable clients.

Often stairs are made of traditional terrazzo or some other composite material that usually deteriorates first on the 'nosing' edges. These can be repaired, or the stairs can be covered with coloured linoleum, or carpet can be used just on the treads. The range of 'nosings' available is wide, they can be of rubber, rubber-based pvc or a 'heavy-wear' reinforced material. A good range is available from

Gradus Ltd
3 First Avenue
Poynton Industrial Estate
Poynton
Cheshire SK12 1JY
(01625 859000)

SKIRTING BOARDS AND JOINS

Traditional skirting boards were hardwood and, as such, are difficult to replace and should be preserved. New wooden skirting boards are usually softwood but many hospitals have hard plaster skirting boards. In sterile areas, flooring will need to be welded to a moulded skirting board; the manufacturers of this are Gradus Ltd (as for stair 'nosings').

WALL PROTECTORS

These should be related to the height of trolleys and chairs likely to damage the walls. A broad painted stripe in gloss paint is the cheapest method to protect walls. Wooden barriers are feasible but there are a whole range of wall, corner, door protectors made by Construction Specialities (UK) Ltd (see 'Entrance area carpets' above). The colours are good and the product is enduring, but it is not a cheap option.

WALLPAPERS

Wallpaper did not evolve until the manufacture of paper and large-scale printing had adequately developed in the eighteenth century. Until then, wallcoverings had been of fabrics or leather but modern wallpapers include delicate iridescent foil papers and pieced rice papers besides plasticised-card papers so tough that they are virtually indestructible.

Two good suppliers of excellent wallpapers and fabrics for the public sector are:

Designers' Guild
3 Olaf Street
London W11 4BE
(0171 229 1000)

Their shop/showroom is at
269–277 Kings Road
London SW3 5EN
(0171 351 5775)
However, if you visit to see their range,
be warned of two things: not all the fabrics
and wallpapers displayed are of the required
fireproofing grade and the prices are retail not
trade so don't faint and totter out believing
they are too expensive – trade prices are
within the NHS specification.

Skopos Designs Ltd
Providence Mills
Earlsheaton
Dewsbury
West Yorkshire WF12 8HT
(01924 465191)

Their London Office and showroom is at
87 York Street
London W1
(0171 402 5532)

Both these firms constantly change and
develop their stock so check the availability of
a design before you specify. There are very
tough, plasticised wallpapers made by various
manufacturers for areas of heavy wear.

PAINT

Paint marketing and usage

The major manufacturers provide most of
their paint for the automobile and decorating
industries (artists, by comparison, account for
only 0.5 per cent of their output). Since the
NHS is one of the largest single employers
in the Western world, its paint requirements
are significant and much expertise has been
involved in creating the product; all that is now
needed is equivalent expertise to use it.

We discuss paint types in Chapter Five and
colour usage in Chapter Six so here we deal
with strictly practical paint application.

Most hospitals paint interior areas on the
simple basis of:

- vinyl matt for flat areas where the surface is
  in bad condition, because it visually
  obliterates lumps and bumps, and where
  people will not make it dirty (like ceilings)

- vinyl silk for other flat areas because it can
  be washed
- gloss oil for woodwork or walls that expect
  heavy wear
- satinwood paint for woodwork in 'posh'
  areas.

This scheme is sensible because gloss paint
washes easily, vinyl silk to an extent and matt
poorly; the areas likely to become dirty are
therefore washable.

Colour coding and identification

Most hospital estates departments use British
Standard colours. There is a discount agreement for British Standard colours (which
include one hundred colours) that have clear,
non-sequential numbers. Who could want for
anything more?

Two factors suggest that this is not enough:
one is the requirements of patient satisfaction
and the other is the marketing possibilities
offered by the European Community. For what
was a *British* standard colour range of 100
colours is now a European standard colour
range of 888 colours. It is called the NCS or
Natural Colour System and incorporates some
of the largest paint manufacturers in this and
other European countries. It operates by a four-
item code that gives the colour, place in that
colour range, the saturation of that pigment (or
hue) and its lightness (or tone). It is Brussels'
answer to colour identification and while no
one would expect any Works Department to
store all 888 colours, they will soon be available
with the same ease as the familiar 100.

Paint colours are identified either by a recognised code, irrespective of the manufacturer,
or by the manufacturer's identifying name or
number, or often by both. Thus in the Dulux
range, 'Regatta' is BS 18 E 53 and Dulux
2959B. Words like 'exclusive' and 'new' speak
for themselves but can indicate that the colour
is testing the market and may not be available
next year.

British Standard (BS) colours

BS colours are widely used and this is the range
stocked by most hospital estate departments.

They are incorporated by several different paint manufacturers so, for example, a colour range made by Albany, Dulux or Leyland will include several BS colours.

A colour is usually identified by the code and not by the name. For example, the BS code 18 E 53 is called 'Chelsea Blue' in the Albany range, 'Regatta' in the Dulux range and 'Gentian' in the BS range; the colour always matches the numbers and letters of the code and the name is variable.

There are one hundred BS colours identified by a number, then a letter, and a second number, e.g. 18 E 53. BS colours are useful and universally available; they can be used to 'touch up' a scheme for years and years but, as a result, they can become over-familiar and dull.

Other paint codes

BS colours relate to Britain while other paint codes relate to the manufacturer. For example, the huge international company AKZO has its own system of ACC-coded range. These are not colours but *identifying codes* for any colour. The most usual colour coding people see is the Dulux Colour Coding range, or the similar Leyland range whereby hundreds of colours can be accurately mixed to a code. Alternatively, the paints developed by Farrow and Ball for the National Trust are a simple but beautiful, subtle range of 1 to 57.

FABRICS

Woven and printed

Furnishing fabrics are basically woven or printed. Woven fabrics utilise a design or a texture on both sides, in other words, they are reversible. The pattern, motives or texture are created as the fabric is woven from the dyed warp and weft threads; tweeds and damasks are designed to make use of this double-sided opportunity. Woven fabrics were commissioned from Marianne Straub in the 1950s for the new NHS cubicle curtains because, of all places, this is where a weave is needed (see 'The origins of this book' in Chapter Eight).

Printed fabrics, whether cotton, trevira or any other material, are printed once the fabric is woven. There is then a clear 'right' side with the pattern and a 'wrong' or reverse side that is no pleasure to look at because it only shows the ink that has managed to penetrate the fabric. That is why printed fabrics are usually lined.

Printed fabrics tend to be less expensive than woven ones because the nature and variety of thread is cheaper, the weaving simpler and not even the cost of printing offsets this. But the cost of lining and 'making up' printed fabric can make their comparison reasonable.

Where to use them

Woven fabrics should be used wherever there is an audience for both sides, such as around cubicles, dividing curtains, door curtains and so on. Weaves consisting of simple stripes and textures are not necessarily expensive, they last and are popular.

Roller blinds

Woven fabric is excellent for roller blinds; compared with curtains, only half the fabric is needed. They are also enduring because while rolled up in daylight hours the fabric is protected from sun and dust; and when down, both sides of the weave can be seen. To decorate the bottom with a 'fancy' edge, shaped by zig-zags, half-circles or any well-drawn shape can add style to the most despairing hospital window. Roller blinds tend to break easily but Roman blinds and Austrian blinds can also be used, the ruching and pleating involved being a pleasant alternative.

Pattern content

Fabric design and manufacture is a massive industry; look at any street market with an overflowing fabric stall, let alone the specialist fabric shops and major stores and you'll see variety unsullied by repetition.

For the purposes of this book we have limited ourselves to recommending two manufacturers (see under 'Wallpaper' above) and they both produce 'collections' based upon some theme or customer requirement.

DOORS

Period doors tend to be of solid wood, usually panelled and often well proportioned and with decent and enduring door furniture. For the last twenty years doors have not usually been solid and consist of a honeycomb core between two panels. They have a different weight, a different proportion and a different look. One of the easiest ways to spoil an older building is by replacing all internal doors with fire-safety doors, and while this is necessary to an extent, one nervous fire officer can do more damage to a building than any other agent. It is up to management to treat fire-safety recommendations carefully and balance extreme advice for ultimate safety with likelihood and environmental quality.

Doors in public areas take tremendous punishment and a door in a hospital will be opened and shut thousands of times in a year. Even the see-through thick perspex doors through which trolleys are driven as battering rams can be well designed.

Door furniture

It is the counterbalancing of the various items of door furniture that gives an impression of care and the placing of appropriate knobs, locks, notices, and viewing windows. Information on doors should be well thought out and clearly presented; there should be no need for or tolerance of hand-written notices.

WINDOWS

Windows, like doors, declare the period of a building and also are immediate indicators of its care and condition.

Window furniture

It is the 'furniture' of windows that is most usually neglected. On old Edwardian windows it is often brass and if anybody can be bothered to strip it and re-attach it, it can look very attractive. Doors and windows of the 1930s often had bronze-type fixtures and again these are indicative of the age of a building and should be treasured if possible. Of course new

locks have to be installed but this can be done subtly; it is all a matter of care and application as with door furniture.

Privacy

Windows in any clinic where treatment is given must have net curtains even if they are not apparently overlooked; it has been known for voyeurs to spy on a family planning clinic with a telescope from a tower block miles away when everyone thought the green field site assured privacy.

Frosted glass is expensive but a cheaper and less permanent solution is to use frosted window foil to make 'mock' frosted windows. Ward names or other door 'titles' can be cut out so that it makes a decorative but impermanent feature, easy to remove.

Viewing windows of unsmashable glass set into doors of either prisons or secure psychiatric units may be unnecessary now that tiny wide-angle 'spyholes' are available. One-way viewing windows that appear as a mirror on the other side have connotations of deceit but straightforward viewing windows, into operating theatres or labour rooms, need neat and smart facilities to obscure them when not required.

Stained-glass windows for 'entrance doors' to hospitals and wards need to be professionally designed but can usually be made locally and are not prohibitively expensive.

Shatterproof

Many windows have to be made shatterproof and this can be done in a fairly cheap manner by affixing an invisible film to the inside of windows or, more expensively, by installing a completely shatterproof glass. Polycarbonate panes can be used but these do tend to get scratched and to loose their shine.

Blinds

Windows can either be left blank, given venetian-type blinds or vertical blinds. Venetian blinds can be used in an interesting way in suitable areas by making the different slats different colours, but they are notoriously hard to clean. Vertical linen blinds are suitable for offices because they cut out sunlight but are not for wards because they rattle disturbingly. Curtains are the most usual requirement because, like carpeting, they make the place feel homely.

Pelmets and rails

Many Edwardian and Victorian windows have pelmets, usually of wood. These were introduced when runners and hooks were in metal and very unsightly. They are not necessary these days with the opportunity to use white or coloured plastic rails and fixtures. It is usual for wooden pelmets to be removed making the window shapes simpler.

Curtain rails need to be fixed to a strong baton and these should be wide enough to allow curtains to hang well back from each window to allow in the maximum amount of light. Curtain poles, with elegant ends and with the curtains on wooden or brass rings, are reminiscent of gracious drawing rooms in National Trust houses but while they look strong, this is deceptive. Staff often ask for them but they are expensive to install and are not robust enough for heavy use.

Suppliers

There are many manufacturers of architectural ironmongery. A modern range for doors and windows in a good range of colours is made by:

Hewi UK Ltd
Scimitar Close
Gillingham Business Park
Gillingham
Kent ME8 0RN
(01634 377688)

Period replacements are advertised in interior design magazines intended for private houses, or come from local suppliers, either from conventional retailers or from salvage yards.

FURNITURE

'An audit of all existing furniture with recommendations on its care, restoration, grouping and uses.' We made this suggestion in Chapter Five because of the frequent wastage and misuse of furniture by hospitals. It could be conducted in the following way.

- *The Audit* to incorporate any existing lists and to discover location of significant items; lists to be supported as necessary by photographs or sketches, then items to be categorised and identified by date, style and condition.
- *Care of furniture* – to see if it has been deteriorating by poor usage that could reasonably be reformed. For example, if furniture is not protected during redecoration and left uncovered to become spattered with paint, if it is left outdoors in the weather or used to prop open doors, such neglect damages furniture.
- *Restoration of furniture* – to assess if items could be repaired, reglued, reupholstered, repainted and so on at a cost that is significantly less than buying new (taking account of new fire and safety regulations whereby some foam stuffing has to be replaced).

  Chairs can be reupholstered and a range of charming fabric is available which is wipeable even though it looks as if it is woven. For example:

The Ambla Collections
Wardle Storeys plc.
Gove Mill, Earby
Colne, Lancashire BB8 6UT
(01282 842511)

- *Grouping of furniture* – whereby components of a 'set' can be assembled as a stylish group, having looked incongruous when scattered; as in clothes fashion, it is items in unison that create quality rather than single items in isolation.
- *Destruction of furniture*
  This may seem an unlikely heading but the unnecessary destruction of furniture by hospitals estates department staff is endemic. Bonfires of bentwood and Lloyd Loom chairs, of 1930s' solid oak desks and of anything that has lost its handles or hinges or staff are simply bored with are

easier than arranging repair. To check around the disposal areas and rubbish bins adjacent to the estates department and furniture stores will probably reveal just how much is discarded. The process of retention and repair is often not well addressed.

- *Buying new furniture*
Choosing furniture should take account not only of safety and suitability but of durability. Tables made of wood can simply be sanded down a millimetre or so when they become stained and old – they have an indefinite lifespan – whereas melamine-covered tops may initially look smart, but once they are chipped they become unsatisfactory to everybody.

- *Buying old furniture*
In Chapter Four we described a unit for elderly people filled with furniture of the type that the old people would have had in their own homes. This meant that hefty sideboards with lots of drawers, solid tables with extending 'leaves', horsehair-stuffed 'wing-backed' chairs, curly cast-iron standard lamps and huge Bakelite wirelesses with knobs on the front were all assembled and proved successful in two ways.

One was that old people actually felt 'at home' because the surroundings looked familiar and also because there were lots of solid pieces of furniture to hold on to; instead of an acre of empty hospital floor to travel to the lavatories, they had a familiar corridor of substantial furniture to grab.

Such purchases are cheap at local auctions and fire and safety issues should be capable of solution.

We have discussed only general, domestic furniture and for this there are many varied stockists; one of the best-designed ranges of heavy-duty, public furniture is:

Primo Furniture plc
Baird Road, Enfield
Middlesex, EN1 1SJ
(0181 804 3434)

FIXTURES AND FITTINGS

The several items we listed in Chapter Five under Mandatory, Organisational and Cultural items are discussed throughout this book and can be identified in the Index. We would observe here that items often bought by hospitals, such as dining-room equipment, are not especially well designed and often a better supplier can be found by looking at another non-health service industry. For example, IKEA restaurants serve numbers of people, including many families, in a stylish, quick and successful way; a visit to look at their fixtures and fittings and how staff use them could be a good starting point.

NOTICEBOARDS

Small pinboards, often coupled with white scribble boards, are widely available in hardware shops and IKEA do a good series. When large areas of pinboard need to be installed, soft-board (or pinboard) made in large sheets is the cheapest material and this is available from any builders' merchant. However, it is very soft and should be 'framed' in softwood to stop the edges shedding. Cork is an alternative, either slabs of it or flooring tiles assembled on the wall.

The best noticeboard material is Bulletin Board made by Forbo-Nairn (see 'Linoleum and vinyl'). This is made in several subtle colours and, being a rubberised material, the holes made by pins close up once removed so it keeps looking smart. It is sold in sheet form that is delivered in a large roll; it is not cheap and has to be stuck professionally onto the wall or a backing-board and framed or the edges will crumble. However, it can create huge areas of smart noticeboard and can be cut to go into odd corners and little spaces.

FIREPLACES

If you want a fireplace and you are dealing with a period building that still has one, fine, reveal and restore it even if you don't light a fire in it. If the building has no such feature, judge the best space for it (sightlines from the door, against an interior wall, etc.) and install a mock fireplace.

There are lots of replicas available in DIY or fireplace shops but they are usually small-scale and of poor design quality. A reclamation yard is best to get an old one or an architect can design one to be built probably from MDF and tiling. If a 'flicker fire' or a video fire is intended, it must be sited near to an electric point.

LIGHTING

There are two aspects to lighting: the type of bulb and the design of the fitting.

Lighting did not evolve gradually over centuries, but all in a jump. The only brief intermediary between millennia of candles was gas lighting before the electric bulb was invented in 1880. This was basically the tungsten bulb and, within twenty years, a growing design industry was encasing it in often elaborate fittings and lamps for industry, entertainment and the home.

The Modern Movement (see Chapter One) rejected these elaborate fittings and regarded the bulb itself as an object to be designed. This had an enduring effect on lighting design, particularly when the tungsten bulb was followed by the post-war fluorescent strip which created light on a different principle, and then the halogen bulb which developed the basic tungsten. The lighting industry has evolved fibre optics and other sophisticated developments while some original problems remain unsolved, such as the requirement for electricity to take away the heat of the lighting it creates. Low-energy bulbs are in the forefront of development due to environmental pressures.

A hospital requires many sorts of specialist and directional lighting, besides domestic and personal lights. There are official recommendations for 'lux' (light) levels for different areas and for spectrum range and reflective values. Fluorescent lights appear to affect some people badly, the rapid albeit imperceptible flickering causing distress. The type of lighting, its encasing and placing require technical, operational and aesthetic collaboration.

SAFETY AND FIRE REGULATIONS

Designers cannot know all the fire and safety regulations but they should know when it is necessary to seek expert advice. There are certain things that hospital estates staff (who are responsible for fire control) do very well and these are the things that can be measured, quantified and assessed. The scientific and statistical evidence of fire behaviour is well documented. Fire officers talk about 'ignition sources', starting at 'O' which is a smouldering cigarette to '1' which is a lighted match, and so on to '5' which is an established fire. One of the worst ignition sources is accumulations of lint and fluff, prevalent in even the cleanest hospital, and a chenille dressing gown, which, while very comfortable, is another.

There will be fire restrictions on interior design schemes that must be observed, and the NHS estates department relevant publications are essential reading. For example, a suspended tiled ceiling cannot be painted with an oil-based paint, or papered with a non-retardant wallpaper and some decor specifications are acceptable in a side room but not on a fire escape route.

The Furniture and Furnishings (Fire Safety) Regulations 1988

These introduced much more stringent regulations that have affected the use of old furniture (see 'Furniture'). Synthetic up-holstered chairs that carry the label 'BS 5852 Part 2' are safe, others may be a fire hazard. Period furniture that is stuffed with horsehair is usually acceptable but if the horsehair is filthy and the item is being reupholstered, it can be washed by putting it into pillow cases and then through the washing machine; the result is piles of beautifully clean horsehair. This, being organic, smoulders and does not melt and spread scalding droplets, like acetate and vinyl.

All fabrics for public premises have to be fireproofed to the standard of B 5678 Part 2. Part 1 isn't good enough and anyone who specifies it could be sued for manslaughter. This is what you would buy in department stores and it is perfectly adequate for normal domestic use. The difference is that B 5678 Part 2 has involved dipping the warp and weft threads in a fire-proofing medium before they are woven; they are then extensively tested by washing fifty or even one hundred times. A fabric can be proofed after weaving but this will not be as good and will not survive washing. Some fabrics can be backed with Pyrovatex and this is effective but expensive. The data given in 'Chapter seven information' under 'Practical care – fire' is for items that will not be washed and is therefore unsuitable for fabric.

Upholstery fabrics have the same strict criteria and it is an acknowledgement of success for such regulations that most of us have not experienced a serious fire in a public building. Some of the disaster fires in, for example, American cinemas in the 1930s meant that hundreds of people lost their lives. Like vaccination, the preventive measures have, to an extent, allowed danger to be forgotten. Some years ago, there was a severe fire in a hospital hall and, although the roof was burnt off completely, the curtains still hung intact like sooty stalactites, a tribute to their fire retardancy.

Fire regulations should be considered as a balance that has to be maintained between sensible precautions and strict regulations. In old upholstered furniture, the stuffing was of poor flammability but the covers dangerous; today, the situation can be the other way around with the upholstery fabric fire-retardant but the foam stuffing dangerous. Both have to be considered.

Wallpapers and the many wallpaper borders are fire-retardant but the effectiveness also depends on the surface upon which the wallpaper is pasted. The 'inorganic group' include brick, blockwork, concrete, plaster and ceramic; these are not flammable. The 'cellulose group' are flammable unless they have been treated; they include all the timbers. The third group of plastics, decorative laminates and thermoplastics, thin vinyl and flock papers are flammable and cannot be made inflammable because they are not porous. There is, however, a development of acrovyn, a plastic laminate, now welded onto high-density fibreboard that is fire-retardant and which comes in large sheets that can clothe an entire room.

Handling of period buildings

An example of fire regulations versus quality can be illustrated with bannisters: in an old building, the fire officer can insist that the bannisters are boxed in – and similarly, all doors can be recommended for replacement because panelled doors are considered hazardous. However, the replacement of all old doors with new fire doors can wreck a period building and managers can insist that only the thin, vulnerable door panels are replaced with specially prepared fire-retardant material (as in National Trust properties) so making a reasonable compromise.

A BALANCE OF SAFETY

There are a great many items mentioned in this book that have safety implications: water features and ponds, plants such as ivy and foxgloves, open bannisters, panelled doors, rocking horses and so on. Medical staff have seen the results of the most unlikely accidents from these and other apparently innocuous items and an aura of fearfulness can be all-pervading.

There was a recent case of a patient lying inhaling from an oxygen mask while his bedside locker was being cleaned with methylated spirits on cotton wool. He took off the mask, laid it on the locker top whereupon it ignited on the residue of spirits. This was a most unlikely accident, but it gave credibility to the motto 'Safety First'.

But life in a hospital can become impossible if safety regulations are allowed to overide all other considerations. This, as with many other matters, is the responsibility of management. Determined managers have insisted, for example, that the recommended number of self-closing fire doors in a corridor would make life impossible for busy staff and have signed a paper exonerating their fire staff from any responsibility while installing only some of the doors.

A scheme of interior decor and art installations can be severely jeopardised by fire and safety staff and the balance of reasonable precautions with public safety must be sensibly and sensitively addressed by those in charge.

GENERAL BIBLIOGRAPHY

Green Building Handbook: A Guide to Building Products and Their Impact on the Environment, Tom Woolley, E and FN Spon (imprint of the Taylor & Francis Group), 1997.
A Visual Dictionary of Architecture, Francis D.K. Ching, Van Nostrand Reinhold, 1997.

TEXT AND ILLUSTRATIONS

Crown copyright material quoted in these chapters is reproduced with the permission of the Controller of Her Majesty's Stationery Office.

Chapter three
Fig. 3.1: Martin Lister ©

Chapter four
Figs 4.1, 4.2, 4.6, 4.7: Photographs and © SH

Fig. 4.3: Winchester and Eastleigh Healthcare ©
Fig. 4.4: Broadmoor Health Authority ©
Figs. 4.5 and 4.15: Chichester Priority Health Care Service ©
Figs 4.8 and 4.11: Photographs Mike Englefield, SH ©
Figs. 4.9, 4.10 and 4.12: Photographs and © Michael Moralee
Fig. 4.14: Susan Macfarlane ©

Chapter five
Fig. 5.1: Forbo-Nairn Ltd ©
Figs 5.2, 5.4, 5.7, 5.8, 5.9, 5.10: Photographs and © SH
Fig. 5.3: Photographs and © MDP (Medical Design Practice (MDP), Anchor Business Centre, School Lane, Chandlers Ford, Hampshire SO5 3TN (01703 271888)), a small company specialising in all aspects of new-build or period renovation of healthcare premises
Fig. 5.5: Photograph and © Michael Moralee
Fig. 5.6: Isle of Wight Healthcare Trust ©

Colour and other factors

CHAPTER

6

PRACTICAL SKILLS AND COMPLEX KNOWLEDGE

Throughout the last two chapters, our advice has basically been practical: for example, how to treat *that* floor in *these* circumstances with *this* product.

We have also many times mentioned the need for design professionals because they will bring not only the extensive practical knowledge of 'how' but also the theoretical knowledge and esoteric understanding of 'why'. How to appoint such professionals, including those for buildings and land, is dealt with in Chapter Nine.

This is therefore not a DIY book on 'how to improve your premises' which could be handed to the estates department with the instruction to implement the advice given in the book and Nirvana would arrive. Instead, this book is a careful investigation into the many subtle issues involved and the educated experience needed to handle them.

Complex activities, such as doctoring or designing, are pursued not just by a set of practical skills and rules. Certainly they are guided by accepted procedures assembled from the experience of others, but it is the flexible application of these coupled with imponderables such as wisdom and invention, besides the aforementioned philosophic knowledge and esoteric understanding, that we now address.

THE AVERAGE HOSPITAL'S POOR VISUAL IMAGE

The two cultures

We would like to expand the point made earlier (and indeed several times in this book) that hospital staff are predominantly from scientific and technical backgrounds. Even apart from clinical personnel, the support professions such as the finance, organisational and management teams are generally from disciplines that depend chiefly on fact and analysis, on observations and evaluation.

The professional disciplines from which designers, arts co-ordinators and artists are drawn are often not seen by those with a science/facts professional discipline to represent any serious discipline; an 'artistic' talent perhaps, a certain inclination for pretty patterns and self-expression maybe, but nothing representing the essential disciplines with which, for example, the catering and technical-engineering professions are ingrained.

This is, of course, nonsense but it does not feel like nonsense to those dedicated NHS professionals fighting for their specialist department.

SUCCESS STORY

A doctor of obstetrics was charged with malpractice and this included 'inconsistency' in her treatment of women patients. In her defence she agreed with this but explained: 'A woman who is six feet tall, well fed and delivering her first child may require different medical procedures from a woman who is five feet tall, ill-fed and delivering her sixth child. It is the flexible application of my knowledge that I seek to apply, call it "inconsistent" if you like.'

Her defence was accepted.

Transfer the 'inconsistencies' to the adroit design-handling of hospital premises and the need for appropriate professionals will be as clear as the need for specialist doctors.

Lack of precedent

Because few hospitals have made provision for good decorative appointment, there are few examples for young staff coming up through the system to remember and emulate. The best publicity is 'word of mouth' and if some premises were of an outstanding quality to please everybody, their influence would be verbally reported and copied. This actually seldom happens because few precedents exist.

Buildings and bodies

Perhaps as a result of this, the reaction of hospital staff to environmental improvements is often unsupportive. There are many possible reasons for this. We have discussed the way in which a sense of being under-resourced can make NHS staff feel that shabby surroundings prove how hard-pressed they are. It may also be that, because the central purpose of the hospital is to treat the human body and it is appropriate, indeed required, for all sorts of invasive procedures to be performed upon it, staff forget the personality raging inside the patient and the need for environmental pleasure and spiritual delight, besides privacy and comfort.

DESIGNERS AS 'PHYSIOLOGISTS'

A building is the domain of the architect, ergonomists and technicians who prepare the building for the job it has to do, but it is the designer/artist who views these different disciplines in practical and aesthetic relationship to each other. Designers are the 'physiologists' of the building world, studying how the whole system works as more than a sum of its separate, specialist parts.

Physiology studies the way in which the whole body system works together. For example, while 'the heart can be studied by the anatomist, then by specialists for blood, nerves and hormones, the physiologist is interested not just in the heart but the heart within a body' (Professor Colin Blakemore, physiologist, in Danny Danziger, *The Noble Tradition: Interviews with the Medical Profession*, Viking, 1990).

For, as the balance of a body is complex, so is the balance of a building; as the efficiency of the heart depends not only on mechanical efficiency but also on subtle elements such as electricity, temperature and adrenalin, so a building depends not only on technical adroitness but also on similarly subtle elements such as abstract and aesthetic qualities. These are recognised chiefly through our sense of sight (Figs 6.1 and 6.2).

ANECDOTE

An arts co-ordinator was hanging large reproductions of Monet's paintings in a hospital corridor. A doctor colleague passed and mildly questioned the choice, saying that she had been looking all morning at prepared slides of brain tissue deformities and perhaps her eyes were not well tuned for Monet or, perhaps, for art of any sort. After an initial sensation of annoyance that her hard morning's work was being (albeit very slightly) deprecated, the arts co-ordinator felt the remark was perfectly reasonable.

The two then had lunch together and the arts co-ordinator learned a lot about brain cell deformities in the course of friendly back-chat.

Later that week, by an unusual co-incidence, this arts co-ordinator was talking to an eminent painter whose work and reputation she greatly admired. In the course of conversation, she reported this doctor's comment, to which the painter replied, 'What an appalling remark. Why do you have to subject your taste to such people?'

Yes, indeed it had been an appalling remark considered while standing in the sophisticated studio of an eminent modern artist. Alternatively, it had been a perfectly reasonable remark when received in a hospital corridor. Both the doctor and the artist were well established within their professions, both were sophisticated and sympathetic but each was, in cultural terms, a million miles apart from the professional aims and understanding of the other.

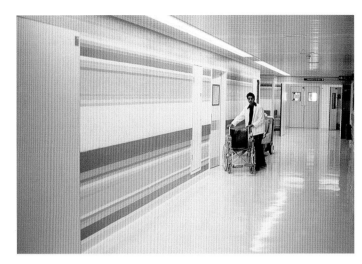

Fig. 6.1 'Yellow Decoration' and 'Blue Decoration' 1987 acrylic on plaster by Bridget Riley. These murals were commissioned for a lift bay and its corridor and a second corridor on two floors of Queen Elizabeth the Queen Mother Wing of St Mary's Hospital, Paddington, London. Typical of Bridget Riley's well-known work, they were painted directly onto the walls and, over ten years later, have lasted quite well.

Our visual vocabulary: the contribution of colour

WHAT CONSTITUTES COLOUR?

Colour exists as light and as pigment; spectral light and coloured pigment are the means whereby we initially recognise our surroundings and they are the prime factors in our potential enjoyment of them.

Light

Spectral light has been studied scientifically ever since Isaac Newton bought a glass prism in Stourbridge Market during his boyhood in the 1650s. The most significant encounter most people have with coloured light is the cunning lighting installed above food displays in super-markets; look at the sleeve of your clothing under the light above the red and then the green fruit and vegetable displays and you will realise what a varying effect they have on appearances.

In a hospital the key need is sufficient light-ing for particular functions. There is something wrong if there is no variation between, for example, the delivery room and the day room, reception or the sluices and this is also discussed in Chapter Five under 'Lighting'. While there are obviously functions for which clinical reason dictates lighting, there are also important emotional factors.

In the ideal world the quality and type of light would be regulated to meet the needs of each area but this is a counsel of perfection to which most hospitals cannot aspire. Adequate and functional lighting which does not distort colours is a more realistic ambition, with obvious attention to providing softer and more attractive lighting in non-clinical areas.

Pigment

Colour pigment is that substance inherent in all material that we visually interpret as 'colour' and it is the most noticeable element of any interior. It can be used imaginatively or in ignorance by those who do not have adequate understanding of its nature and properties, and colour use – above all – is too important to be left to amateurs. There is a vast literature about colour from many disciplines but we have here endeavoured to compress the material into a useful précis for the purposes of this book.

USES OF COLOUR

Colour exists only in the presence of light. Colours do not therefore represent constant values since light affects the nature of the colour, and light itself is not a constant quality. It is therefore important to understand that the tint and shades of different colours need to be handled carefully and chosen in the light at different times

Fig. 6.2 'Falling Leaves' by Sian Tucker in the Chelsea and Westminster Hospital 1993. This 75ft mobile consists of ninety separate elements, each individually pivoted. It is constructed from painted Foamex panels suspended on stainless steel rigging and movement mechanisms.

A commission as dramatic and successful as this does not occur in isolation. It was planned and made for a specific space with all the necessary sophisticated technical resources to support it and within the context of a well-established and highly professional Arts Project.

of the day, and also the artificial lighting under which they are to be seen.

Since there is some evidence that colours influence mood and mental state, they are a powerful factor in any environment. So the first matter to consider is the medium in which colour is most often manifest, which is paint.

Is there more to paint than 'Magnolia'?

The most popular paint colour bought for interior decoration is magnolia. This was once called cream but it has enjoyed the same linguistic reformation whereby a difficult patient has become a challenging client and a local hospital is now called a community care centre. This 'popularity factor' is based not only on sales statistics supplied by the paint trade but also on the evidence of our own reliable eyes. Peer into people's front rooms, look at banks, stores and (of course) hospitals, and cream – rechristened magnolia – greets us as an unchallenged sea. Study any colour chart and you will find buttermilk or champagne, apricot-milk or magnolia, but never, ever pure cream. For cream, along with rat-catchers and dustmen, has been relegated by marketing maestros to a distant and rougher age.

The subtle variety now available in paint ranges is due to a dazzling renaissance in the chemistry of colour, the opportunities of mass manufacture and intensive marketing. The continuing popularity of basic magnolia may be due to negative rather than positive forces. It may be used simply because it is difficult to dislike rather than like. Customers and colleagues are unlikely to be annoyed by anything so bland; they may be bored but not enraged, so those who make these decisions play safe and magnolia is chosen again and again and again.

'Those who make the decisions'

This is an important issue that has already occurred many times, and will do so again before we suggest the solution in Chapter Nine. We are not expecting many people to read this book from end to end like a novel, but to dip and skim as they require. Therefore, these points that are essential to our whole theses are occasionally reintroduced.

In most hospitals, decor decisions are made by the staff who occupy the premises due for redecoration or sometimes by the painting firm who will carry out the work. But selecting paint colours is not the same as applying them to the wall; it is about having design knowledge, expertise, experience and skill. Therefore, what are the relevant areas of knowledge and understanding needed to select the ingredients for a successful interior intended for specialist and mass use?

The practical matters concerning paint techniques, paint types and their trade availability are described in 'Chapters three/four/five information'. However, the more abstract matters of colour theory and knowledge are also important.

BELIEFS, MYTHS, THEORY AND KNOWLEDGE OF COLOUR

Beliefs in the healing power of colour is a part of what used to be called fringe medicine, but was then reassessed as 'alternative' and is now graced with the grudging approval of 'complementary'. It contributes to the holistic or 'whole' approach to people's mental, physical and spiritual needs. It includes practices associated with other cultures, such as acupuncture, or other ages, such as dowsing and healing.

So far, so good. But does it work? Need a busy NHS manager take any account of such matters? This depends on whom you ask so let us briefly look at available evidence. There are basically three sources of knowledge and information about colour: the beliefs and experience of therapists and healers, the knowledge of scientists and psychologists, and the understanding of artists and designers.

Colour therapists and healers: their beliefs

Colour therapists base their therapy upon the belief that every human is surrounded by an aura which is apparent to clairvoyants and which can be affected by the person's state of mind and health. This belief was described by a theosophist called Charles Leadbetter who, in 1902, published a book called *Man Visible and Invisible*. This purported to illustrate several examples of the human aura as it is affected by our mental condition: for example, black indicated hatred, red on black is anger, yellow denotes an intellectual and so on. Leadbetter is best remembered for the influence he had on the artist Kandinsky who was the first Western creator of completely abstract painting.

It is this simplistic symbolism of colour that tends to undermine the credibility of colour theory. For example, red means stop in Great Britain, but in China (until recently) it meant 'go'. If navy blue is always and invariably the colour of authority, as colour theorists claim, is this the reason why the police, porters and prison officers wear it? Or do we see it as representing authority because they wear it? This in itself may have depended on cheap and available dye-stuffs at the time uniforms were initiated, as happened when 'early medieval blue dyes . . . faded, and ran; only workers in rough, often-soiled garments wore blue. In Europe, blue has ever since been the customary colour of worker's clothing; overalls . . . and "blue collars" survive today alongside American blue jeans' (Margaret Visser, *The Way We Are*; 'Wearing blue', Viking 1995).

On the other side of the 'blue' coin, 'As a sky goddess, the Virgin Mary's colour is blue. Her starry mantle is a figure of the sky . . . The reason for the symbolism is also economic, however, for blue was an expensive paint pigment, obtainable only from crushed lapis lazuli imported from Afghanistan' (Marina Warner, *Alone of All Her Sex: Myth and Cult of the Virgin Mary*, Weidenfeld & Nicholson 1990). Traditionally, Mary was transfigured into the 'blue' sky, and blue is associated with maleness (blue is for a boy) because a son was seen as a gift from heaven and girls were merely of the flesh and therefore awarded pink.

The anecdote, history and myth surrounding colour show that rigid and ingenuous associations of colour with characteristics may be based on little more than cultural and personal programming, or economic chance. The study of colour is almost as controversial as the study of space; both astrology and astronomy involve studying space but the bases of interpretation are profoundly different.

Scientists and psychologists: their evidence

Circumstantial responses

Some of the most reliable experiments available on the effect of colour on attitude and behaviour have been done by NASA. Their aims could be advantageously transferred straight to any hospital or home where people are cooped up for a long time in one place and are still expected to co-operate and behave well. This is one such example:

The investigation and use of colour in space system design is necessary in helping to provide visual stimulation, volume enhancement and in creating moods to relieve the monotony of prolonged confinement. Colour schemes are planned in relation to room volume and function, the purpose of the mission and desired behavioral aspects.

(*The Study and Application of Colour in Extraterrestrial Habitats*, collective findings published by the Habitability Technology Section at the manned Spacecraft Centre)

This sounds ideal for hospitals as well as space ships, so what are the colours that can achieve this? The conclusion of NASA's work was:

The association of colours with definite mental conditions and moods is general. No absolute relationships have been established and the subject is open to individual interpretation . . . The problem of individual differences in habituality concerns the colour of living areas. Personal preference depends on such factors as the individual's familiarity with certain colours and colour combinations and the emotive connotations they may have for him.

(*Ibid.*)

In other words, if as a child you were scratched by a ginger cat or had an unpleasant aunt who wore a violet dress, you will remain conditioned to dislike these colours. This does not augur well for the universality of colour reaction.

Physiological responses

However, in spite of this cautious acceptance that colour is too dependent on personal programming to offer any general guidelines of effect, certain general reactions seem to be common to most Western people. There seems to be some consistency in colours associated with attractive smells and tastes, which are different pinks, pale yellows and greens. 'Warm' colours appeared to benefit requirements of social interrelations, and 'cool' colours apparently encouraged introspection and contemplation. There are other colours associated with overestimation and underestimation of time which again could be as useful in a hospital ward as in a spacecraft. These observations were very general but there are a number of experiments on the effects of colour.

In another interesting series of experiments the physiological responses to colour were investigated and reported in *Physiological Response to Color* by Peter Kaiser (York University, Ontario, Canada, 1984).

The electroencephalogram, galvanic skin response, blood pressure, heart and respiration rate and eyeblink frequency constituted the gamut of tests given to subjects. Amongst the conclusions quoted was the view that subjects seemed to be naturally divided into two groups, visualisers and non-visualisers:

- a 'visualiser' is one who regularly employs vivid visual imagery
- a 'non-visualiser' relies on other identifying factors.

The results of colour tests between the two were significantly different and this is quoted to show that not only is colour variable but so are people's responses.

Colour 'hue', 'tone' and 'type'

One problem in ascertaining uniformity in tests such as these is in the difficulty of maintaining colour consistency. For every colour has a three-way range, one range denotes hue, the other tone and the third is purity or colour 'type'.

Hue is the degree of dye or stain in the suspending fluid: for example, in an egg-cup full of red paint, there could be just one gram of pigment or one hundred grams or anything up to saturation point when the solution might theoretically become as thick as treacle. This would alter intensity and opacity but not the 'type' of colour and not, unless the pigment amount was dense (that is, in the treacle stage), the tone. However, if white is added, this alters the 'tone', that is the dark and light of the colour.

The primary colours – red, blue and yellow – all have the constant opportunity to grade off into the secondary colours on each side of themselves in the classic colour circle: for example, red tends on one side to purple through the blue and the other into orange through the yellow. They are like amorous neighbours, quite unable to leave each other alone. A pure primary colour is therefore one that shows no inclusion of its neighbours and this is difficult both to identify or maintain. So pink, for example, can range in hue and tone from near invisibility to its parent, red, while altering its appearance all the way from near yellow to near purple while remaining pink, of a sort. Asking for 'pink' without specification could result in a wide range of unexpected results.

Does the experimental literature support the claim that colour affects human behaviour? Yes, perhaps, but not consistently because of individual and cultural variance. However, there is enough evidence to suggest that reds can trigger epilepsy and, from other data, it also appears that oranges and blacks may stimulate depressive and

'Clink pink' – a cautionary tale

In a large general hospital in southern England, premises were recently allocated for an Assault Clinic. It was to be, and indeed is, run in partnership with the local police force for the interviewing and treatment of rape cases, both women and men, and other victims of violent assault. The police advised that pink was a colour likely to induce relaxation so the nursing sister in charge ordered walls, doors, everything to be in plain, bright pink selected from the BSC chart. Apparently the basis for this advice was that restraint cells in America were painted pink. What the nursing sister did not know was that subsequently it had been found in America that pink had a significantly destabilising effect after the short initial period during which it had appeared to be soothing. It is now known pejoratively in America as 'Clink Pink'. Used here without checking the information, it actually increased the tension it was designed to relieve. Even magnolia might have been better!

Recently some health authorities have issued directives that green is a colour to be used for its supposed calming effects. There is no more basis to believe that green is beneficial rather than pink, and such oversimplifications ignore both innate colour subtlety and the requirements of different circumstances.

aggressive reactions so it may be better to avoid strong use of these colours in health settings.

The third source of information about colour is from artists and designers. How do they help the debate?

Artists and designers: their understanding

In 1991 the Arnolfini Gallery in Bristol hosted a conference on 'The Nature of Colour' which focused on the aesthetic use of colour in contemporary and historic context. The scientific data available was presented for its interest value; for example, it appears that while that area of the brain that detects colour has been identified, the mechanics whereby it does so remain inscrutable. In the tradition of such conferences when they are at their best, conclusions evaded those assembled but the overpowering result was to convince everyone that colour is one of the most mysterious and joyous ingredients of human life (but not of animal life, as apparently horses don't see colour but snakes do, which seems unfair). The sheer energy with which colour has been used and developed over the millennia to express belief, emotion and vision is persuasion enough to realise that there is more to life than magnolia. So, how can this combination of mystic beliefs, scientific knowledge and passionate enthusiasm be used positively in designing health settings?

Colour complementaries

One of the necessary lessons to be learned is the use of complementary colour. This can best be explained by reference to the usual colour chart which shows the complementary or opposite to each colour that we all see briefly as a retinal after-image. There is one important instance in which hospitals use this and it is in operating theatres which are traditionally green to offer the staff visual relief from the sight of red blood (see 'Operating theatres' in Chapter Four). This principle is valid and could be extended: different greens could be used in an interesting way. Van Gogh wrote 'There is no blue without yellow and without orange' so even Clink Pink might be jollied along with a little pale green as a complementary colour.

Qualities of dissonants, discords and tertiaries are also part of the colour vocabulary of specialists. These, with primary and secondary colours and their complementaries, constitute the 'language' of colour which needs to be used, as does any language, by those who are educated in its usage.

Monotony relieved by colour

If we could refer again to the NASA intention to use colour 'To relieve the monotony of prolonged confinement', the relevance to hospitals is obvious. Most people who are in hospital do not want to be there; their lives were interrupted by an accident or conditions that few would seek and their conditions of confinement can be ameliorated by the visual interest of their surroundings. It is more interesting to look at two colours than one, three than two and so on, although the point at which variety becomes a muddle is usually dictated by educated common sense. However, using the textures of paint techniques (rolling, dragging, splattering and so on), introducing wallpapers, tiling, fabrics, upholstery, pictures and mirrors can help patients to perceive the medical and social world they are in more favourably.

So far the discussion has referred to public areas where the contention is that design principles should prevail. However, many healthcare premises have single rooms for long-term patients and it is obviously right to allow them to choose, as far as possible, their own decor and furnishings. This depends on the patient's circumstances and even though the outcome may seem appalling to others, in such cases the aim is to comfort the patient by allowing individual preferences. Even in an open ward, accommodation for 'personalising' the space can be offered with accessible locker tops and pin boards.

CONCLUSIONS

Colour is important because it is a powerful idiom that can affect not only our mental condition, mood and perception of time, but also our perception of volume, shape, space and perspective. Proportions of one colour to another and their relationship also alter our perception of them.

The time and cost of applying colour is the same, whether it is one that gives pleasure to some, many or none. Where an inappropriate colour has been chosen by people with good intentions but lacking the professional skills, the results will probably fail to give positive pleasure and may be actively unpleasant. As Kenneth Edwards pointed out, 'These details should not be left to the abilities of the maintenance man or the taste of the hospital sister' ('The environment inside the hospital', *The Practitioner*, vol. 222, June 1979). Once a colour has been applied as a paint or wallpaper it will probably be there for some time, and in many cases for years, so we suggest that the additional cost of professional advice is a worthwhile investment.

Proportion and spatial relationships

MENTAL HARMONY VERSUS MUDDLE

Many hospital walls present a mass of fluttering bits of paper, signs that can be contradictory, mandatory fire equipment and emergency lights, smoke detectors, leaflet racks and telephone booths. Most of this is in some way necessary but it is not efficient because we become overloaded with information we cannot deal with, and there is seldom a sense of mental harmony when you are in such a state.

The practical aspects of noticeboards are dealt with in Chapter Five ('Noticeboards') but here we are considering them aesthetically as one visual ingredient in an interior. For if we are uncertain about the effect of colour on people, we are even less certain as to the effect of proportion and spatial relationships. However, the fact that we do not fully understand something is no reason to dismiss it and there is enough precedent to believe confidently that the spatial relationships between objects within an interior are important and should be handled with consideration.

'GETTING IT RIGHT'

One account of the part spatial relationships play in our everyday lives has been written by the critic Ernst Gombrich in his 1955 classic study *The Story of Art* (Phaidon):

Anybody who has ever tried to arrange a bunch of flowers, to shuffle and shift the colours, to add a little here and take away there, has experienced this strange sensation of balancing forms and colours without being able to tell exactly what kind of harmony he is trying to achieve. We just feel that a patch of red here may make all the difference, or this blue is alright by itself but does not 'go' with the others, and suddenly a little stem of green leaves may seem to make it all come 'right'. 'Don't touch it any more' we exclaim, 'now it's perfect.'

Not everyone is quite so careful over the arrangement of flowers, but nearly everyone has something they want to get 'right'. It may be just a matter of finding the right belt which matches a certain dress, the right tie for a particular sports jacket, or nothing more impressive than the worry over the right proportion of, say, custard and pudding on one's plate. In every such case, however trivial, we may feel that a shade too much or too little upsets the balance and that there is only one relationship which is as it should be.

This deceptively simple explanation of balance and relationships is part of Gombrich's explanation of the sophisticated, even mathematical, structure of paintings throughout Western art. In an art gallery, we might see paintings of a 'Landscape with Centaurs' or a 'Madonna with Donors' and find them satisfying without realising that it is their qualities of spatial relationships and colour that help make them so. In other words, it is their abstract qualities that 'speak' besides their literary or 'story' content. Only during the twentieth century has art discarded its literary mantle and been presented simply as a set of relationships. This is 'Abstract Art' which can be difficult to understand because it offers no 'story' to distract, enchant or humour us.

Our hospital walls consist of these abstract qualities, in one way or another this is what they are, and they are capable of subtly providing mental harmony as well as necessary information about where to go for an X-Ray or wait for the doctor.

Form and function

THE BEHAVIOURAL INFLUENCE OF DESIGN

The relationship of form to function is a time-honoured debate. It must be assumed that there were always some forms which were more effective and appropriate for particular functions than others, and that people of the time realised that getting the right form could contribute to improving efficiency; in objects the size of a castle to a finger ring, from a mansion to a teacup and from a whole hospital to a door handle, generations of people have given thoughtful consideration to how to design and make them.

Witness the keyboard on which this book was created; the letter arrangement was established by the inventors of the first typewriters, taking account of the frequencies of use of each letter in the major European languages, the finger span of the average hand and the focus range of the average eye. These elements have not changed although the technology has developed beyond all recognition; what was clockwork has become word processor electronics but the keyboard design works for both. Its moulded light-grey casing displays those keys in matching grey and subtle donkey, each identified with sans serif black letterform; a perfect example of functional form.

However, the behaviour of any writer who simply sits down to work is not likely to be dramatically affected by an item as small as a keyboard, but designing large buildings for many people is entirely different.

We are now demolishing tower blocks because they apparently encourage behaviour that is not socially acceptable; the form was not compatible with the function they had to fulfil (see 'The Modern Movement' in Chapter One) or perhaps they were developed with too much regard for land and building economy rather than the variety and quality of personal and family life. We might therefore reconsider the teachings of Rudolph Steiner who, in a time of post-First World War despair, taught that behaviour is influenced by architecture and artefacts; for example, his buildings avoided the rectilinear. It is in another context that the suggestion has been made that patients with some sorts of mental disorder find the right angles of a door or cupboard, especially as they point in perspective towards you on approach, uncomfortably menacing. The current interest in Feng Shui is another aspect of our belief that form matters and influences our feelings and behaviour (see Chapter Three). None of these theories needs to be adapted wholesale but those who design, appoint and furnish premises for the public should be aware of the teachings of the past as well as the opportunities of the present.

FASHIONS IN FORMAL FUNCTION

Different ages have combined function with form in different ways. Baroque designers gave even a simple object like a candlestick a mass of protrusions and concavities, swirls and curls; the Bauhaus simplified everything down to the cone, the cube, the sphere and the pyramid. Everything around us reflects some design ideal, however feebly, and in a public place like a hospital perhaps only two ideals should dominate.

One is consistency: if you are in a Victorian workhouse or a 1960s' concrete block, design its interior in sympathy. A fine Victorian hospital can perhaps use luxurious colours with its restored carved woodwork in a period corridor (Fig. 4.4); in contrast, a modern hospital used the opportunity of its cubic lift bays for a most imaginative commission from Bridget Riley (Fig. 6.1).

The other is to keep function and form obviously linked. For example, an architecturally interesting new way to flush the lavatory, turn on the taps, find the soap and dry the hands can confuse a patient who is already stressed. There is enough mystery in modern health care, with all its baffling technology, without introducing a different sort of door handle. The best designs retain clear function and adapt shape to modern materials and methods of manufacture.

Conclusion

Our discussion of these matters is, we realise, brief compared to the hundreds of books about colour, proportion and spatial harmony and other design issues. However, we hope we have conveyed the essence of each subject and its importance so that readers will recognise the complexity of the issues involved and can commission the painting, embellishing and furnishing of their buildings by professionals who are expert and experienced. We devote the whole of Chapter Nine to describing how this may be done but first we look at whether hospitals are really suitable venues for art and, if so, what sort of art?

CHAPTER SIX INFORMATION
Colour and other factors

The nature of working as an interior designer for a hospital is peculiar in that it combines what amounts to lavish 'shopping' sprees with a degree of intellectual enquiry. That is why there are some subjects in this book which we consider from an academic point of view, such as the 'aesthetic'; while for others we merely offer practical advice, such as a smelly ward, trampled grass, a broken window.

The intention of these 'Information' sections is to give the necessary contacts and data to put into effect our practical advice described in the preceding chapter. This is easy when we are specifying a bacteriologically sterile floor or a way to fend trolleys off the walls, but does not readily lend itself to a line of theoretical enquiry involved in the discussion of the qualities of colour, space, proportion, form and function. All these are the essential building blocks of the 'aesthetic' that we identified early in Chapter One.

Hence this particular 'Information' section is short and consists simply of a bibliography of writings from which we have not quoted directly but which have influenced our understanding.

BIBLIOGRAPHY AND ARCHIVES

Designing for the Handicapped, ed. Kenneth Bayes and Sandra Franklin, George Godwin Ltd, 1982.

'The Art and Science of Colour' unpublished paper prepared by the Arnolfini Gallery, Bristol, 1990.

'What color reveals: A therapist's point of view', *Color Research and Application*, Jose Raul Bernado Vol. 8 No. 1, 1983

Out of the Blue The Independent Magazine. Andrew Graham-Dixon, 17 July 1993

The Art of Colour, Johannes Itten, trans Ernst Van Haagen, Van Nostrand Reinhold, New York, 1961.

Know Yourself through Colour, Marie Louise Lacy, The Aquarian Press, 1989

Sense of Order, Ernst Gombrich, Phaidon, 1988.

Colour Archive; Faber, Burin and Eric Danger; data deposited at the South Bank University Library. See MARU South Bank University, Chapter One Information.

Colour Archive at Royal College of Art Library, including educational videos on colour. RCA, Kensington Gore, London SW7 2EU (0171 590 4444)

ILLUSTRATIONS

Fig. 6.1: Public Art Development Trust ©
Fig. 6.2: Chelsea and Westminster Hospital Arts Project ©

Arts and decoration

From high art to humble memorabilia

CHAPTER

7

The effect in sickness of beautiful objects, and a variety of objects, and especially of brilliancy of colour, is hardly at all appreciated.

Such cravings are usually called the 'fancies' of patients . . . But much more often, their (so called) 'fancies' are the most valuable indications of what is necessary for their recovery. . . .

People say the effect is only on the mind. It is no such thing. The effect is on the body too. Little as we know about the way in which we are affected by form, by colour, and light, we do know this, that they have an actual physical effect.

Variety of form and brilliancy of colour in the objects presented to patients are an actual means of recovery.

(Florence Nightingale, *Notes on Nursing*)

THE ISSUES INVOLVED

The world of hospitals and the world of art are very different and, since they do not generally get along well, it takes considerable skill to bring them together.

Hospitals are difficult places to run; like prisons and palaces, the inhabitants cannot easily escape, the staff have many tasks to perform and public expectation is high. The buildings are often huge and messy and it is surprising that they inspire so much affection.

Art is a tricky customer which constantly redefines itself. Its boundaries float and merge and it is not easy to teach, administer, accommodate, promote, purchase, evaluate, explain or install, least of all in a hospital.

One function of art is to challenge the 'status quo' of society's functions and beliefs and this can make its audience uncomfortable. As patients are usually already stressed, is a hospital an appropriate venue for these cultural 'challenges'? Yes, sometimes, if the other qualities of delight and invention, surprise and consolation are allowed full rein. That is why this chapter includes 'Decoration in hospitals'.

'Art in Hospitals' is currently a popular subject of discussion and advertisements for arts co-ordinators are increasingly seen in the press. We shall enquire:

- What purposes can be achieved through such appointments?
- How do such appointments turn out?
- Why are the decorative, alternative and historic arts not generally included?

HOW IMPORTANT IS ART IN A HOSPITAL?

We suggest two 'answers' to this: the first is whether art as a global, human product and activity is important. In this context we shall assume that because art is a universal product and activity with recorded expression from earliest times throughout all cultures and circumstances, it is somehow necessary for the human condition. It may be especially necessary in times of personal stress and therefore have a special place in hospitals.

The second 'answer' is local and practical: is it important in your hospital? The answer is yes, it is, but ways must be found to incorporate it appropriately. Art carries with it responsibilities of selection and maintenance which involve financial, practical and legal considerations.

Aims of an art scheme

- To show a range of varied work that is intriguing, distracting and enchanting and which the professional person will know is good and the general public will suspect so.
- To demonstrate that there are informed and receptive minds at work and that care and professionalism are of a high standard, implying a quality of universal care.
- To influence the entire hospital ambience, including uses of land and choices of furnishings, and to raise standards in every respect.

- On a practical level, to identify different areas of a large and confusing building by visual effect.

Can the benefits of 'art' be evaluated?

Since classical times, art has been associated with hospitals and healing but the literature that attempts to evaluate and identify the benefits is slight. There is plenty of anecdotal evidence and some surveys of the benefits of involvement with the arts for the mentally handicapped, sick and the elderly, but otherwise research is scant. We would prefer that it was otherwise, but this is the sad truth.

In Chapter Two we described the evaluation carried out to demonstrate the benefit of trees and growth, but no serious parallel study has been done for the visual arts. Art schemes therefore usually operate on the basis of hope, faith and considerable charity. However, there are useful ways in which you can to some extent check that your arts scheme is worth the time and effort involved, but this is linked to a complete environmental programme and not just a picture here and there. In Chapter Nine, under 'Criteria for success', we discuss how such schemes can be evaluated but for the moment we shall look at the content of an art scheme.

What sort of art?

The world of art can, in this context, usefully be compared to the world of animals. The strength, size, danger and sheer drama of the hammer-headed whale or the tiger is marvellous to contemplate but you would not want them at home lying on the hearth-rug; that role is best filled by a contented cat or a polite puppy. We often admire art but say 'I wouldn't want to live with it', but this may be a judgement of homeliness and scale rather than quality. Goya's *Black Paintings*, Picasso's *Guernica* or even Michelangelo's *Creation* are highlights of human inventive capacity but they are not of a domestic scale, either in imagination or in feet and inches.

A critic's view

The art critic Richard Cork, commenting on hospital art installations, wrote:

> The danger with 'hospital art' is an overwhelming urge to play safe and produce art which is forgettable and just bland. You don't want Francis Bacon's all over the place and Damien Hurst's dead animals in formaldehyde wouldn't go down too well. But I would have thought that there was room to explore a few alternatives . . . Works that are about energy, and savouring and relishing life are what you need when you're lying in your hospital bed, or walking around feeling exhausted after an operation.
>
> (Richard Cork, 'Art in healthcare', *Health Service Journal*, 2 November 1995)

TASTE AND SELECTIVITY

Personal taste versus professional judgement

Aesthetic preferences are sets of judgements that we consciously and unconsciously develop over time by comparisons, peer discussion, intellectual enquiry and practical experiment. Naturally, those who are professionally involved with the arts

HYPOTHETICAL SUCCESS STORY

A hospital is offered money to buy a work of art. Management suggest a boardroom portrait of the Chairman, or a painting of the hospital frontage; the arts co-ordinator wants a sculpture that the intelligentsia will envy; but the nurse representative wants a mural done by the mums of child patients.

What does an arts co-ordinator do?

The Machiavellian solution might be to keep your head down, watch while management and nursing staff compete, and then congratulate the winner and side with them.

The intelligent and responsible solution is to agree that everyone has a point, then go away and treble the money by sheer hard work and cunning (see Chapter Ten, 'Fundraising'). That way all three schemes can be done but you should control the commissioning of each with a rod of iron; then you will scoop up any gratitude and credit that may result.

spend more time and attention on developing this set of judgements than those in other, unrelated professions. While the statement 'I don't like it' is fine as a personal judgement, it is limited, while the professional response asks, 'is it appropriate, is it good of its sort and will it enrich an overall art scheme?'

Elitism versus popularity

The main jibe received by anyone running a hospital arts programme is 'Why do we have to accept your taste regarding the art shown in our building?' There is no short answer, only a long one.

Divisions in history

There are fundamental problems between 'elitist' art and popularism. The main one is that artists, from medieval times to today, have not believed it to be their role to please the general public. Indeed, it is a foundation stone of Western artistic beliefs that to pander to the ignorant is the road to perdition.

This attitude was given a new thrust by both the French and American Revolutions which established the ethic that man's condition would improve and advance as time progresses, and that artists had a duty to be in the vanguard of that advance. Therefore, it didn't matter if the general public didn't like their work because they were fulfilling a superior role, one which history would recognise eventually and which, frequently, was the case. Look at Van Gogh and, while we're looking, consider how psychotropic drugs might have 'calmed' him out of his painting.

The 'unsophisticated' arts

One result of this was and still is that there is a gulf between the way majority popular taste fulfils its need for beauty and diversion in those unsophisticated arts called 'popular', 'vernacular' and 'folk', and the sophisticated high art's definition of beautify and diversion. The overwhelmingly obvious example is that of 'pop' music and culture.

A second reaction occurred when the Industrial Revolution permitted the mass production of objects including 'substitute art' or 'kitsch' aimed 'to give pleasure to the eye and sentiment to the heart of the naive' (Ernst Gombrich, *On Pride and*

Prejudice in the Arts, published by the Art and Architecture Society (See 'Chapter one information') 1998).

Sometimes objects created for the popular market and manufactured by a dark satanic mill made the difficult journey upmarket: Staffordshire pottery and Wedgwood tableware for example. But our whole attitude to art and artefacts is now becoming more sincerely egalitarian, and the current nature of museums and antique shops, sales and collections exhibit this as never before.

Broad areas of excellence

These divisions, as they are generally agreed by informed consensus, have always existed and excellence usually lasts while trivia usually vanishes. Many creations are deservedly unpopular and the experimental is not the same as the merely execrable; unfortunately, the ability to distinguish them is difficult and sometimes only time will tell, so may we briefly consider the reasons why we do not get tired of Shakespeare?

'Sweet Swan of Avon' – how do you help?

Shakespeare started out as a 'popular' artist, churning out his plays to an urgent deadline with a requirement of filling the house with 'the vulgar' and the middle classes besides attracting the patronage of the intellectual, powerful rich. He avoided political trouble (the rack, that 'bed of ease' which claimed some of his colleagues), he made enough money to offer employment to many and ease to his family, he became acceptable in every social sphere and he died in his bed after a happy drinking spree up the Bidford Road with Ben Johnson and Michael Drayton.

Many artists have done as well in worldly achievement but the difference is that we have not got tired of Shakespeare's work. One reason is that it was from the beginning both popular and elitist. As a result, his plays are loved and adapted by every age; the sad ones are given happy endings and the salacious bits are weeded out for school texts before everything is restored in a new edition checked by computer for stylistic authenticity. We see his plays produced in Japanese, in Xhosa, all in white or all in black, 'hi-tech' or fairylike, spoken with the original Warwickshire vowels which no one understands outside Warwickshire or adapted for film, animation and television. In short, there are as many things you can do with Shakespeare as you can do with an egg; how does this 'man for all seasons' relate to a hospital arts programme?

It should in such circumstances be possible to demonstrate that popular and elitist arts can co-exist; that by presenting quantities of dramatically varied material, everyone who is willing to be pleased can be so.

Female icons

Hospitals are strange places that can attract unexpected expression of people's needs. The portrait of the Queen, young and regal, used to suggest more than monarchist loyalty and it was ubiquitous in hospitals; now Princess Diana's portrait has replaced it. One reason may be that, in our monotheistic and masculine age, we need a female deity. After the Virgin Mary was banished by the Reformation, we had Queen Elizabeth and sometimes borrowed Joan of Arc; then there was a long wait before Florence Nightingale and Marilyn Monroe came along and now that Princess Diana has died at the height of her beauty and influence, her position is currently unassailable.

The 'King's Evil'

The circumstances of her death are already the stuff of powerful mythology and aspects of her life and behaviour echo the ritual of royal touching for the 'King's Evil'; this vestigial belief is manifest in the protection of the modern monarch from casual touch, hence the Queen's inevitable gloves.

> 'The "healing touch" was an old English belief . . . and to heal by touch was the King's sacred prerogative.'
> (C.V. Wedgwood, *The King's Peace*, Collins, 1955)

But this power could, by popular if not establishment belief, be transferred to the spouse/deity, as it clearly was to Diana who went bare-headed, sometimes barefoot and often ungloved and was generous with her touch.

This section may seem contrary in a chapter about 'art' but we have included it to encourage anyone who works in hospitals to observe and respect oddities like this. Healing has many dotty aspects, and this is one of them. The image of a female icon, such as the hundreds of portraits of Diana in hospitals, is as different as it is possible to be from the sort of art that wins the Turner Prize but it is there because it is necessary and some such powerful necessities must be intelligently absorbed or that bright, correct and modern young arts co-ordinator had better go and work elsewhere. There is no snobbery like arts snobbery and if you can't 'take' the Princess Diana portrait in its frilly gold frame or a concrete garden donkey with geraniums in its panniers, you'd better go and work in a Bond Street gallery.

'Culture clash'

Many hospitals give as the reason for avoiding aesthetic issues that these are personal matters and that you might paint a wall or hang a picture which someone hates. The result is that walls are magnolia and pictures are chosen for blandness and uniformity, while the result of this is infuriating to anyone who knows or cares about what can be achieved. Avoiding a 'culture clash' leads to 'culture starvation'.

'Arts at the one pole, scientists at the other and between the two a gulf of mutual incomprehension – sometimes dislike, but most of all a lack of understanding' (C.P. Snow, *The Two Cultures*, CUP, 1959/64). These two worlds are very different and they need help to understand each other. A hospital that seeks to introduce art into its premises needs to appoint someone of considerable experience and ability, of the same high calibre as the head of any other important department.

Art in context

Hospital managers who admire the atmosphere achieved in other public premises where decor, decoration and art are used in a way which gives pleasure and creates a positive impression, will probably not have the time or knowledge to achieve something similar in their own buildings. The single most important action such a manager can take is the appointment of someone with specialist knowledge, skills and experience to lead the task of transforming bricks and mortar, often crumbling and shabby, into the kind of buildings where patients, staff and the public feel positive about their surroundings.

Range and variety

We earlier suggested that high quality linked to visual range is the best way to establish a hospital arts scheme. So we now look more carefully at this question of 'range'.

CONTEMPORARY ART

Contemporary art has a bad public press. This is partly because the media love to simplify complex matters and present art as controversial, inexplicable and preferably offensive. The fact is that, frequently, contemporary art *is* controversial, inexplicable and possibly offensive, but so it has often seemed to its immediate audience. The Impressionists were regarded with anathema by the society of the time. So, do you risk it? Yes, providing you have appointed a capable arts co-ordinator.

STUDENT ART

If you ask the local art students to display their work, the results will be at least as satisfying as student surgeons taking on an operation; it is good to give learners a chance but you may need to do a lot of clearing up afterwards. Of course students, whether artists or surgeons, need to be allowed to take the floor and show what they can do, but this should be under the supervision of someone who knows what it is all about. 'Don't go wild lad,' said the surgeon to the medical student doing his first appendectomy, 'it's not the place.' Excellent advice which could be applied to many art students, especially since the nature of art itself is to redefine itself every day, challenge our assumptions and stir us all up. Students tend to exploit this opportunity and may well decide, for the sake of it, to shock the ladies in the WRVS shop and the local lollipop lady. So, by all means invite them to cheer up your hospital but do it through the mediation of your specialist staff.

LOCAL ARTISTS

County cricket clubs have had to tackle the question as to whether they could include cricketers from outside the county. The conclusion was that if you wish to present the national best, you cannot be confined to geographical accident. Excellence is more important than proximity.

However, within the main body of an art programme, there is a significant place for local artists because they help reinforce a sense of place and local pride. A 'send-in' art competition for a hospital's catchment area is fun, albeit exhausting, to organise. 'Span' is the key to success; include not only the endless local landscape watercolours but the 'naive', the nostalgic, the unusual, the hidden, like pictures of kittens knitted in felt and fluff, the Union Jack all done in matchstick heads, the Queen portrayed in glitter string and nails, pictures done by ex-service men of far away places drawn on the backs of old maps, and so on and on. Look hard enough and the odd and the lovely besides the ordinary will crowd in. Marshall and organise it, display it intriguingly and then throw a party and everyone will be better disposed to admire their hospital or, if necessary, forgive its shortcomings.

At the other end of the scale, it is useful to remember that even famous artists have to live somewhere and they will probably have local affiliations to their hospitals like anyone else. It is well worth finding out if this is the case and then making a courteous approach for the possible gift or loan of work. In return, they will want reassurance that their work will be well and safely displayed, insured and acknowledged. Your reputation for handling such matters will affect their willingness to co-operate in this way.

DECORATION IN HOSPITALS

While 'art in hospitals' is a widely recognised subject, 'decoration in hospitals' is not usually discussed.

What is 'decoration'?

Decoration is a visual quality rather than a category of objects (Fig. 7.1). It often implies temporary embellishments such as celebration bunting, festoons and Christmas displays (for a discussion of Christmas decorations, see 'Chapter information').

Decoration is an essential ingredient of the traditional popular arts inherent in fairgrounds, pub signs, caravans, circuses and the folk arts of any nation. It is also associated with design for the theatre, with some filmic and exhibition design, with puppets and toys, all of which suggest ephemerality and enjoyment.

Fig. 7.1 Detail from a 90ft long hand-painted tile frieze 'The Chase' installed in the Charing Cross Hospital, London, 1881 and now restored and in the Jackfield Tile Museum.

Decorative qualities include those of immediate charm, accessible content, controlled use of shape and colour, repetitive pattern and visual wit. These qualities are usually applied 'to' an object so you get a decorated boat, an embellished stage, a patterned book.

'Decorative arts', 'popular arts' and 'applied arts'

The term 'decorative arts' used to be interchangeable with 'popular arts' but times have changed; as countrymen no longer wear smocks, children no longer rely on Punch and Judy for entertainment and ships don't need figure heads, so these popular arts are now in museums rather than daily currency. The 'decorative arts' are now linked with the 'applied arts' which include those practical, usually domestic items such as furniture, furnishings and fittings that have inherent decorative qualities and also those purely useless items, such as ornaments, that embellish a pleasant and comfortable life. It is because decoration is 'applied' that the two terms are now linked.

Decoration, the fine arts and architecture

During the twentieth century, much mainstream art has been involved with political and social ideas expressed in often abstract terms; the exploration of materials, concepts of consciousness, of self, of freedom, of the environment, of expression itself have created work that has spun off into the 'isms' of 'expressionism', 'minimalism' and 'conceptualism', into 'land art', 'body art' and 'performance art'. While these are significant to our age, demonstrations of these avant-garde forms may not offer much consolation to worried patients. It is the 'private turds in public places' syndrome.

Compare the Albert Memorial to the 'Political Prisoner' maquettes of 1944 (an international sculpture competition prompted by the discovery of the concentration camps and other prisons during the liberation of Europe). Many young and later eminent sculptors took part and, while it was famously won by Reg Butler, many of the submitted maquettes, which broke with much established sculptural tradition, are now as well known as the winner.

Comparing these commemorative sculptures, it will be clear that, during less than a hundred years, standard decorative embellishment became generally irrelevant to the avant-garde fine arts. It has similarly become irrelevant to architecture: compare the rich ornamentation of Westminster Abbey or the Bank of England to the rigorously unornamented Shell Building or West Point, although some decorative features are creeping back into the creations of some architects (see Chapter One).

Factors such as this make much late twentieth-century art hard to display to a non-specialist audience and especially in situations of human distress, such as hospitals. It can be done, but requires great care, skill and sensitivity and we suggest that decoration is a significant but neglected alternative. Decoration is essentially merry and light-hearted, and should be just what you need to look at when you are ill. So, how do you employ it? The answer will emerge during the remainder of this chapter (Fig. 7.2).

FINE CRAFTS

The term 'crafts' encompasses traditional crafts, like thatching and domestic crafts like potting and wood turning. 'Fine crafts' have adopted many of those practical skills to make objects which may have no use at all but which explore aesthetic qualities for their own sake in a way most usually connected with painting and sculpture. For example, some bowls are still useful things out of which to eat your fruit salad but others have developed into small 'sculptures' intended only for enjoyment. This has more of a historic tradition than is generally realised but it is mainly a late twentieth-century development that has seen textiles, ceramics, wood and metal handled in original ways.

How does a hospital assemble material for an art scheme?

Some discussion of the financial implications are given in Chapter Eight but we would like to emphasise that the main expenditure should be the salary of someone who has the acumen and knowledge to assess what may be freely available.

FREE MATERIAL

Existing hospital material

Older hospitals sometimes own plans, maps, photographs and portraits linked to their history and a display of these can include related material photocopied from the county archives.

Sometimes a county archive will accept deposited material and offer photocopies and even a small grant for display as a 'swap'. Other items accumulated over the years, like silver cups and trophies, donated collections of shells, minerals, fossils, stuffed animals, insects, stamps, coins, old surgical instruments and hospital equipment, can all be made into intriguing displays (Fig. 7.6).

Fig. 7.2 Detail of the 'Leopard' from the mural (Fig. 2.13) showing the wooden shutter-boarding used to make the window bay part of the design, and the careful integration of planting with the painting. 1988

Display

It is an advantage if, whoever handles this, has some experience of working with the discipline of museum archives besides the razzmatazz of theatre design. The imaginative display of such material can be an opportunity to introduce 'decoration' into hospitals.

Valuation

The accurate valuation of these items for insurance or resale is best done by one of the major auction houses that have local branches or agents (Christies, Bonhams, Philips). Twentieth-century objects are especially difficult to value. Odd items that baffle everybody can be identified by the local museum staff but not valued.

Gifts

Hospitals tend to attract gifts which are prompted by gratitude or 'in memoriam'; these can be appropriate or otherwise so, like all aspects of a hospital's work, it needs a clear policy.

We suggest that either you accept everything, or closely specify an agreed design or a specific piece of equipment or refuse everything except money. The worst scenario is to accept a gift and then ignore, damage or lose it. The gift of pictures is fraught since they are usually of poor quality but not always; the Richard Dadd pictures owned by Broadmoor are now of great value. The consequence of accepting everything is, however, a risky policy and we do not advocate it.

Possible resale value

Merit and value are not the same thing; the Richard Dadd pictures mentioned above always had merit but they now also have value. Hospitals acquire odd things and the perceptive handling of them can reveal the possibility of resale value.

Patients' work and children's work

Both these have a significant place in an art scheme and can best be shown as changing displays in permanent showcases and frames in a specific location. There is usually enough of both these categories to allow changing displays; work should generally be returned to its source rather than kept, except possibly for unusually good examples which the hospital could negotiate to retain.

PURCHASING

Paintings and drawings

Aim for as great a variety as possible in date, size and value of 'originals' in the sense that they are 'hand-done' and not reproductions; they therefore need to be treated with some respect and displayed to their best advantage besides being protected from damage.

Prints

This is a ubiquitous term meaning anything produced either by mass printing, by batch printing or by artists' own printing. Mass-produced prints are often called 'posters' and sold from poster shops. 'Poster' used to be a derogatory term implying cheap, transitory paper prints. Modern laser printing now makes excellent quality poster/prints very cheaply available on the mass market and these include all manner of subject-matter from Old Masters to current images. Batch-produced prints occupy the 'middle' market and are better quality but of less varied subject-matter. Artists' prints are the most expensive because they are in a sense 'hand-done'

and produced in limited editions, but an artist's print can have considerable resale value.

Illustrated books can be cut up and displayed (if you buy two paperback copies) and these can run along a wall as a series.

Photographs

Photographs are surprisingly difficult to buy because of copyright protection. Professional photographers tend to work in the publishing, advertising or packaging industries where massive mass production is expected, and the purchase of prints in any other capacity is not seriously catered for.

Photographs singly printed as a signed edition are sold and, like artists' prints, the high price reflects this. There are picture libraries and agencies from which photographs can be reasonably purchased. Their addresses are found through the British Association of Picture Libraries and Agencies (BAPLA) which publishes a new catalogue each year.

Photographs of animals are enduringly and universally popular; photographs of astronauts or people doing things such as sports, gardening, sailing are excellent; space, the night sky and seascapes besides the inevitable landscapes bring a vigorous and normal view of life into fraught circumstances and are especially appropriate in psychiatric units.

The cheapest and easiest way to achieve displays of photographs is simply to buy two copies of a magazine (such as *BBC Wildlife*) and chop them up for display, or to buy photograph/posters from the listed outlets.

Brass rubbings

These can be bought from brass-rubbing centres but are not often very good. Rubbings are especially popular if they are from a local church and they need not be black silhouettes of praying figures. This is an ideal commission for an artist or student who is used to handling colour and texture on a large scale, as a rubbing can include colour and incorporate lettering and medieval motifs to make a decorative panel.

Once complete, a rubbing is best dry-mounted onto a stable base and laminated for protection. It can then be screwed up as a permanent display and perhaps 'finished' with a painted border surround.

Maps

Old maps of the immediate area can be found in local book and junk shops or from the Map Shop (see 'Chapter information'). Displayed beside a contemporary map with 'You are here' marked in red, an old map can be an intriguing diversion for bored people in a waiting room. Maps of the night sky, planetary or moon maps, historic maps in reproduction are all available.

Religious material

Religious reminders of any sort are very much out of fashion. This may be because those involved in art schemes are usually quite young and have not yet confronted physical mortality. Reminders of the great faiths need not be confined to the chapel, the synagogue, the shrine or temple.

However, visual material relating to Christianity is amazingly ill supplied; even the large cathedral shops are disappointing and there are no relevant catalogues of either historical or modern material. The chain of SPCK shops have some material and if you want a poster of a puppy saying 'I tumble for the Lord' that is where you will find it.

Lettering/calligraphy/poetry

Calligraphers who produce lettered silk-screen prints can be found in registers and indexes. The scheme of poetry displayed as posters on London's underground is described in *Poems on the Underground*, but poems can be simply produced with a large letterform on a word processor and displayed. The Arts Council poetry library now in the Royal Festival Hall and 'Poetry Please', the weekly Radio 4 programme, are both excellent resources and indicators of quality.

Other items

Cartoons and caricatures, stencils, silhouettes and scraperboard, old souvenir editions of newspaper and magazines, collages, origami, kites, anything from holograms to stamps, interesting wrapping and packet material, cut-outs and models can all be used for displays. Paper itself is a decorative medium; marbled, pierced, layered and lacy papers are beautiful and, if folded and fanned, can in themselves make a display.

Textiles

Tapestries are expensive to purchase, but impeccable historic tapestry facsimiles are available at a reasonable cost. Other woven textiles make effective wall-hangings and they can include rugs and simple weavings, reproduction 'throws', printed and embroidered panels besides macramé items. The field of contemporary textiles, including tapestries which can be obtained on loan, is particularly inventive and intriguing.

Tiling

Tiles are comparatively expensive but are hygienic and enduring so, in capital terms, are an excellent investment. From Victorian times until the late 1930s, municipal swimming pools, museums, education institutions, labour exchanges, indeed anywhere where the public were invited to congregate would tend to be protected and enhanced with tiling decoration (Fig. 7.3). Many of these tile schemes are now enjoying recognition and restoration.

Ceramic glazed tiles can offer either simple hard-wearing wall 'cladding' with decorative embellishment or narrative 'picture' panels in the style of the day. Hospitals had a particular tradition for Victorian and Edwardian 'nursery rhyme' panels (Fig. 7.4). These have recently been extensively researched, some rescued for museum care (where they can be seen) and some even reinstated in their original hospitals. This work is carefully compiled and published by the 'Tiles and Architectural Ceramic Society'.

However, many panels have not survived fabric alterations, staff carelessness and fashion changes. The political correctness scrutiny now applied to nursery rhymes has led to the destruction of many such panels.

Apart from historic tiles, modern tiles are available which are either mass-produced by a commercial manufacturer like Pilkingtons or batch-produced by a designer studio; there are a number of such studios but the best-known and one which has been producing tiling for hospitals for many years is Kenneth Clark Ceramics in Lewes (Fig. 7.5). They produce complex panels but also several border designs that can edge an area of plain tiles to give it interest; or a small decorated panel could be let into a plain area, which is well worth considering when upgrading drab premises.

Fig. 7.3 Seymour Children's Ward, St Thomas's Hospital, c.1910.
 A charming ward for children; this photograph shows a terrazzo floor, white painted iron cots with brass knobs, enamel medicine cabinets and electric lighting while heating was from a large fireplace. The tiling scheme, which covers the walls from floor to ceiling and incorporates several nursery rhyme panels, has the inscriptions along the top, 'These panels were given by Alan Johnston Douglas 1902'.
London Metropolitan Archives

In design terms, the commercial range tend to be disappointing although Pilkingtons have recently collaborated with Skopos Fabrics to make a unified range for children's premises.

Mosaics

Mosaics are labour-intensive and are subsequently comparatively expensive and vary enormously in quality. However, this is one of the few art forms where 'quality' (implying exactitude of technique and sophistication in design) can be happily irrelevant if the overall design has enough verve and energy. It is especially suitable for a team undertaking because everyone can do as much as they feel capable, some parts are repetitive and some creative so it unites contributors of varying abilities. Mosaic is an enduring medium but any scheme has to have professional planning because a panel has to be secure both overall and in part (Fig. 7.10).

Fig. 7.4 A nurse shows a child the Dick Whittington tile panels.
London Metropolitan Archives, c.1910

Fig. 7.5 'Boy and pigeons' detail from a tile mural 'Brighton Town': designed and produced by Ann Clark of Kenneth Clark Ceramics for the outpatients' department of the Royal Sussex County Hospital, Brighton. 1992

Boxed displays of three-dimensional material

Historical, reproduction and decorative objects can be safely displayed in perspex boxes or conventional display cases. Small domestic items like buttons, fans, feathers, laces, ribbons and all sewing materials can make a comforting display in a women's ward. Gloves and small fashion accessories like beads and inexpensive jewellery, kitchen items like jelly moulds, small pots, decorative plastics or glasses, also puppets and theatrical masks, ships in bottles, toys, cut-outs of all sorts, historical reproductions like royal seals, and sport, hobby and gaming material are all feasible besides natural items such as feathers, seeds and shells displayed perhaps in the manner of a Victorian 'curiosity cabinet' (Fig. 7.6).

Paper sculptures

These are usually available from the artists who make them but they tend to be comparatively expensive as they are 'one-offs'. Other paper items like huge Chinese fans and lanterns are produced in quantity at low cost, especially at Easter and Christmas.

Mobiles

Mass-produced mobiles made of a light, laminated and non-flammable material are available in variety and are not only of the usual, nursery subjects such as balloons or parrots, but use designs by artists such as Alexander Calder and Joan Miró. Artists' mobiles are expensive but worth investigating; they are also the sort of work an 'Artist in Residence' can produce with patients.

Mobiles are sometimes produced by inventive therapy or art classes, and simple chinese fish in quantity can be made by the children's ward; these will need professional assembly and display like other patients' work. Hospitals tend to be rather hot and heat rises so any hanging object hung high is likely to have plenty of moving 'airstream'.

The value of nostalgia/knick-knacks

Art schemes, even if professionally run, can tend to be over-serious and narrow in what they include.

'Cosiness' is important in interiors and while no one advocates a tide of trivia, appropriately

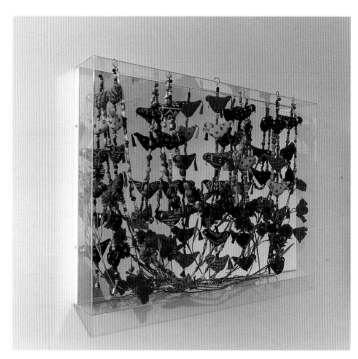

Fig. 7.6 Two decorative cases sited in hospital corridors. The shells were a collection given to the hospital and stored for years until they were assembled into this display. The Indian fabric birds and silk flowers displayed in a perspex case are simply meant to please, amuse and reassure people. The cost of both displays was negligible. 1989

selected and placed objects such as sea-side memorabilia or a plasticine elephant made by someone's grandson can have comforting qualities. Nostalgic items and 'cosiness' need not be confined to 'appropriate' wards (such as those for geriatrics or children) but used widely.

HIRING AND ADVISORY AGENCIES

There are a number of organisations that exist to loan pictures and other works of art to hospitals and hospices. The earliest was the Red Cross service started during the last war when large numbers of people were hospitalised. It still exists, but the main national ones are 'Paintings in Hospitals' and their parallel scheme for hospices, and the Arts Council. These, with schemes run by the regional arts boards, are largely subsidised by the complex network of government arts funding. There are others which are more commercially orientated and, as a result, more expensive.

THERAPEUTIC ARTS

The focus of this book is on the physical environment and does not discuss art, music, drama or literature either as therapies or as 'visitors' to a hospital because these activities do not make any direct contribution to physical surroundings. But the work of all therapists is valuable and makes a difference to patients, especially those in long-term care.

Several of these therapies are promoted by an 'umbrella' organisation and some are long-standing; the Council for Music in Hospitals (which currently takes 3,500 concerts into hospitals each year) was founded in 1948, and SHAPE in 1974, but there are many others (often started to fulfil a local need) that are active for as long as they are needed. They can be found through the usual local channels. Local groups working on Reminiscence Therapy sometimes have links with the local branches of the Oral History Society.

There is plenty of precedent for the involvement of the performing arts; dancers from the Royal Ballet have visited cancer wards and *King Lear* was performed at Broadmoor. To show that the arts and, in this case, music are known to have beneficial effects, we are quoting from a letter Haydn wrote in 1802:

Often, struggling against the obstacles which oppose my labours, a secret voice whispered to me: 'There are so few happy and contented people here below; grief and sorrow are always their lot; perhaps your labours will be a source from which the care-worn, or the man burdened with affairs, can derive a few moments' rest and refreshment.

COMMISSIONING

Hospitals often have specific art requirements best filled by a commission. First of all a clear brief is necessary saying exactly what you require; this is not to deny artistic opportunity but merely to tell the proposed artist that you know what is involved and are going to match their professionalism with yours. For the full necessary details of such an undertaking, please refer to the 'Contract of commission' in 'Chapter information'. Sometimes, what starts as a simple commission becomes a major series and those who make commissions of any sort should be prepared for sometimes greater results than they anticipated (Fig. 7.7).

Murals

Murals have a long tradition in hospitals and some fine examples survive: Hogarth's murals for St Bartholomew's Hospital are still in their original location on the stairs to the Great Hall.

Murals have enjoyed considerable 'vogue' in recent years in public buildings generally but the problem they present is that, once on a wall, they are immovable and we urge that they should be painted onto movable panels so that when the hospital closes or the department moves, the painting can be transported. The appointment of an artist to paint a mural can come under any category – an artist especially contracted or 'in residence', community artist and so on (Fig. 4.10).

One concern seldom expressed is that murals can present conditions of 'claustrophobia' in the same way as lifts and other enclosed spaces; a corridor may be transformed into such an

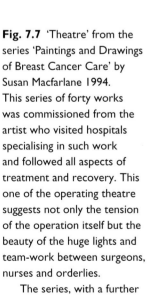

Fig. 7.7 'Theatre' from the series 'Paintings and Drawings of Breast Cancer Care' by Susan Macfarlane 1994. This series of forty works was commissioned from the artist who visited hospitals specialising in such work and followed all aspects of treatment and recovery. This one of the operating theatre suggests not only the tension of the operation itself but the beauty of the huge lights and team-work between surgeons, nurses and orderlies.

The series, with a further set 'Living with Leukaemia' (see Fig. 4.14), has been exhibited widely and remains a unique documentary of modern cancer treatment.

HORROR STORY

A modern Midlands hospital purchased a lifesize sculpture of a camel in unstained wood and it was installed in a small courtyard. Because it was made from several wood sections, it carried the practical requirement (legally agreed in the 'Contract of Purchase') that it would be annually treated for protection by the hospital maintenance staff with clear cuprinol.

Unfortunately, one year the sculpture was accidentally treated with dark-stained cuprinol instead of clear so the whole sculpture became Jacobean oak instead of natural pine. This constituted 'damage' to the work and implicated the staff in negligence and breach of contract. The camel was eventually restored and reworked under the supervision of the artist who had to be paid by the hospital to supervise the work (Fig. 7.8).

'enclosed space' by a large mural that overpowers and crowds, giving a feeling of being closed in and possibly engendering negative reactions which are hardly appropriate in a caring environment.

Sculptures

Unlike a convenient panelled mural, sculptures are usually heavy and expensive to install and insure. They tend to attract vandalism and this may be because they have a strong physical presence and do not fight back. They are seldom purchased because they are so expensive, but more usually hired either from their maker or from one of the organisations listed in 'Chapter information'.

Because they are usually sited out of doors, sculptures also have a particular requirement of care and this can cause problems (as in the 'Horror story').

Stained glass

One traditional use of this is for the commemoration of people or events in the solemn precincts of church, chapel or boardroom (Fig. 7.9) but it can easily be used in a more domestic way. A simple stained-glass panel in a door can be cheap to make to a good design but protection from breakage is essential. Alternatively, some of the most adventurous (and costly) recent hospital commissions have been of decorated glass, engraved or coloured, and these large panels need constant surveillance (which is why they tend to be in reception areas). But small panes, perhaps in a ward's entrance door and incorporating its name

or logo (such as oak leaves for 'Oak Ward') can be sandwiched between sheets of unbreakable glass which gives them necessary protection.

COMPETITIONS

A professional competition for a commission is a serious undertaking. It is costly, because of advertising in 'trade' magazines and papers, and demanding in time and space. It can be useful as a public relations exercise but it is not necessarily a way of finding the best artist for a specific commission. Arts organisations now have such a sophisticated network of registers and information that careful scanning and a follow-up enquiry are usually revealing enough for a suitable artist to be selected.

Fig. 7.8 'Camel' wooden sculpture by Chris Campbell, Milton Keynes Hospital 1983. For the adventures associated with this camel, see above and Chapter Nine.

Fig. 7.9 Stained-glass window dedicated to Alexander Fleming and his discovery of penicillin in 1928 while working at St Mary's Hospital, Paddington. Lower light in a window at St James's Church, Sussex Gardens, London.

There are few public memorials to men or women who have saved life by science or philanthropy, in comparison to those who have, by war and conflict, destroyed it.

RESIDENCIES AND COMMUNITY ARTISTS

The key to success in these appointments is, as with most things, ensuring that realistic expectations by the employer are matched by clear understanding on the part of the appropriate employee. An agreed contract which has had management attention and reasonable pay forwarded promptly are essential.

Community artists can be in any field, literature, music, dance, drama, pottery, art and so on. There is usually a strong requirement for staff and patient involvement and the artist will probably be expected to illustrate daily events, or work with untrained people in the production of work that is of common importance.

This is not easy to organise in human terms or bring to fruition in aesthetic terms, but if it is well done the results can be superb. Fig. 7.10 shows a fine example of a community mosaic produced in Manchester. There has recently been some

excellent work done in the creation of gardens for long-term patients by involving them and their staff in making sculptures and benches, paths and low walls with ordinary materials that come to hand in the tradition of vernacular gardening.

An 'Artist in Residence' has a different undertaking, and the incumbent will be free to pursue his or her own work with little inter-ruption except for the observation of interested parties.

This may sound a 'soft option' but it is not so because there are high requirements of success and such artists are usually appointed because their work in some way reflects or is significant to hospital life.

COST GUIDANCE

It's all relative

The cost of anything is relative; the NHS itself was introduced during a national 'State of

Fig. 7.10 'Head for the Hills' is a mosaic in the entrance to the Mental Health Unit at Manchester Royal Infirmary. It was made by the residents under the organisation of the Artist in Residence, Langley Brown, who took them on a day out in the hills; they drew their red mini-bus and the countryside and then collectively assembled this mosaic. 1985

Emergency' and during fears of bread riots in the aftermath of war.

Compared to the total budget of a hospital, the relative cost of even an ambitious art programme is minimal. It is a question of scale and the framing bill in one national hospital with a well-established art scheme in 1994 was £25,000 out of a total budget of £70 million. An art scheme can be started on a proportionately tiny sum.

A candidate for fundraising

An art scheme is an ideal and usually successful scheme for fundraising. It is preferable for the hospital to contribute something rather than rely solely on fundraising, to show their commitment and involve them in plans and choices (see Chapter Ten, 'Fundraising').

Art as a financial asset

Art itself can quietly become an asset. St Thomas's Hospital has been buying works of art throughout this century and now has an asset of considerable interest and value. This is a course of action that can be started at any time but expert advice and highly informed judgement are essential.

Capital and revenue expenditure

The money for a project is usually found somehow, by fundraising, special allocation, forgotten funds and so on. Then the work is done and applauded and, all too often from that day, deterioration begins. The problem is that hospitals do not allocate either money or the responsibility of care to anybody in particular and so the bright new scheme gradually becomes an embarrassment until perhaps several years later it is guiltily removed.

These projects should be well maintained; then they act as an asset and as a magnet for public confidence and further funding. Unhappily, this is rarely the case.

What can go wrong?

PERSONNEL PROBLEMS

The public

Damage and theft are the main problems here. Damage can occur simply as a matter of wear and tear, for which obvious precautions can be taken, or intentional vandalism against which there is little protection. Similarly, casual stealing can be deterred but determined theft may have to be accepted. Protective coverings and secure fixings and framings are part of the answer; vigilance is the remainder.

The staff

Anyone who cheerfully assumes that hospital staff will invariably be grateful for all this 'artyfication' is in for disappointment. All sorts of resentments surface for all sorts of reasons. As a result, staff have been known to react to an art programme as follows:

- Remove items without authorisation and hide them
- Resite items inappropriately
- Stick notices/chewing gum onto them
- Draw rude messages/faces on them with pen/lipstick
- Obscure them with furniture/equipment/drinks machines
- Steal them/damage them/complain about them
- Run services (wires/pipes/switches) over them
- Alter the surroundings dramatically and without notice
- Allow the surrounds to decay or become neglected
- Add their own material to an agreed scheme
- Refuse to pay hire fees/insurance
- Contravene copyright/contract
- Lock off the area (room/courtyard) and refuse access.

LEGAL PROBLEMS

Most of the above violations could involve legal difficulties either with the artist or the agency who supplied the work.

Original works of art have some protection against violation and alteration and this cannot be lightly ignored. Similarly, many of the loan agencies hang works of art on the contractual agreement that the installation will not be altered without consultation, so the mischievous actions listed above may constitute a breach of contract.

Solutions

The overall solution is responsibility; from the Estates Staff to the Chief Executive, an art scheme requires this and fails without it. If key management staff leave and even if the vacant post is redefined and altered, the ongoing responsibility remains and the legal and contractual obligations remain.

A practical solution is to write into somebody's job description to check works of art at agreed intervals and provide the care and maintenance required. However, 'the buck stops' on the desk of the legal head of the organisation.

Help is at hand

WORKING PRECEDENTS

There are currently about sixty art co-ordinators working in the NHS and, although their effectiveness varies greatly, there are a lot of ideas and energy being expended. Any good library that conducts a computer search will demonstrate the frequency with which the subject is reported in journals published papers and the media.

The identifying names roll before us: *Arts in Hospitals* and *Arts for Hospitals*, the *Healing Arts*, the *Soothing Arts, Action Arts, Art for Health's Sake, Artery, Arts in Action, Action Arts, Medart, Arts Update, Arts Medicine, Celebratory Arts* and so on. Some of these journals become well established and by this we mean they survive for over five years or so, but others vanish, often in the wake of health service reorganisation.

Establishing professional contacts

An arts co-ordinator will need access to a good medical and management library (which most hospitals provide) and an art library (the local art college/department is usually willing to give access). 'Arts for Health' in Manchester is a central base for information insofar as there is one. The regional arts board is a key contact.

ARTS SUBSIDY NETWORK

There are ten regional arts boards in England with responsibility for arts activities across the country. They get their money from two sources: their local authorities and, by far the largest contribution, from the national bodies, the Arts Council of England and the Crafts Council. They should be the first 'port of call' for any new scheme, although the quality of their service varies enormously across the country. They and the art departments of the county and district councils will be most likely to give 'start-up' grants and the staff will also probably be very helpful in specialist terms.

However, even a generous grant will still leave a 'shortfall' which only fundraising can cover. Since this is the key to success, fundraising is the subject of Chapter Ten.

And finally . . .

The ineffectiveness of isolation

It is not uncommon to be walking through a hospital, perhaps not better or worse in its decor than any other, and suddenly come across pictures and installations that are obviously the work of an arts co-ordinator. It is like finding an island of art college or art gallery culture, all by itself and unrelated to anything else around it. Perhaps, on enquiry, one is then told that there is indeed such an appointee and is directed to their room/studio.

And there one will find an arts co-ordinator, probably very committed and intelligent, working hard but well aware that the life of the hospital is going on all around as it ever has. Because they are not integrated into the system arts co-ordinators are not able to make any significant or serious difference to the 'delight and comfort' of the place.

This can be a sad waste of potential and this is why we advocate the appointment of a 'Design Team' who are not just expected to beaver away in corners, but to become part of the decision-making process. Anything less will be unlikely to make any significant difference.

We are addressing this chapter to those health authorities and trusts that have no significant art scheme, but there are many that are well-established and even distinguished in their material and organisation. These include the art schemes at the Chelsea and Westminster, St Thomas's Hospital, the Hammersmith, historic works at Guy's and a fine modern collection including many specific commissions at St Mary's on the Isle of Wight. There are many others of note but it is the hospitals with nothing that we hope to help.

Purchase: where can you buy art?

ART VENUES

The local galleries of whatever type or size will be advertised in local tourist information or by the regional arts board. The method and manner will vary throughout the country but all galleries want the public to know their whereabouts so publicity will be available. The availability of work and prices will vary but there are an increasing number of 'art sales' that are aimed at a wide market and an average buyer (see 'Fairs' below).

The major public galleries generally carry poster-prints of work in their possession, such as the Liverpool Walker Art Gallery or the London National Portrait Gallery. A gallery that specialises in a particular artist, such as Salford Gallery which has the Lowry collection, will have the best collection of that artist. For further material, see the Poster Art Catalogue under 'Mail order catalogues'.

Contemporary Art and Crafts Fairs

At the top end of the market are the two Contemporary Art Fairs held annually at Bath and London and the Chelsea Crafts Fair run by the Crafts Council each autumn; a well-established fair that combines them (and there are many) is the Waterperry Annual Art Fair. While these are interesting for those seriously concerned to see what is going on, items are usually more expensive than most hospital schemes can contemplate, but this is not always so and it is a useful place to see artists who might be successfully commissioned or employed in some capacity.

Student Art Shows

Students working in practical art subjects to degree standard exhibit their work annually in their graduation shows which are open to the public. These can be traced from the county education authority or from the publication *Careers in Art and Design* by Linda Ball and Noel Chapman (Kogan Page, 1996) which lists all art and design courses.

Local Art and Crafts Societies

Information about these will be found as for any other local amenity; ask the Citizens Advice Bureau and look for notices in the libraries and information centres; the arts board may have listings. Established professional artists who live locally can be traced from arts registers and indexes and the arts board will direct you.

THE ARTS PRESS

There are many art and craft magazines and, like all professional journals, they tend to speak to their own kind. The most attractive, colourful and chatty, offering ten issues a year, is *Arts Review*, available from

Hereford House
24 Smithfield Street
London EC1A 9LB
(0171 236 4880)

Artists' Newsletter is a well-established magazine for arts information, advertising, news and views and so on, covering every aspect of the contemporary art world, and it has comprehensive exhibition listings. It is produced monthly by

AN Publications
PO Box 23
Sunderland SR4 6DG
(accounts, orders, subscriptions: 0191 514 3600)

AN Publications' excellent booklist specialises in practical matters for those with professional involvement in the art world; several are mentioned in the course of this text.

Crafts, the main magazine for fine crafts, is published by the Crafts Council and is an elegant, attractive and serious magazine about the making and marketing of contemporary crafts (see under 'Help is at hand').

The whole span of art magazines will be found in bookshops run by major arts centres and galleries, such as the three Tate Galleries (London, St Ives and Liverpool).

INDEXES AND REGISTERS

The Crafts Council houses a Register of Makers from around the country that includes folk and restoration crafts. The Index is a slide library of selected craftspeople working in textiles, ceramics, glass, wood, metals and jewellery, bookbinding and basketry.

The ten arts boards in England run registers which between them represent a countrywide archive of who is making what, and they should direct you to other registers, such as the Women's Art Slide Library, or other self-defining groups.

MAIL ORDER CATALOGUES AND MUSEUM SHOPS

This list is neither complete nor exhaustive but includes those of national distribution that have supplied successful material. Many of them operate a discount scheme for the NHS of 10–25 per cent off advertised prices.

BAPLA – British Association of Picture Libraries and Agencies
18 Vine Hill
London EC1R 5DX
(0171 713 1780)
This is the major trade association for picture libraries, representing 335 members. These vary from small specialist collections to large international stock agencies; it lists members by name with an account of what they stock, and can give contacts by subject-matter, such as aerial photography, food, animals, sport and so on. It publishes a catalogue every year and is invaluable in picture research for those buying photographs for display.

British Library bookshop
Euston Road
London NW1 2DB
Within the new British Library complex that houses the library and some fine exhibition gallieries, is this shop which sells excellent historical reproductions.

Pioneer Project (Celebratory Arts) Ltd
32/34 Main Street
Bentham
Lancaster LA2 7HN
(015242 62672)
This is an association of artists who work in alliance with health practitioners, schools and members of the community to promote positive health. They produce postcards and poster-prints on issues of health, such as 'heart' and 'lungs', that are witty and graphically brilliant.

'Flensted Mobiles' is a firm providing quantities of varied mobiles in paper and laminate; some are enchanting designs for children but many others are intriguing abstract designs. They are on sale in big museum shops but there is an English agent:

Anna Sixsmith
29 Point Hill
Greenwich
London SE10 8QW
(0181 691 2660)

Hines of Oxford – importers of tapestry replicas. Catalogue (£5) and shop:

Kenneth Clark Ceramics
The North Wing
Southover Grange
Southover Road
Lewes
East Sussex BN7 1TP
(01273 476761)

Weavers Barn
Windmill Road
Headington
Oxford OX3 7DE
(01865 741144)

Replicas of eleventh- to eighteenth-century tapestries which are impeccably printed from a photographic transparency onto a woven base of appropriate scale for the image. They are deceptively accurate reproductions and the most successful are those that respect, even if they do not duplicate, the scale of the original. They are not cheap (a replica four feet square is about £400; an NHS discount scheme is in operation) but are highly popular.

Imperial War Museum.
Mail order catalogue and shop:
Lambeth Road
London SE1 6HZ
(0171 416 5000)

Recommended: reproductions of wartime public relations graphics for cooking, transport and so on.

London Transport Museum
Mail order catalogue and shop:
Covent Garden
London WC2E 7BB
(0171 379 6344)

Reproductions of past and current transport posters.

Map Centre
22–24 Caxton Street
London SW1 OQU
(0171 222 2466)

Current worldwide maps and also historic maps, maps of the night sky, space and so on.

The National Trust
Head Office:
36 Queen Ann's Gate

London SW1 H9AS
(0171 222 9251)
Mail order catalogue: 01225 790 800.

Recommended: replicas, decorative items, 'harvest boxes' displaying shells, seeds and flowers, sampler 'kits'.

The Natural History Museum
Mail order catalogue and shop:
Cromwell Road
London SW7 5BD
(0171 938 9123)

Recommended: textiles, inventive items based on animal forms.

OXFAM Fair Trade Co.
Information Service:
Oxfam House
274 Banbury Road
Oxford OX2 7DZ
(01865 313600)
Mail order catalogues:
Freepost Ex151
Exeter EX4 5HQ
(01392 429428)

Recommended: textiles, woven, embroidered and printed, paintings on silk and paper works, fans and mobiles.

'Past Times'
Mail order catalogues and several shops:
Witney
Oxon OX8 6BH
(01993 770440)

Recommended: replicas, decorative items, textiles, trays, kites, 'naive' paintings, historic maps.

The Poster Art Catalogue
produced by the Art Group
Head Office
146 Royal College Street
London NW1 OTA
(0171 482 3206)

Distribution Centre:
Booth Drive
Park Farm South
Wellingborough
Northamptonshire NN8 6GR
(01933 400 555)
Freephone for sales only: 0800 289 899.

Over a thousand well-produced poster-prints of varied design and photographic images including historic material.
Science Museum
Mail order catalogue and shop:
Exhibition Road
London SW7 2DD
(0171 938 8000)
Recommended: imaginative and unusual items.

Victoria and Albert Museum
Mail order catalogue and shop:
Cromwell Road
London SW7 2RL
(0171 938 8434)
Recommended: replicas, decorative items, textiles.

MULTISTORES AND SPECIALIST SHOPS

IKEA. There are IKEA stores at Warrington, Gateshead, Leeds, Nottingham, Birmingham and in London at Brent Park and Croydon; the Croydon branch is the largest but they are all enormous.

For a catalogue with addresses and contacts, ring 0181 208 5600.

Recommended: 'Marketplace' rugs and textiles, clocks, china, glassware, perspex and paper, wood, basketry and many inventive and unusual items. Some lines are available for a limited time, others continue for years. These items are not 'nostalgic pastiche' but use recognisable design elements inventively. Prices are famously cheap and the reason is massive mass production and popularity. A few words of caution: the catalogue is not a complete list from 'Marketplace', delivery is not available (not even of heavy items, although private firms offer such a service from some of the stores), the ordering or reserving of goods is difficult. IKEA operate strictly on the principle of customers coming to buy and taking their purchases. At Christmas and Easter they have special lines that are worth the journey.

Other relevant stores are Reject shops, Habitat, Boots kitchen and gift departments and SPCK shops for Christian material.

HISTORICAL MATERIAL

Such items, whether replicas, reproductions and so on are available from several of the outlets we have already listed.

Brass Rubbings

The key publication to finding their where-abouts is *Monumental Brasses in the British Isles* by Mill Stephenson (1926) available in reference libraries and you can thereby find local brasses. Other selected listings are published but many churches have banned brass rubbing because it damages the latten. The diocesan offices of your nearest cathedral will give you contact numbers of churches and their incumbents and will also be able to tell you whether there is a brass-rubbing centre which houses replicas. The objection to these is that some 'replicas' have reduced the original size; this, in our view, so far negates the quality of the original brass, in which the silhouette and detail were directly related to proportion and size, as to render it pointless. However, the best replicas are very fine and there is a good collection at Westminster Abbey and St Martin's in the Fields.

London's Museums of Health and Medicine

The London Museums of Health and Medicine Group was formed in 1991. Its aim is to raise awareness of the outstanding resources offered by listed museums through joint undertakings such as publicity leaflets, lectures and research.

The leaflet *London's Museums of Health and Medicine* lists sixteen museums in London that provide a dramatic insight into the social and medical history of health and disease. Conducted tours are available. The leaflet is available from the Wellcome Institute Marketing Department (0171 236 1180; or see 'Chapter one information,) or contact the Group at:
The Old Operating Theatre Museum
(0171 955 4791).

Another good publication is *Weir's Guide to Medical Museums in Britain*, published by the

Royal Society of Medicine
1 Wimpole Street
London W1M 8AE
(0171 290 2900)

Diploma in the Philosophy of Medicine and Diploma in the History of Medicine are two part-time Saturday morning courses run in London over 20–25 weeks by

The Society of Apothecaries
Apothecaries' Hall
Blackfriars Lane
London EC4V 6EJ
(0171 236 1180)

Hiring and borrowing

The Red Cross set up the first picture loan service specifically to supply hospitals during the last war; it is in operation in very few areas now and has been largely superseded by other agencies.

NATIONAL AND REGIONAL AGENCIES

'Paintings in Hospitals'
The Sheridan Russell Gallery
16 Crawford Street
London W1H 1PF
(0171 935 0250)

Two-dimensional work of all sorts, mainly paintings and prints, is bought and displayed at this gallery where hospital staff can visit any time by appointment and select a minimum of five works and a maximum of forty. There is a fee per piece and insurance. The agency insists that works are hung for patients' benefit and not in offices. 'Paintings in Hospitals' now also supplies hospices.

Hospice Arts, Forbes House
9 Artillery Lane
London E1 7LP
(0171 377 8484)
This organisation does not have a 'library' of pictures to lend but works instead to encourage and develop opportunities for hospice patients to share with artists in the creative process.

Arts Council Collection
The South Bank Centre
The Royal Festival Hall
London SE1 8XX
(0171 921 0875)

This was started in the 1940s and purchases from a wide artistic spectrum have been made consistently ever since. It is now housed at the South Bank and administered by the South Bank Trust (as is the Poetry Library); its huge collection is 'tiered' in its availability.

Both 'Paintings in Hospitals' and the Arts Council collection have requirements of insurance and care which are all too often neglected; both organisations complain of the frequent negligence with which works of art are often treated which has led to tightening of conditions and increased fees.

There are other loan collections across the country and the arts boards have information (see 'Help is at hand').

Display materials and equipment

The best displays are done by someone with the accuracy of a bookbinder and the aplomb of a theatre designer. Basic tools are a large work surface, clean storage, a cablefree drill, an aluminium stepladder and well-equipped toolbox; the use of trolleys and vans is also necessary.

FRAMES

Quality frames

Good-quality frames for the prestigious pictures can be specified from any frame-maker; a recent, technological development is for a picture to be scanned into a computer and then 'printed out' in a variety of frames for the customer's selection.

Basic frames

Buying frames from a mass-production line or any of the large stores is cheap but they are of standard sizes and tend to be flimsy. A local framer may make them on discount prices but secure picture frames in which pictures can be changed is the best solution, although not the cheapest.

Secure frames

The best 'tried and tested' secure frame is constructed with a backing 300mm deep (made from hardboard edged with aluminium) which is screwed to the wall. The shallow perspex 'box' top, containing the picture, is then fitted over this and screwed around the edges.

This frame has been used for years in general and psychiatric hospitals. The frame can be adapted for secure units and special hospitals by using fireproof foam and wood backing and security screws, while the basic design can also be made into deep boxes up to about 1500mm deep for the display of three-dimensional items. The picture or contents can be changed simply by unscrewing the perspex top while the base remains fastened to the wall. They are enduring and overcome theft and fading.

This basic design can be made by any firm that deals in perspex and display matters, and these firms will advertise locally or will be known to the local museums and galleries.

SCREENS AND CASES

All equipment will last longer if carefully handled and stored and it is worth making protective calico covers to be used during all removal and storage.

General exhibition material is available from specialist manufacturers or 'made to measure'. Two well-established suppliers are:

Click Systems Ltd
5 Tanners Drive
Blakelands
Milton Keynes MK14 5BU
(01908 617788)
and
Marler Hayley
Little End Road
Eaton Socon
St Neots
Cambridgeshire PE19 3SN
(01480 218588)

A cheaper scheme can be devised by purchasing a set of basic display panels (honey-comb boards are best, several thicknesses available but all substantial and light) from any supplier of museum services and assembling them with 'Klem clamps' – aluminium clamps that you tighten with an Alun key so that they can be linked at angles between 90 and 180 degrees to make a 'zig-zag' of panels. The firm also supply clamp-on spotlights and leaflet holders:

Klemetric Displays Ltd
11 High Street
Wansted
London E11 2AA
(0181 530 3785)

The relative merits of glass and perspex are discussed below under 'Light' and 'Fire'.

SERVICES AND MATERIALS

Services such as dry-mounting, laminating, photography enlargement, labels, and purchase of items like display cases and screens can be found under 'Exhibition Services' in your Yellow Pages. Alternatively, you can ask your local museum or art gallery display departments for recommendations.

Fabrics: felt, hessian, etc.

Local shops normally stock only that intended for small, domestic projects. The main suppliers are:

B. Brown Display Materials
74–78 Wood Lane Edge
Hemel Hempstead
Herts HP2 4RF
(01990 340340)

Water-based adhesives

Adhesives stick things together in one of three basic ways: a water-based glue such as 'Gloy', flour paste or 'Polycel' penetrates the material each side and then evaporates; once dry it is enduring and stable in that it is 'inactive' and has no effect on its adjacent material. Preferably it should be dried under pressure but this is not always feasible. Valuable items treated in this way should be stored or mounted onto acid-free paper or card (which is like distilled water, free from all impurities). Traditional brown sticky tape is similarly a water-based adhesive.

Glue size, traditionally made from animal hooves, and its derivative Scotch glue are in this category but they are messy to use, have to be applied hot and they do not last, as anyone will know who has seen wood joints of old furniture fall apart scattering a mass of dry crystals.

Petroleum-based adhesives

Petroleum-based adhesives (such as Cow Gum and Copydex) are viscous and also penetrate, to an extent, their contact surfaces. They are effective for material heavier than paper because they are strong but, even when dry, they are not inactive and their oils continue to seep into their contact surfaces, eventually staining them with an oily shadow. Over many years they harden and darken so should be used with discretion.

Sellotape and double-sided Sellotape come within this category and should be used invisibly on any permanent display; masking tape is better. The strongest double-sided Sellotape is the heavy-duty carpet variety but, once on a surface, it is difficult to remove. If you want to discourage theft by gluing down items, this is ideal.

Other adhesives act like a binding 'sandwich'; they penetrate very little of their contact surfaces but adhere and dry mainly either by the absorption of oxygen ('Bostik') or by chemical reaction when mixed together ('Araldite'). They were first developed during the last world war when aircraft depended on adhesives and are, consequently, extremely strong and impossible to remove.

Aerosols and others

Aerosol adhesives such as 'Trademount' are useful for mounting light material, but are neither strong nor enduring. Blue-tac is handy but its oil spoils absorbent contact material, and Pritt, while convenient and solvent-free, is not strong. Sometimes the best solution is dressmaking pins, button and nylon thread, panel pins and tiny screws.

Permanent displays of paper items should use cut mounts and secure material invisibly with brown sticky tape or masking tape; larger items of any value should avoid having any adhesive attached to them and use threads and pins. Impermanent displays can get away with anything.

Christmas decorations

While everyone likes a brave display, the damage that is done to walls, ceilings and doors by staff attaching decorations with Sellotape and Bostik remains throughout the remaining year to depress everyone.

Alternatives to adhesives

Decorations can instead be attached to existing fittings, pillars and so on with cotton or nylon thread, fine string, fuse wire or heavier wire made into hooks. These and a determination to take decorations down thoroughly, may avoid the situation whereby leftover tufts of glitter are left, stuck out of reach, to discolour gradually during the year's remaining eleven months (see Chapter Eight, 'A patient's comment').

Practical care

PHYSICAL ASPECTS

Placing

This involves safety, convenience and aesthetics and is subjected within hospitals to a host of difficulties; the statutory notices plastered up after you have completed a display or the sudden installation of a dispensing machine or a set of new fire hydrants can negate your best efforts. The only answer is consultation with relevant staff; firmly, professionally and consistently.

Light

Fading occurs because light is energy that batters at vulnerable fabric and eventually destroys it; witness any newspaper left in the sunshine for a week. Light hours are called 'lux hours' by museum curators so, if your material has to be protected, either have low lighting (which may be suitable in a museum but probably not in a hospital) or display it under perspex which cuts out 93 per cent of ultra-violet light. Valuable material can be covered with ultra-violet protective perspex which eliminates a further 3 per cent of light or you can invest in ultra-violet 'sleeves' for fluorescent lights.

The simplest solution is to display all paper-based material under ordinary perspex and keep anything valuable or old out of direct light as heat is also a damaging factor.

Heat

Fading relates mainly to paper items but anything hung above a radiator will suffer. Large paintings and hangings should be hung securely avoiding direct heat and light. Even a tile mural can be damaged if placed above a radiator and, worst of all, beneath a top grill blowing cold air; the combination can make the adhesive and grout crumble, tiles fall off the wall and land you in a 'safety' dispute.

Theft

There are two main types of security: one is to render theft near impossible (the Crown Jewels have never been stolen from the Tower of London) and the other is to deter the passing, opportunist thief. It is only for this last category that we advise.

Casual theft can be discouraged by using the secure frames and boxes described above, by strong fastenings (mirror plates) with either ordinary slot-head screws or posidrive/Philips screws or security screws (usually these require an Alun key), or by concealing screw caps (available from any DIY store). Try fastening or gluing down everything possible (see 'Adhesives') to make theft difficult. For example, ceramic pots containing dried flowers can be filled with sand or sawdust so if anyone takes them, they will be embarrassed by a tell-tale trail from a hole in the pot base. Empty vessels (decorative pots, silver trophies and so on) can be filled with water and no thief wishes to be soaked. Valuable items should be within sight of staff and not near any exit.

Fire

The standards applied by fire officers are not always consistent, even within one authority, for some allow perspex picture frames on an 'escape route' and some do not. Large areas of perspex (over 1 metre square) that have air underneath them can reasonably be seen as a hazard so either install uncovered material (such as paintings or textiles), or use glass and, to avoid splintering if smashed, use a transparent adhesive; a local supplier will be recommended by any security firm or architect who deals with public buildings.

A military development that was made available for the Gulf War is a non-toxic fire-retardancy fluid called Environgraf 321 that can be applied to anything that is absorbent (such as paper and fabric) which then becomes equivalent to 'O' rating (the highest degree of fire retardancy). It is now used extensively in theatres and exhibitions and it has made possible displays of greater variety in public places.

There are many Environgraf products, coatings for wood and metal, plaster and cable coverings but the relevant one here is Environgraf 321. This is a non-toxic liquid with which you treat all the goods that no fire officer would previously allow in a public place.

Environmental Seals Ltd
Environgraf House
Barfreston
Near Dover
Kent CT15 7JG
(01304 842555)

This is a central dealer who will refer you to local distributors who will probably be able to treat large items for you.

Any item that is absorbent should be saturated, either by applying with a paint brush or from an ordinary plastic 'spray bottle' or by immersing it in a bowl or bath and then allowing it to dry thoroughly. Unstable dyes can run so apply by spray and keep the item flat. Once dry, that item will not burn but once washed or cleaned, retreatment is required. The product is not cheap but represents release from prohibitive fire regulations.

ORGANISATIONAL ASPECTS

Safety of the public

The laws of safety that govern public places apply to an art scheme as to anything else. If an artist is commissioned to create a new work, safety consideration should be implicit in the contract (see 'Contract of commission') subject to the normal care expected of the client.

There are particular safety problems with any form of water (see Chapter Two, 'The inexpediency of a water feature'); fountains that spray water in droplets are thought to be prone to Legionella disease so only fountains that trickle or dribble are feasible. It is confidently stated that 'anyone can drown in an inch of water' and wild ducks tend to settle on water and the faeces of any species is viewed with alarm by safety staff.

But water features are often requested and ducks do not seek permission before inhabiting a pond, so it is up to management to decide how far to allow these remote, lethal possibilities to influence their installation.

Damage

Serious damage to a significant item can be claimed against insurance. Any damaged work of art made by someone still alive should be referred to them for repair (explained in 'Contract of commission' below). The 'Help is at hand' list will refer you to agencies such as the arts boards who should be able to refer you to specialist advice, but any damaged item should be dealt with immediately as damage breeds itself.

Insurance

You can reasonably decide not to insure items you own as the premiums are high for anything displayed within reach of the public, but loaned material usually has a condition of insurance.

The insurance of really valuable items is expensive so either display them as suggested above, confine them to the boardroom or sell them.

Basic advice

Advice covering identification, care and display of historic material (over fifty years old) and also ethnic, archaeological and natural material can come from the local museum service staff. For modern material and technologically based material (film, holograms and so on) appropriate advice will be given by the regional arts board or they will refer you to someone who can help.

For valuation and insurance advice use local or national auction houses or the arts boards.

Legal care

Many problems have a legal basis, not least so those encountered in an art scheme and these relate primarily to:

* contractual agreements of commission/purchase/hiring
* copyright protection of work.

CONTRACT OF COMMISSION/ PURCHASE/HIRING

A contract is simply an agreement between parties that is intended to be binding. While it can be verbal, problems are avoided if the terms of any important agreement are written down (as Mae West is supposed to have said, 'A verbal contract ain't worth the paper it's written on'). A contract of commission should include the following and the basics adapted for purchase or hiring.

The client's obligations

* *Money*
  Total price, inclusive or otherwise of VAT, materials, research and travel fees, installation costs and help. Whether payable in instalments or one lump sum (it is customary to give one third on acceptance of the contract, one third half-way through the project and one third on completion).
* *Making the work*
  Is an initial maquette or sketch to be proffered?

EXAMPLE OF COPYRIGHT CONTRAVENTION

The mural 'In the Garden of Eden Adam Names the Animals' (Fig. 2.13) was painted by one of the authors in 1988 and she retained copyright. It was an awkward site as there were two large windows dissecting the wall which were 'disguised' as two glass trees by framing them in shuttering plywood cut into tree silhouette shapes. These two windows looked into an office and, during winter, bright-blue plastic was installed over the glass as draught excluders.

These two bright-blue windows interrupted the colour theme of the mural and, while it was in place, a photograph was taken of the mural for the cover of the annual report. While this was a compliment, no permission had been sought and the resultant photograph showed the mural in a condition that was not the artist's intention.

She therefore arranged for the blue plastic to be replaced with clear plastic and used the copyright fee for a new photograph to be taken under her direction. It was then used, as intended, on the annual report and everyone was happy. However, the hospital had not realised that they had contravened the law both by subjecting the mural to 'derogatory' treatment and photographing it without permission. This is the sort of situation that can lead to costly legal claims.

(It is customary that once such evidence of the artist's intentions has been accepted by the commissioner, the final work is bound to be accepted providing it relates adequately to the initial design.)

If work is to be done on site, access and work conditions.

- *Future care*
  Future care and maintenance of the work, the artist's or owner's right to oversee repair if it is damaged, protection against alteration, poor display, reallocation of its site, etc.
- *Copyright*: who owns this?

The artist's obligations

- To honour all the terms of the contract.
- *Safety of the object*
  Will it injure or fall onto anybody, is it technically safe (i.e. will not fuse all the lights), will it obscure light, stop up drains, strain or damage the floor and so on?
- *Durability of the object*
  Will it disintegrate, fade and blow up or down?
  If maintenance is required, are details supplied?

COPYRIGHT

This is the protection of writers, artists, composers and other creators of original work from having their work copied or plagiarised to the extent that it might reasonably be mistaken for the original, and from reproducing pictures of it. There is also some protection from abuse and alteration of work.

Copyright is a separate legal entity from the object itself; you can own a picture or sculpture but not necessarily own its copyright. If a contract of sale or commission does not specify, it is assumed the artist owns the copyright but much trouble is avoided if you make clear specification from the outset. Artists who are in employment (such as an artist in residence) usually concede copyright rights to their employer but again it is best to specify.

Copyright exists from the moment of creation and covers all works of artistic creation. It does not require registration and exists for fifty years from the death of the creator. As an example of this, J.M. Barrie left all royalties from *Peter Pan* to Great Ormond Street Hospital for sick children and this lasted until the copyright expired during the 1980s.

If the artist retains copyright, it allows the artist the exclusive right to authorise reproduction (or copying) of a work which can only take place with consent. Permission is normally granted by payment of a fee which allows artists to make some income from their work.

The copyright also allows the artist some moral rights over the work, which include the right to claim authorship and the right to object to any derogatory treatment.

Advice on copyright can come from the arts boards or the Arts Council or, for the artist, from membership of DACS:

Designer and Artists Copyright Society
Parchment House
13 Northburgh Street
London EC1V OAH
(0171 336 88111)

ARTISTS IN RESIDENCE

Many hospitals employ an artist in residence for some scheme and the items listed earlier under the employment of an arts co-ordinator and above for commission and purchase will apply. Basically, success depends on everyone knowing what is expected either side, but copyright also is an important element, especially if patient work is involved and if the artist is 'employed' rather than 'commissioned'.

It is usual in all these cases for the trust to own the work and accept the obligation of care, repair and maintenance to be clearly understood, even when staff are replaced. The creator or artist usually retains the copyright. The hospital's solicitor should be involved in drawing up this agreement.

Help is at hand

Government subsidy for the arts is administered by a network of publicly funded organisations consisting of the arts and crafts councils and the regional arts boards.

NATIONAL BODIES

These will be most useful for advice on salary scales, copyright, contracts, and contacts for the regional arts boards.

Arts Council of England
14 Great Peter Street
London SW1P 3NQ
(0171 333 0100)

Arts Council for Wales
Holst House
Museum Place

Cardiff CF1 3NX
(01222 394711)

Scottish Arts Council
12 Manor Place
Edinburgh EH3 7DD
(0131 226 6051)

The Crafts Council
44a Pentonville Road
Islington
London N1 9HF
(0171 278 7700)

Register and Index slide library of crafts-work is available; *Crafts* magazine is published ten times a year.

REGIONAL ARTS BOARDS

There are ten arts boards in England which provide a specialist service across the country. Most of them run registers of artists and while, as with anything, the standard of service varies, they are the only national network catering for the contemporary arts.

They will put you in touch with art commissioning agencies in your area with whom a hospital would probably work directly.

They should be your first contact if you want either funding or guidance on any of the arts, whether live music or dance, literature in any form, film and video or visual arts.

Eastern Arts Board
Cherry Hinton Hall
Cherry Hinton Road
Cambridge CB1 4DW
(01223 215355)

East Midlands Arts Board
Mountfields House
Forest Road
Loughborough
Leicestershire LE11 3HU
(01509 218292)

London Arts Board
Elme House
133 Long Acre
London WC2 9AF
(0171 240 1313)

Northern Arts Board
9–10 Osborne Terrace
Jesmond
Newcastle-on-Tyne NE2 1NZ
(0191 281 6334)

North West Arts Board
Manchester House
22 Bridge Street
Manchester M3 3AB
(0161 834 6644)

Southern Arts Board
13 St Clement Street
Winchester SO23 9DQ
(01962 855099)

South East Arts Board Union House
Eridge Road
Tunbridge Wells
Kent TN4 8HF
(01892 507200)

South West Arts Board
Bradninch Place
Gandy Street
Exeter EX4 3LS
(01392 218188)

West Midlands Arts Board
82 Granville Street
Birmingham B1 2LH
(0121 631 3121)

Yorkshire and Humberside Arts Board
21 Bond Street
Dewsbury WF13 1AX
(01924 455555)

OTHER AGENCIES

We are listing only those organisations that are nationally relevant and which have been in operation some years. For reasons of space we are not listing the several dozen further addresses for hospital arts activities but would refer readers to the comprehensive booklist and listings in the book *Helping to Heal* (see below).

Arts for Health
Manchester Metropolitan University
All Saints
Oxford Road
Manchester M15 6BH
(0161 236 8916)

This was founded over twenty years ago by Peter Senior and is the most stable and reliable agent, library and archive on the subject. It aims to assist in improving the physical and social environment of healthcare buildings and advising on the starting of an arts programme. Membership entitles subscribers to the Information Pack, free telephone advice, information and contacts, access to the library and their magazine *Artery*.

Public Art Development Trust
3rd Floor
Kirkman House
12–14 Whitfield Street
London W1P 5AD
(0171 580 9977)

This organisation exists to advise and facilitate the placing of art in publicly owned spaces and this includes hospitals. They also undertake research and feasibility studies and offer information on all aspects of art in public places. They operate in Greater London only but they have an extensive library and slide library and will advise any applicant.

BIBLIOGRAPHY

Much of what has been written on this subject is in journals produced for the health management profession (listed in 'Chapter one information') or in one of the art magazines (listed above under 'Arts press'). Books have generally been published by one of the major charitable foundations such as the Gulbenkian or Carnegie Trusts because it is not a subject likely to hold its own in the commercial market place. Our selection of these and other books used here is as follows:

Helping to Heal – the Arts in Health Care, Peter Senior and Jonathan Croall, 1993 (Gulbenkian Foundation, 98 Portland Place, London WIN 4ET; 0171 636 5313).

Art in Hospitals: A Guide, Lesley Greene, 1989 (King's Fund, 11–13 Cavendish Square, London W1M OAN; 0171 307 2400).

Art and Mental Health Hospitals: Art as an Effective Element in the Care of the Mentally Ill and Mentally Handicapped, ed. Malcolm Miles, British Health Care Arts, 1991.

Artists in Residence in Hospitals: the Contributions of Artists to the Quality of Life in Acute and Long Stay Hospitals, ed. Malcolm Miles, British Health Care Arts, 1991.

The Unsophisticated Arts, Barbara Jones, The Architectural Press, 1951.

Twentieth Century Ornament, Jonathan Woodham, Studio Vista, 1990.

Percent for art: a review, ed. Alan Haydon and Isabel Vasseur, 1991. Published by the Arts Council, 14 Great Peter Street, London SW1P 3NQ.

Brightening the Long Days: a study of Victorian and Edwardian hospital tile pictures, ed. John Greene (this publication is currently out of print but worth tracing through libraries).

ILLUSTRATIONS

Fig. 7.1: The Jackfield Tile Museum, The Ironbridge Gorge Museums ©

Fig. 7.2: Photograph Mike Englefield and © SH

Figs 7.3 and 7.4: Guy's and St Thomas's Hospital Trust ©

Fig. 7.5: Kenneth Clark Ceramics Ltd ©

Fig. 7.6: Photographs and © SH

Fig. 7.7: Susan Macfarlane ©

Fig. 7.8: Photograph and © David Wright

Fig. 7.9: St James's Church, Sussex Gardens, Paddington, London ©

Fig. 7.10: Hospital Arts and START, Manchester ©, photograph Jack Sutton

The human factor

INTRODUCTION

Throughout this book the subjects we have discussed have decreased in size. We started off by describing whole hospitals and huge sites and then the components of hospitals, those rooms and areas we all recognise, before we examined the features that comprise them, such as the ceilings, floors and walls. Then we discussed the pictures on the wall besides those qualities of colour and shape that surround them; now we hone down to those particular qualities of hospital care that affect the single patient lying in a hospital bed. All those who deal with the very young, the very old or the very ill know that for these people life centres around their bed and that they perceive the world from it.

This book is not about the quality of professional care. Excellent nurses, doctors and therapists can triumph over poor-quality buildings, decoration and design but our argument is that they are too often required to do so unnecessarily. Most patients do not carefully analyse which aspects of their experience delight or depress them in the way that we are doing in this book, but nevertheless they can have the impression of being well cared for or sense that things are not quite right.

AUTHOR'S ANECDOTE:
THE ORIGINS OF THIS BOOK

When I was an art student in the early 1960s, I fell ill and was admitted to my local hospital for several weeks. The ward was a Nightingale design in a wartime hut and the regime was as described in Chapter Four under 'Patient wards', but it represented excellent care. The responsibility for this rested with the ward sister to whom I owe, if not my life, certainly my sanity and happiness during that painful period. She was a delightful woman, probably in her late thirties, and she had calves like Guinness bottles and curly hair like a painted Botticelli angel; she attended to me beyond the call of duty and, on the first day that I was able to walk any distance, she took me on her 'day off' to her own home and gave me a lovely, non-hospital dinner.

During this time, new curtains were allocated to our ward and Sister chose them, with the chief doctor backing her hurried choice. I lay in bed, imbued with art-school values, frantic with frustrated understanding of the qualities of drawing, of printing, of the scale of repeats, of colour gradations, and knew that I *knew* what was needed was a woven design so that those in bed could have the benefit of the design quality – as well as those outside. 'Oh no, dear,' they said when I revived enough to sit up and tell them so, 'we can't have those because the Works Department haven't any samples.'

Eventually, as I lay in bed looking at the wrong side of a poorly printed fabric, badly drawn and shoddily made (too few hooks and an inappropriate Rufflette tape), I also knew that darling Sister, who was good at pretty well everything else, was no good at choosing curtains. By then I had been kicked out of my cosy and curtained position, which was reserved for the very sick up by her desk, and been sent down to the convalescent end with the geraniums and the 'outlook' and a set of faded reproductions of Degas' ballet dancers lent by the still active Red Cross Picture Service. Some other wilting dame was occupying Sister's attention (how *dare* she, and how could Sister get through the day without *me*?) but the seeds of this book had been sown, even though its gestation and growth took thirty-five years.

One day, after a painful treatment and a long sleep, I awoke to find the curtains drawn around my bed and the window open. It was a spring evening and distant church bells were just audible in my curtained area, cocooned within the peaceful ward; visiting hours were

Fig. 8.1 Times have changed since Sister wore a hat like a sailing ship and ran her ward with military precision besides serving the meat and two veg. at dinnertime. Unknown hospital; July 1941. RCHME

and one day I would rejoin it. Then a nurse brought me a fried egg, a small salad and an orange drink. It was delicious. (SH)

Would these ward conditions be likely or even possible today?

THE SAME HOSPITAL TODAY

Architecture, layout and land

Those huts have been rebuilt as single-storey wards and the layout is now that of bedded bays. The architecture is good, albeit rather ordinary, and the wards are very hot in summer, the 'very cold' in winter being offset by heating but the energy loss must be considerable. They look out onto grassed banks, frequently mown noisily, and a few heavily pruned shrubs before surrounding car parks stretch as far as the eye can see. The landscaping is utterly uninspired, the allotments having long since been banished as they were considered 'unsightly'.

Ward conditions

Ward windows are fixed so that they open only a few inches (necessary for today's security) so, while those particular church bells still ring, a patient would be unlikely to hear them, partly because there is so much other noise going on, like the grass cutting outside and the constant movement of cars and tooting of horns.

Wards inside are dominated by radio and television from which there is no escape; headphones are seldom compulsory and, in the children's ward, video games and loud television mean that even children regaining consciousness after an anaesthetic are denied peace. Visiting hours are almost continuous and ward discipline appears now to be guided by the principle of *laissez-faire*.

Hierarchical discipline is out of fashion and the days when Sister wore a hat like a sailing ship and exerted detailed discipline over staff besides serving the meat and two veg at dinnertime have long since gone (Fig. 8.1). Personal responsibility has replaced it, which may not be the best way to run a ward where the people have a short stay under conditions of intense personal discomfort.

Decor

The interior design was specified by the architect and, while a fairly good job was made of it, it

for two hours a day, afternoon and evening, so the ward was usually quiet once 'rounds' were done. There were allotments nearby outside and the sense of people quietly growing things assured me that normal life elsewhere continued

displays poor knowledge of daily hospital life and no inspiration, and certainly no 'delight'. When any refurbishing is done, the decor is chosen by the nursing staff who, while they are good at pretty well everything, are not necessarily great at choosing curtains. The pictures, range of library books and selection of newspapers are poor.

Food

Today there is more choice and greater variety. In the 'old days', if you were something weird like a vegetarian, the diet was cabbage, cabbage and yet more cabbage. We discussed 'food' in Chapter Four under 'Patient wards' but we would mention here that, since jobs have been clearly defined, it is unlikely that a carefully cooked egg could be provided when a sick patient felt like it.

Could Sister take a patient home for a meal?

This kind gesture would be unlikely today because of insurance implications: supposing that patient got hurt and decided to sue, supposing there was a question of assault or abuse? Today, the occupational therapist takes some patients home on a planned pre-discharge visit to make sure that they can manage to cook a meal, walk upstairs and bath safely. 'Safety first' said the Headmistress in *The Prime of Miss Jean Brodie*. 'But safety does not come first,' answered the impossible but inspired Miss Brodie, 'Goodness, Truth and Beauty come first.'

The quality of treatment

The technical aspects of medical and nursing treatment have improved and changed since the 1960s and most patients stay in hospital for only a short time. In some ways, the caring and hotel qualities of care have not kept pace with technical aspects.

Where hospital stays are short, the gratitude patients feel for having received free treatment and the strong national affection for the NHS mean that in 'Satisfaction Surveys' this gratitude is expressed and rightly so. However, if we enquire and question this 'gratitude barrier,' we hear about those aspects of care which patients feel could be improved.

Patients generally expect that the treatment they receive should be the most appropriate for their medical condition; they would choose good medical and nursing care above better food in an attractive ward. Implicitly, they often make this choice and we can hear of it in the stories they tell about their hospital stay: wonderful staff and treatment, such a pity about the poor food, noise and dinginess. In a prosperous country at the end of the twentieth century this is not a choice that the NHS should have to offer and it is often an unnecessary choice, as this book has shown.

A PATIENT'S COMMENT

The day room should have been a warning of things to come. Under the 'No Smoking' sign, which spelled out the trust's commitment to promoting health, were two ashtrays overflowing with cigarette stubs. I sat myself down on one of the four serviceable chairs and looked over to the washbasin which, in mid-spring, was stuffed full of Christmas decorations that no-one had put away.

From then on, my stay in hospital became a clear demonstration of the gap between the rhetoric in trust mission statements and the reality of the growing squalor of many of their hospitals.

This was no London teaching hospital or a crumbling inner-city Victorian building. This was a hospital in the leafy suburbs, built less than twenty years ago and supposedly catering for a district of middle class and therefore vocal clients.

I was admitted to a ward where the beds were so close you could reach across and touch your neighbour. Around the curtain rail trailed cobwebs, laden with dust. I pointed out the dirt and dust under the bed to a cleaner. 'Oh yes', she said, 'you could grow potatoes under there.'

I was in for a fairly routine toe straightening operation and, when the consultant came to see me later in the day, he was horrified to find the leg weighed down with bedclothes. I needed a cradle to take the weight off, so could I ask the nurse for one? No, said the nurse, there was no cradle available so I would just have to keep it uncovered. They found one eventually.

Then came supper. The man who had been in my bed previously – yes, this was a dreaded mix-sex ward – had not ordered any food so there was none for me. I could have an orange juice but not a sandwich or a piece of fruit.

At breakfast, they said there was no toast and offered me disintegrating buttered bread. The care assistant explained it was difficult to separate the ready-buttered loaves that arrived on the ward. And could I fill in my menu card for the person who was to have my bed later that day, please?

I was meant to stay for four days, but discharged myself on the second. As I prepared to leave, clearly unable to walk, I asked for a wheelchair. No, said the nurse, there was no wheelchair available and no porter. I could use crutches and 'hop it', she said, without a hint of irony. I hobbled down the ward and out to my husband's car while he worried about the ticket wardens telling him, 'You can't park there, you know.'

Having worked in the NHS for twenty years and subsequently in health service management, I thought I knew my rights and how to get them . . . I wrote to the chief executive. Two months later he wrote back to apologise and explain how seriously he took my comments.

The point of this story is simple. There was no-one to blame for the inadequate organisation and management of the ward and I do not believe this was a resource issue. I want to know not who set the standards in food, hygiene, catering and equipment, but who was accountable for them? Who was in charge here? . . .

The trust had various mission statements and placards announcing its wish to deliver the highest quality care and asking for patients' comments. The trust listed among its ward staff ward managers, a service manager and a patients' relations manager. If it is not their job to close the gap between the words and the experience, then whose job is it?

(Naaz Coker, Fellow in health and clinical services management, King's Fund College, 'Smoke and dust', *Health Service Journal*, 17 July 1997)

The five senses

We have five senses, hearing, smell, sight, touch and taste, through which we know the physical world. As we experience our surroundings, we add feelings to the information which our senses supply. The colour which gives you a feeling of happiness because it is linked to a happy experience is the same colour which makes me

anxious because of its unpleasant personal links. The sounds which you hear and enjoy as good jazz music are the same that I hear as disturbing noise. The fabric which you feel as soft and comforting I find itchy and unpleasant. In our private lives we choose experiences which give us pleasure and seek them when we can.

It is easy to assume that people who are critically ill are less aware of their surroundings, although we have enough accounts from patients who seemed unhearing and unseeing that they could indeed see and hear. New techniques for studying brain activity will give us much information about whether the unhearing hear and the unseeing see; the evidence emerging so far is that our senses and the messages they bring us are important for normal development far sooner in life than we thought possible and also in brain states in which we have tended to think there was no consciousness. We can test the hearing of babies at birth by studying their brain activity when we generate noise, and we know that even very young babies respond differently to the face and voice of familiar people.

People with conditions that lock them out of our world because they cannot communicate are easy to discount. 'Me. The stiff one, old clay-boots with his clay head and old clay balls, a scarcely breathing hotch-potch of skin and bone who flexed not the smallest extremity, not even a toe, who lay all night like a corpse himself, who had not spoken a word in anyone's living memory' (Paul Sayer, *The Comforts of Madness*, Constable, 1988). This is a story of a catatonic man who actually recounts his own death. However, more fortunate cases are beginning to use technology to tell us that they can in fact hear, smell, see, touch and taste. When caring for such patients, we should assume that their senses are as acute as ours and indeed are likely to be accentuated because their world has become contracted and focused through illness.

This morning, with first light barely bathing Room 119, evil spirits descended on my world. For half an hour the alarm on my machine that regulates my feeding tube has been bleeping out into the void. I cannot imagine anything so inane or nerve racking as this piercing beep-beep-beep pecking away at my brain. To make matters worse, my sweat has unglued the tape that keeps my left eyelid closed, and the stuck together lashes are tickling my pupil unbearably.

To crown it all, the end of my urinary catheter has become detached and I am drenched. Awaiting rescue, I hum an old song by Henri Salvador; 'Don't you fret baby, it'll all be alright.' And here comes the nurse. Automatically, she turns on the TV. A commercial, with a personal computer spelling out the question: 'Were you born lucky?'

(Jean-Dominique Bauby, *The Diving-Bell and the Butterfly*, Fourth Estate, London, 1997. Translated by Jeremy Leggatt).

HEARING

We can hear while in the womb and hearing is thought to be the last sensation to fade when dying. Whether we perceive those vibrating air waves that are interpreted by our cochlea as communicative 'sound' which we understand or as unwelcome 'noise' which irritates us depends on our age, gender, culture, social situation and mental and physical state. Noise that we cannot tolerate is a major source of stress, but we are able to excuse unpleasant sounds when we can identify them and feel they are necessary.

Gender differences in noise perception

There may be gender differences in the perception of noise: women appear to forgive background noise of anything provided that it is of an even level, but are distressed by sudden loud noises, and men dislike background noise but can accept loud and uneven noise. One would like to conclude that these reactions are cultural and relate to the traditional life styles of men and women; men are able to tolerate cannon shot while being infuriated by child chatter which disturbs the concentration necessary for tracker-hunting, while women accept benign household hubbub but are distressed by loud retorts that denote danger. However, the individuality of response to sound should be borne in mind.

'Unnecessary noise is the most cruel absence of care' (Florence Nightingale)

Hospitals are noisy places. From a ward bed you will hear a constant stream of noise; there will be bangs, squeaks, footsteps, thudding, clattering, clicking, shuffling, equipment humming and bleeping, voices loud and all too clear, voices muffled when only a word or two is audible,

coughs, sighs, laughs, greetings and farewells, bells, radios and televisions.

It is generally assumed that 'sound' is inevitable and acceptable, but that 'noise' is avoidable and not acceptable.

Certain criteria help transform sound into noise: noise is sudden, unfamiliar or unexpected while sound is communicative, useful and appropriate; noise may be monotonous, endless and meaningless while sound can be intriguing and attractive.

Tolerance to noise is generally lower during illness and the sickroom quiet is one of our oldest traditions in caring for the sick. The control of noise should be an important part of the health environment, but disturbing noise is one of the most frequent complaints patients have about their hospital stay.

The King's Fund hospital noise surveys

The King's Fund conducted two surveys into 'Noise control in hospitals' in 1957/8 and 1960 and followed them up in 1973 with a report as to whether improvements had been achieved. The causes of noise were listed as follows:

- telephone and medical equipment
- the conduct of cleaners and cleaning equipment
- furniture and doors
- radio and television
- the conduct of staff and visitors
- other patients
- traffic outside.

The conclusion of the King's Fund Report on 'Noise control in hospitals' was: 'Our experience is that the greatest single factor in controlling noise is staff discipline.' The term 'staff discipline' implies an all-powerful matron insisting on silence, but it should mean staff self-discipline, an awareness of the value of quiet and the damage done by noise. Caring staff can put themselves in the place of the patient who is unable to control the irritation or assault of noise and less capable, while ill, mentally to filter out the unacceptable noise.

When the 1973 King's Fund second survey on 'Noise control in hospitals' was done, wards might have had one television; TV programmes closed down during the night and the shirt-pocket radio was a fantasy. Nearly thirty years later, there are more complaints about noise than any other

'It was the noise I couldn't stand; there never seemed to be a moment when there wasn't someone banging something, or feet walking up and down the ward with squeaky shoes, or doors slamming somewhere.'
(Patient's comment)

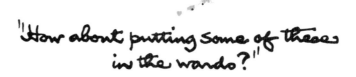

Fig. 8.2 Selection from a series of nine poster cartoons by 'Fougasse' (Cyril Kenneth Bird) commissioned by the King's Fund during their survey *'Noise Control in Hospitals'* 1957/8 and 1963. These were reproduced as A4-sized posters and distributed to hospitals as part of a campaign against noise.

Fougasse is best remembered today for the series of wartime posters 'Careless talk costs lives' which he produced for the Ministry of Information; these use the same red border and white space surrounding the drawing in order to isolate them from all the surrounding noticeboard paraphernalia.

single cause and this may be largely due to the proliferation of individual and communal television and radio sets in the wards.

> There seemed to be TV everywhere; there was a big one down one end of the ward which was on a lot and was very loud, and the woman next to me had her own and asked me if I minded and I did but you can't say so, and there was one in the lounge on all the time too.
>
> (Patient's comment)

Radio and television: entertainment or invasion?

In many daily lives background television and radio are the norm. Work with children who exhibit delayed language has shown that turning off this background noise improves speech and language.

If children live surrounded by words and noise which have no relevance or meaning for them and to which no one is paying any attention, we should not be surprised if they infer that words and language are not important and not worth their attention either.

When people are ill, it is unlikely that being exposed to the random effect of radio and television will be beneficial, but this can be controlled. Now that it is easy to record programmes and buy videos, timed viewing is feasible and headphones for all sets are compulsory in some wards. Some airlines are considering introducing 'technology-free zones' (like smoke-free zones) and this idea could reasonably be adopted by hospitals.

Hearing and the elderly

The majority of people in hospital are older people. As we age, our hearing deteriorates; we lose the ability to hear faint sounds and this gradual loss is linked to increasing difficulty filtering out background noise to focus on the sounds we wish to hear. Many older people find it difficult to hear well enough to carry on a conversation where there is background noise, although they can enjoy the same conversation once the background noise is removed. It is therefore paradoxically even more important to reduce noise when we are caring for older people so they can hear and respond to speech.

Current techniques enable us to measure stress levels in response to noise, but this is an area where we should not need the sophistication of a randomised controlled trial. Care, common sense and imagination are enough to remind us that noise always annoys (Fig. 8.2).

In new buildings good acoustics should be an intrinsic part of the design. In older buildings it is usually too expensive to improve the acoustics radically but these buildings are often so well built that noise is anyway less of a problem than elsewhere. Improvements can be made with thicker, lined curtains, noise-absorbing floor surfaces like linoleum and carpet and acoustic ceiling tiles. The design team should be able to specify how to use these in a way that improves noise control but without an ugly appearance.

SMELL

Unattractive smells

One of the achievements of the twentieth century in hospital care is the absence of smell. The most common smell in hospitals used to be that of antiseptics but modern antiseptics no longer smell. Wound dressings have also developed so that the smell associated especially with wartime hospitals has also faded. Modern continence products and care mean that the unwelcome urine and faecal smells should also be a thing of the past, providing sensible choices are made about floor coverings and cleaning is regular and thorough.

One source of smell that has had consistent attention for years is that of smoking. A national 'non-smoking' policy is now so universal that it needs no discussion here, but some place should be set aside for smokers other than outside. The most usual is the space between the outer and inner automatic doors at a hospital's entrance, but a sea of cigarette butts and a small group of furtive smokers at the entrance to a place dedicated to health is not an encouraging first impression.

Desirable odours

Pleasant smells are difficult to introduce because the pollen of any scented plant can aggravate respiratory complaints. However, there are some smells that are almost universally liked, often to do with cooking.

Modern methods of food production and ventilation in small kitchens mean that in most hospitals there is no smell of cooking and, for those who remember the bad old days when the smell of boiled cabbage began to reach the wards soon after breakfast, this is an achievement. But there is also a loss; we have visited small hospitals where the smell of scones baked in the after noon was clearly a pleasure to everybody, and in some old people's care homes, meals are prepared while pleasant cooking smells stimulate appetite. Patients can enjoy involvement in the preparation of meals and the link between food smells and a sense of well-being is very strong.

A recent example of recognising the positive contribution of the sense of smell is the use of aromatherapy, massage with scented oils, which combines the sense of smell and touch. Perhaps it also alerts the 'sixth sense', that of being attended to as an individual in a caring and competent way. Aromatherapy is used for the terminally ill in hospices and increasingly also in general hospitals. Although there are no randomised controlled tests of its benefits, it appears to give delight, improves sleep and reduces the need for medication.

SIGHT

In a way, this whole book is about sight. Throughout the chapters we have shown that, to a significant extent, what we see makes a diff-erence to our confidence and sense that we are in good hands; this is quite apart from the further capacity of what we 'see' to offer or deny potential 'delight'. There are one or two further specific points about sight that we need to include here.

Today, we are much more conscious of the need to preserve individual dignity, and we try to offer privacy to hospital patients in situations where they would expect it in their own homes, such as during toileting, undressing or while feeling too much pain or being too ill to be seen. We also try to protect patients and visitors from distressing or unattractive sights, although this may be impossible to achieve completely, but the effort recently to offer separate Accident and Emergency waiting rooms for children so they do not have to see accident victims is humane and sensible. Medical staff are so used to gory sights that they forget such things can distress others.

Visual disturbance and sensitivity

Many illnesses are manifest by sight disturbances that may result in someone losing balance, feeling

or actually being sick or fainting. Our persistent advocacy of the use of professional designers is so that these factors can be taken into account without compromising standards of interest and variety.

Bright light which we cannot control and avoid is excruciating and doubly so when we are ill. Flexible, controllable lighting is an important part of good design.

Hospitals are visually alien places. When we wake up in a hospital bed, we will see nothing like the sights we see when we wake up at home. If we are drifting in and out of consciousness and we see and hear nothing familiar, our confusion remains. If we are lucky, a familiar someone-we-love will be beside the bed calling us back to consciousness but, without that attention, there will be nothing: no known wallpaper, quilt cover, bedside lamp, curtain or picture. The longer our stay in hospital, the more important it is for us to build a sense of pleasant familiarity so that we are no longer in an alien world. A well-designed environment can help us do this, especially if we have a few familiar objects around us.

TOUCH

Active and passive touching

Nursing journals briskly explain that there are two sorts of touch: the necessary touching which is to investigate, treat and communicate (active touching) and the unnecessary, optional touch which is solely to comfort (passive touching). Massage, used extensively in hospices, is a structured and acceptable form of passive touching. All nurses have to engage in active touching but passive touching implies the nurse actually wants to touch the patient.

Patients know which sort of touch they are being given and most interpret the second as a personal gesture of comfort and sympathy: 'She just took my hand and sat with me'; 'she held me and cried too'. However, in order to handle the unusual intimacy of the service that nurses and doctors do for patients, rules about touch have evolved and are implicit in medical training.

The healing touch

Spiritual healers depend upon touch and the only explanation that is consistently offered is that it transmits energy. The successful healing touch is as mysterious as it is rare but the National Federation of Spiritual Healers is gradually persuading conventional doctors to take healers seriously and some work from NHS hospitals and surgeries with apparent success.

Touching animals

Animals have traditionally played a far greater part in everyday life than most of us in the 'post-horse' era can remember. Chickens in the garden, a pig in the sty, a watch-dog and cats for the mice, possibly a parrot on a perch in the hallway, all these were an accepted part of many a domestic arrangement, and 'tame animals' were 'tame' when you could touch them freely. Then mass food production and shopping opportunities put paid to the chickens and pigs while parrots and dogs make 'messes' which microbiologists assured us were 'injurious to health'. Shakespeare's 'humble necessary cat' hung on in the popularity stakes but animals generally joined other time-consuming but delightful domestic items such as open fires and lamp-light into banishment.

Before long, nostalgia and revised attitudes to mental health voiced by behavioural psychologists began to describe the benefits that 'tame' animals bestow. Physically it appears that stroking fur (and, one supposes, feathers) can reduce symptoms of stress and slow the pulse. Tame animals provide many mental benefits; they present opportunities for safe projection of feelings and are non-judgemental, non-argumentative and non-combative, while they can receive and return unconditional affection.

Animals have a long tradition as part of the psychiatric hospitals' environment, both as part of the economics of a largely self-supporting farm and also as deliberate therapy.

Pets have been kept in homes for the elderly and on children's wards, and under one paediatrician, each child was allocated an animal during their stay in hospital. One problem is that, surprisingly, these animals are often neglected. They are seen as a patient benefit, not as creatures deserving of care, and so they tend to get overweight and under-exercised, are given unsuitable food and denied contact with their own kind. However, schemes such as 'Pat a Dog' and visiting pets are successful and the question of infections being passed on should not arise with healthy animals who are wormed and groomed regularly.

'The NHS is usually excellent at treating the severely sick, but at its margins it is prone to falter.'
(Sandra Barwick, the *Independent*, 10 October 1992)

TASTE

We have discussed the appearance and presentation of food in Chapter Four. Here we would mention that in many illnesses we feel we have a nasty taste in our mouths, a furry tongue, an un-fresh feeling, a dry throat. Having a constant supply of something to drink is important, and maintaining fluid intake matters. Drink has to be accessible: a jug of water and glass at the back of a locker is no use, neither is a carton of drink that a patient cannot open. Few hospitals can offer cups of tea or coffee when we feel like it, although 'drinks trolleys' are a frequent and welcome 'marker' in the day, but the taste quality is inevitably institutional.

'Mouth care' is a term used in nursing for gentle cleaning of the teeth and mouth, and it can be the greatest relief when the mouth feels dry, furry and sour-tasting. There is the question of the doctor's 'bitter brew' and pharmacists have successfully replaced many sour liquid medicines with pills and injections; that 'spoonful of sugar helps the medicine go down' is no longer necessary.

THE SIXTH SENSE AND SISTER SENSES

Predictions, prognostications, telepathy and other ill-understood manifestations of foreknowledge can be conveniently 'dumped' into this category along with other baffling aspects of human perception and responses. When a reasonable explanation of something is eventually presented, that manifestation is then removed from this useful category of the sixth sense and popped into some physiological classification like 'meteorological and barometric responses'.

Many people report increased stiffness and pain linked to weather changes, and climatic conditions have been associated with mental conditions, bleeding rates in post-operative patients and the onset of labour, as reported in 'Influence of the Full and New Moon on the Onset of Labour', *Journal of Midwifery*, March/April 1988. From studies like this, it does appear that some 'old wives' tales' have more credibility than once thought likely.

The spiritual 'aesthetic'

Our intention in including this rather odd 'aside' is to emphasise that it is in hospitals that people are observed under conditions of illness, injury and sadness and that the best observers need to take into account qualities that cannot necessarily be measured or quantified and react sympathetically.

This has been our message in many different guises throughout this book, regarding colour, plants, noise, and so on, and it refers us back to our opening definition of 'the aesthetic' and the spiritual aesthetic which engenders hope, contentment and peace.

The aim of a hospital is to heal disease, banish despair and soothe agitation, and it appears that the last two are the most difficult to achieve.

THE EXPERIENCE OF ILLNESS

The experience of acute illness cannot be conveyed but only implied; when you feel so ill that you would sincerely prefer to die than live, when only water is acceptable because all other drinks are too complicated, when balance is destroyed and light, food, noise and movement are unbearable, when you cannot tolerate any pattern, picture or visual agitation, this is a degree of distress that is often accommodated when it accompanies a life-threatening situation but not when it is not.

Hospices are normally better geared to this degree of pain. It is in a hospice that you realise that a door-stop that stops doors banging has been invented, that the application of an oil-can stops trolley wheels squeaking and that radios, televisions, kitchen noise and talking can be controlled. The hospice movement is widely admired for its handling of terminal illness and all its associated needs by these simple expedients. Some of its practices could well be adopted by the average hospital.

Other human influences

Many architects and designers are confident in their abilities to produce designs that are fine until, once complete, people start to live and work in them. In their eyes, it is the people who degenerate the vision, to which the sceptic might reply that if people, with all their messy and illogical habits, are not comfortable then the building has failed. Hospitals, of all public buildings, are prone to 'person stress' because there are so many people involved in often urgent and messy matters (Fig. 8.3).

THE IMPACT OF PEOPLE

People as pollutants

People are major pollutants as any keeper of premises open to the public will endorse. They quietly breathe, sneeze, shed skin and sweat moisture into the atmosphere and, in the hot and crowded conditions which hospitals tend to offer, a human being can give off an amazing quantity of water in an hour. Their clothes exude corrosive substances, like acid rain, and flatulence releases methane. Anyone in charge of conservation in picture galleries knows well the polluting power of even the best-behaved visitor.

In a hospital there is even more to contend with than methane, dust, water vapour and the wildlife that thrives on them. Floors and walls receive body fluids frequently and in plenty and the fashion for universal carpeting and the 'contracting out' of cleaning services have contributed to doubtfully clean hospitals.

Vandalism and theft

Vandalism can take place either inside or outside. From outside come all the forces of people who treat the premises badly for various reasons. Perhaps they didn't expect to come to hospital. They might have been on their way to a football match or to visit their grandmother, then had an accident, or were taken ill, and now find themselves in hospital. To express their resentment at the interruption of their daily lives, they take it out on the premises. Vandalism can also be an expression of resentment, grief or sheer boredom.

There have been enough studies of people's reaction to interiors to show that, in decent premises, if damage is repaired immediately, then vandalism does not accelerate but gradually peters out or is at least much reduced. There are other factors, such as 'The Hawthorne Factor' that demonstrate that if changes of any sort (even inconvenient and unnecessary changes) are made to premises regularly, people react well and respect the changes. Just to alter the arrangement of furniture and noticeboard displays could fulfil this.

The second sort of vandalism comes from inside the organisation and emanates from the

Fig. 8.3 Weighing babies at the baby clinic (top). Patient interview prior to discharge (bottom). These are two out of a series of over one hundred drawings made by Stephanie Fryer when she was Artist in Residence with the Southern Derbyshire Community Health Services Unit. A selection was reproduced and used as postcards. 1987

staff themselves, often from hurry or unawareness of their surroundings, such as the ubiquitous use of Sellotape, blue-tac and drawing pins used by staff for their many notices. A more dramatic example was a case of a surface conduit of electric wire and new switch being placed right on top of an Edwardian tile mural, right in the middle of a duck, completely ignoring that it was a charming mural put up only for reasons of pleasure. One brisk drilling from an impatient electrician ruined it forever.

However, the average hospital is not an island and if it is within a community where despair and boredom have created a climate where vandalism is routine, it will be hard for any public building to be immune. Some inner city clinics and surgeries have to maintain virtual fortifications to protect staff and premises, but this kind of vandalism is a community issue and affects everyone.

There is no solution other than providing a good environment and maintaining it determinedly.

Patients: 'a time, a name, a number'

While many hospitals endeavour to provide 'delight' and 'comfort' for their patients, not all patients are comfortable or delightful. Providing a service which will satisfy this varying multitude and their visitors is endlessly difficult albeit essential. Whatever stereotype we have of the grateful, reasonable, compliant patient will not survive long because the patient in prospect is different from the patient in reality.

Flawlessly typed, and spaced
At the proper intervals,
Serene and lordly, they pace
Along tomorrow's list
Like giftbearers on a frieze.

In tranquil order, arrayed
With the basic human equipment –
A name, a time, a number –
They advance on the future.

Not more harmonious who pace
Holding a hawk, a fish, a jar
(The customary offerings)
Along the Valley of the Kings.

Tomorrow these names will turn nasty,
Senile, pregnant, late,
Handicapped, handcuffed, unhandy,
Muddled, moribund, mute.

Be stained by living. But here,
Orderly, equal, right,
On the edge of tomorrow, they pause
Like giftbearers on a frieze.

With the proper offering
A time, a number, a name.
I am the artist, the typist;
I did my best for them.

(Ursula Fanthorpe, *The List*, *Selected Poems*, Penguin, 1986)

CHAPTER EIGHT INFORMATION

ILLUSTRATIONS

Fig. 8.2: King's Fund for London © (see also *The Good-tempered Pencil* by Fougasse, London: Max Reinhardt, 1957)
Fig. 8.3: Southern Derbyshire Health Authority ©

Conclusion

Fig. C.1: S. and C. Calman ©

Professional appointments
The 'design team'

CHAPTER

9

INTRODUCTION

The common theme throughout this book is that far too many hospitals generally lack those aspects of the 'aesthetic' that we defined in our first chapter; these include 'comfort and delight' which, as we have seen repeatedly, are important to busy staff and stressed patients alike and which our last chapter ('The human factor') emphasises especially.

Staff in the NHS want to offer a good service in an attractive and sympathetic environment and the management's responsibility should be to ensure that there are systems in place which help them do so. However, few NHS organisations have such a system whereby this is achieved.

Many managers reading this book will be working long hours and are faced with myriad pressures and problems of making the NHS work within a fixed budget. A modern health authority is amongst the most complex of modern institutions; the idea that a manager of such an organisation will be expected to find time or the opportunity to achieve 'delight' may reasonably raise a groan from those who occupy the position.

Apart from staff who may become inured to a shabby hospital and patients who are so grateful to be treated that they are disinclined to complain, the new non-executives of trusts and authority members often notice the poor 'aesthetic' and feel very strongly that something must be done about their hospital. They comment about its depressing image, poor signposting and generally uncared-for appearance. But somehow this interested concern does not often get translated into action. This may be because the suggestions appear too daunting, too lengthy, too costly or too hard to imagine happening in a familiar hospital. It may also be that, because no practical solutions are offered which can be put into practice quickly, there are few suggestions which a hospital manager could start within a

week or a month, within current budgets and with existing circumstances.

WHAT TO DO

These aesthetic qualities *can* be supplied though, not as an afterthought or an extra, but as an integral feature in the full functioning of a modern health service.

Achieving 'comfort and delight' depends on the most senior management in two vital ways, both of them realistic and effective. The first requirement is for the chief executive and the chairman of the board to show they care about these qualities; to notice when they are achieved; to comment upon their absence and to keep asking questions aimed at making everyone aware that they matter.

The second requirement is to build into your system the expertise which knows how to achieve the whole range of aesthetic qualities and takes responsibility for doing so, so that they become an integral feature of your service. The most effective way to make sure your organisation will provide comfort and delight is to appoint a design team.

THE DESIGN TEAM

An estates department of a large hospital may well have architects and perhaps landscape architects employed for special projects, but they are unlikely to be permanent staff. In order to achieve the qualities we have discussed, an average-sized hospital should appoint a design team consisting of:

- a landscape architect
- an interior designer
- an arts co-ordinator.

These three core members of the team do not necessarily need to be full-time if the organisation is small – they could even be 'shared' with another site – but they need to be available on a consistent

'People and perfect processes make a quality health service; a poor quality service results from a badly designed and operated process, not from lazy or incompetent health care workers.'
(John Ovretveit, *Health Service Quality*, Blackwell Science Ltd, 1992)

basis. For example, an average to large site in poor condition will need the full-time attention of such a team to instigate a significant difference.

The three staff should be appointed as a team, not as three individuals, and they should have sympathy for each other's values. For example, it should not be beneath the attention of the arts co-ordinator to consider the design and placing of radiators, or the landscape designer to consider the selection of pictures, or the interior designer to consider installing climbing plants. If you are careful to appoint an integrated team, the site will benefit from a co-ordinated approach and there will be continuity if one team member leaves, the others being involved in their replacement.

Status of the design team

When a new system is introduced into an organisation, it requires senior management support until it is embedded. The investment in a design team is more likely to be successful if a key role for the chief executive and a board non-executive is built in. This might be a quarterly progress meeting which both attend and an annual report from the design team to the whole board, which could be a 'before' and 'after' slide show of hospital changes achieved rather than only a written document.

Below the chief executive, the day-to-day reporting should be to someone with enough authority and overview to show that the design team is not an optional extra but an important and integral part of the overall approach to providing a quality service. This will mean that the design team are involved with each and every upgrading, alteration and development inside or outside the entire premises and that no casual alterations to careful schemes are subsequently made. Such a degree of control and such

a change in procedures require the endorsement of authority and also the co-operation of the estates department staff.

The design team and the estates department

That this relationship is positive and mutually helpful is essential. Conflict can and does arise because of a lack of appreciation of the other team's aims and priorities and uncertainty about seniority and ultimate authority.

Possible solutions to conflict

Incidents like that in the 'Horror story' arise from mutual mistrust and poor management structures.

A solution might be for staff from each team to spend one full day 'shadowing' staff from the other team to see exactly what they do and why. The design team can then see the complexity of the service areas and the range of requirements that these have to fulfil, probably viewing some of them from vertiginous catwalks high up in the roof areas, and understand that the estates staff can risk their own safety in, perhaps, keeping emergency generators going during a crisis. Similarly, the engineers and surveyors could spend a day with the design team and see the range of contacts they establish and complexity of arrangements they make while doing highly professional work that depends upon educated judgement consistently applied, and not based on ethereal whim.

Problems can also arise because estates staff are usually men and design team staff are often women. This factor, and the question as to who has ultimate authority over management of land and buildings, must depend on management handling and way the teams are briefed.

HORROR STORY

An interior designer specified that the new metal windows on an undistinguished extension to a period building should be painted a dun colour instead of bright white like the large sash windows in the adjacent fine building. This was so that the extension, which was also to be covered in creepers, would be visually muted. It happened that the professionally required undercoat for this colour was turquoise. The painters complained to the Estates' Manager that this was a ridiculous colour – windows were always white and certainly never turquoise – so he countermanded the instruction and the windows were painted white; he also forbade the creepers because of the alleged damage they would do to the brickwork, even though clear agreement with all relevant staff had previously been reached.

FINANCING THE DESIGN TEAM

Salaries

If the budget for your trust is £50 million, you can build a design team into your system for 0.2 per cent (£100,000) of your budget, and you can make a good start even with 0.1 per cent (£50,000) of your budget.

The salaries should be commensurate with each appointee's experience. As with any other appointment, if you pay peanuts, you get monkeys. The recruitment and selection process should aim to make appointments of well-qualified staff with some years' appropriate professional experience in their own field. Contracts should give some stability, perhaps three years subject to a satisfactory performance against agreed objectives; ideally, such a team should live locally, but if this is not feasible, they should be required to spend adequate time on site.

Capital expenditure

It may reasonably be feared that such a team, once in position, will devise expensive schemes for site improvement but this should not occur for two reasons.

Any hospital will have basic budget allocations for the buildings, the interiors and the land and it will depend on the invention and experience of the design team to use these existing budgets in the best possible way. We have made many suggestions throughout this book for the imaginative use of existing facilities, which depends on the quality of the design team; this expectation should be part of the job description.

However, there is a limit to the use of ordinary opportunity and new schemes will be devised that require capital expenditure. These should be the subject of fundraising. It is axiomatic in many professions (in arts organisations, including theatres and galleries, and museums and nowadays also educational establishments) that funds are raised to fulfil the most innovative and exciting work. Staff are expected to become accomplished fundraisers and this should be part of the design team's brief.

Chapter Ten is devoted to fundraising as a hospital presents many opportunities. Our suggestion is that any money the team wish to spend over and above the existing budget, they raise from external sources.

ACCOMMODATION OF THE DESIGN TEAM

Premises

Since the nature of the work will be both administrative and practical, the premises need to be a studio as well as an office to accommodate three busy, creative people.

The design team should have direct access to outside for deliveries, daylight should be good and blackout facilities should be available. There should also be storage space and, above all, once the premises are established they should not be altered. One arts co-ordinator had eight changes of premises in four years in one trust which was wasteful. Once everyone knows where the design team are, they can establish their premises with all their equipment and material. There may also be a need for outside premises such as greenhouse, storage rooms and so on, and security will be an important item.

Tools and equipment

These will cover the different disciplines of administrative work (hence word processors, fax and phone) *and* creative work (needing large tables, drawing desks, spades and drills, stepladders and cameras).

These requirements are basic to achievement in this complex field and start-up costs are no more than for any other significant department.

Criteria for success

A series of clear criteria for success should be established, linked to a time programme that might look like this.

AFTER THREE MONTHS

By then the design team should be established so that all senior staff and those with whom they work regularly (team leaders and heads of departments, also estates, cleaning and maintenance staff) know who they are and their location and extension numbers, besides understanding the basic nature of their work. All board members should be aware of them and have received a brief but clear 'Plan of Action' giving a programme for the next year.

AFTER ONE YEAR

There should be available a series of 'before' and 'after' photographs showing the work of each team member, some working in collaboration with each other, and of several site improvements inside and out. These should receive staff and patients' comments showing that change is noticed and generally appreciated. The team should have presented a plan for the next three years which is updated annually.

The design team should have established a good dossier of varied samples associated with their work which they can show to staff. A record of their contacts is to be handed on if a team member leaves. The premises of studio/offices should demonstrate the professionalism involved and the range of the work, making the place a cultural 'hub' which attracts visits from staff, casual or purposeful, and from those who are interested, involved or just nosy.

The local press should also be taking regular notice and reporting the changes favourably; likewise the local radio station.

AFTER THREE YEARS

Site success

By this time there should be a significant number of site improvements, well documented by before and after photographs.

Some of these developments should be merging to create continuous areas of significant improvement, resulting one way or another in visual 'delight'. Not only should they have been created but they should also have been successfully maintained.

Staff, patients and local reputation

The team should be accepted by staff and be integrated into people's way of working and thinking. Staff and patients should by now be demonstrating not only by comments but by their actions that they like the improvements. A play garden should be full of children, a 'relaxation room' should be in use, and so on.

Local press should be giving regular coverage and local organisations that are in any way associated with the work (e.g. garden trusts, art organisations) should be involved in some way.

Critical reaction

Some national newspaper, media and specialist magazine coverage should have been achieved. By now, members of the design team should have been recognised as experts in their field, and be giving talks to conferences, writing articles for papers and so on.

AFTER FIVE YEARS

Site transformation

By this time the hospital site generally should be so improved in all visual and environmental aspects that it is established as an item of local pride and as a national professional example. The effect of 'delight' will show in the popularity of the place with staff (who want to work there) and patients (who appreciate this element during their visit or stay and express their appreciation).

Critical success

Schemes should now be entered for, and winning, national awards and prizes. The work of the design team should be receiving significant media notice (magazine articles and so on) while members of the design team are being acknowledged as experts in their field.

If any of the team leaves, a replacement should be easy to find as the reputation of the team's work should attract candidates of calibre.

Continuing financial viability

While the full-time salaries continue to be paid by the authority, the capital expenditure raised consistently from outside sources should be considerable and many donors should be pleased with the result of their funds. General capital and maintenance expenditure should not have risen beyond expectation.

Fundraising

CHAPTER

10

Hospitals . . . get first priority . . . there are four hospitals in the suburbs, just outside the town. The idea of this is to prevent overcrowding, and facilitate the isolation of infectious diseases. These hospitals are so well run, and so well supplied with all types of medical equipment, the nurses are so sympathetic and conscientious, and there are so many experienced doctors constantly available that, although nobody is forced to go there, practically everyone would rather be ill there than at home.

(Thomas More, *Utopia*, 1516 trans. Paul Turner, Penguin Classics, 1965)

Money plays a part in achieving Utopia so we conclude our book with advice on how to obtain it for 'comfort and delight'.

INTRODUCTION

The requirement of the design team to raise money for site development and improvement will probably become a significant part of the job. It is hard work raising substantial money; it requires consistent application, determination and time. When we advocated in the last chapter that the three members of the proposed design team should be experienced at fundraising, this was one part of the reason. It is one thing to have bright ideas; it is another to raise the money to undertake them, then make everyone get on with the work involved and ensure the schemes are maintained after the initiators' departure.

Each of the three members of the design team should have a good knowledge of the administrative and financial structures around their professional discipline, and know where to start in raising funds to develop their work. There may be precedents within the local health services for fundraising that will be useful, either from lots of small fundraising efforts in several departments or, if the matter has been well organised, possibly under one charitable umbrella.

Money is raised from a combination of local and national sources, both charitable and commercial, and the new possibilities of winning lottery money for capital expenditure and the opportunity to apply for European funding have introduced new elements into an already complicated game.

The hospital as applicant

Hospitals are generally successful candidates for fundraising, partly because everyone is afraid of illness, and to help them is an oblique expression of self-preservation; also because the needs and schemes can be very diverse and so take advantage of many opportunities. There should be no question that money is sought to fill gaps in statutory government funding but instead you can suggest that the appeal is to enhance a system that needs only a bit of help to become perfect.

INHERENT BENEFITS AND PROBLEMS

Professional fundraisers

Apart from the role of the design team, a hospital may appoint a professional fundraiser. Some of the best are those with experience of giving grants on the basis of 'poacher turned game-keeper'. A professional fundraiser can be offered an income which is a percentage of what they raise, which is an excellent incentive to success. If office facilities are provided (premises, telephone, word processor, fax and photocopier) this percentage can be lower than if they are working independently but, as with anything else, you get what you pay for. Any salary, if part-time, should be 'pro rata' for the experience of the person, supplemented with a 'pump-priming' fee for stationery and photography, equipment and postage. For a specific project, like a scheme to buy a CT body scanner or a staff swimming pool, a professional fundraiser may be appropriate.

Legal requirements

The 1992/3 Charities Act sought to control the activities of fundraisers by making obligatory some requirements for all those in this work; the most important of these is that you are obliged to have a clear contract of employment and also that you state to any charity from whom you seek funds what commission or salary you draw.

Why form a charity?

Some hospitals were originally founded, from medieval times on, as charities receiving bequests. They are not now in this legal category since the foundation of the NHS which was a 'nationalisation' of health care. The creation of NHS Trusts has rearranged their status but not altered it in this respect; an NHS trust should found a 'charity' within its organisation if it needs to receive funds from charitable sources.

Many hospitals have therefore created small charities for the single purpose of receiving money. This is because many charities have a legal stipulation that they can give only to other charities and if this sounds like 'the big fish feeding the little fish', that is exactly the situation. By stipulating this condition, they ensure that their money does not go on commercial enterprises or schemes that are government responsibility or to individuals, however deserving; instead, they finance 'charitable' activities which are basically educational, humanitarian, social or cultural.

An 'Art Scheme' or a 'Landscape and Garden Scheme' will probably fulfil these criteria and you will expect to apply to appropriate charities to fund them. So, if your hospital does not contain such a charity under whose auspices you can operate, you will need to form one. There are also advantages regarding income tax and VAT once you are registered.

When and how to register

If you expect to have a continuous, ongoing scheme of fundraising for the many projects a design team would expect to initiate, it is sensible to form a charity. Prepare your 'aim', which must come within the charitable brief, and apply to the Charity Commissioners for registration. Acceptance is not a forgone conclusion and neither is the procedure quick. Excellent help lines are available as is an invaluable publication

(*How to Form a Charitable Trust*) from the Directory of Social Change (see 'Chapter information' for address).

Problems of organisational 'inter-politics'

Within even a small hospital, there may be several fundraising efforts going on and they can undercut each other and confuse the issue by multiple appeals; the children's ward may be campaigning for play equipment, the library might be appealing for a colour photocopier while the design team are advocating several schemes simultaneously, and they could all write to the same people and exhaust potential good-will. There needs to be co-ordination whether by a professional fundraiser or by the chief executive's office.

PREPARATION OF A SUCCESSFUL APPLICATION

The 'attractive' versus the 'not so attractive'

It is easiest to raise funds for children, sight, experimental technology or anything rare and interesting (especially if it might threaten us all like cancer or Aids). Ecological schemes are also attractive and there are charities that exist for very particular subjects, such as the Clothmakers Guild which once gave money for hospital curtains. It is most difficult to raise money for anything that appears not so attractive (like middle-aged mentally handicapped patients), familiar (like the common cold) or anything obscure, boring or disgusting.

Success breeds success and once you have raised some money, used it well, acknowledged all the donors, invited them to see the result of their donation, held a party and advertised their generosity, you can start the next undertaking well primed.

The content of an application

Whether this is a single A4 page for local distribution or a lengthy form for a major charity or the huge form for a lottery application, there are four criteria: clarity, detail, attractiveness and lastly an assurance that the money will be well spent.

'Clarity' simply means stating what the project is, what it will cost, what other efforts you have made to fund it, when it will happen, how you will keep it going and who will look after it.

.'Detail' is the ability to describe briefly but fully the nature of your organisation and reasons for the appeal.

'Attractiveness' is the quality that will make the recipients sympathise with your organisation and your handling of the appeal, and it is both a verbal and visual quality. Visually, all forms, letters, odd material and photographs can be neatly mounted and encased in an inexpensive but attractive folder that will stand out lying in someone's 'In Tray' and refuse to be forgotten. The staff who select and judge these applications get bored with mediocrity and are usually delighted with an imaginative scheme professionally presented.

An assurance that the money will be well spent is more difficult and it is the major problem faced by those who give money; some of the major charities ask that the application is endorsed by the chief executive or Chairman so that responsibility for expenditure is directly attributable. This is one reason why we advocated the close involvement of these senior people in our description of how to set up a design team.

Large organisations will have guidelines for applicants and these should be followed to the letter. If they want three copies of everything, oblige; if they specify nothing larger than A4, obey; if the application has to be endorsed by the Chairman, corner that person and get the signature.

Many donors will impose conditions; the most usual is that the money is used within a certain time, evidence of completion is submitted and that full acknowledgement is published. Whatever the conditions may be, fulfil them scrupulously because you could be made to repay the money if they are flouted.

HELP IS AT HAND

'You are everyone's competitor and they are yours'

Colleagues engaged in a similar line of work may be disinclined to share their experience because you will all be competitors for the same goodies; when a rabbit finds a good clover patch, it seldom wastes good eating time by going to tell the other rabbits. However, some colleagues may be generous enough to share information and all of them will probably have to publish a list of their donors. These are excellent leads, but there are

official sources of help such as the Charity Commissioners and the Directory of Social Change (see 'Chapter information' for addresses).

The Charity Commissioners

Their work is to register and further the work of the several thousand charitable trusts that exist; they monitor applications for those wishing to register, oversee their conduct and maintain a full register of them for public access.

The Directory of Social Change

This organisation is set up to help the voluntary sector in matters which include fundraising. It publishes a set of paperback books on all aspects of moneyraising that are without equal for intelligent clarity and knowledge. The staff have done the donkey work and the books are the sifted results that save everyone a lot of time. The Directory has premises in London near Euston Station (see 'Chapter information') and their book list should be the first acquisition of anyone involved with fundraising.

Where does the money come from?

A simple scheme may need only one good donation but a complex undertaking may end up with several dozen donors, all coming from one or another of the following categories, unless there is a huge lottery grant that solves all problems (see 'Success story' at the end of this chapter). For donors, look at the 'Acknowledgements' for any large art exhibition or theatre production; then consider that for every successful application probably twenty others were made that failed and the scale of the undertaking will become apparent.

Money comes from:

- national sources
- international sources
- local sources
- sources pertaining to hospitals
- specialist sources.

NATIONAL SOURCES

The National Lottery Charities Board

Lottery money is often of a significant amount and it has altered the landscape of fundraising. It has injected a great deal of money into the system but there are, as ever, some disadvantages; some people have become 'addicted' to the gamble and donations to charity generally appear to have fallen but many good enterprises have benefited. A lottery grant is therefore worth pursuing but it is a demanding exercise.

The National Lottery Charities Board is an independent body set up by Parliament to distribute funds raised by the National Lottery to support charitable, benevolent and philan-thropic organisations throughout the UK. It is ultimately responsible to the Culture Minister at the Department of Culture, Media and Sport. Twenty-eight per cent of the money raised by the National Lottery goes to good causes that are divided between these five categories:

- The Arts Councils for England, Wales, Scotland and Northern Ireland
- The Sports Councils for England, Wales, Scotland and Northern Ireland
- The Millennium Commission (currently being run down)
- National Heritage Memorial Fund
- Charities Board.

A sixth 'good cause' category is in the process of being introduced: the New Opportunities Fund to benefit health and education.

These five categories are administered by five committees which handle applications for schemes that are deemed to be of national significance and not geographically specific. For example, the West Pier at Brighton bid for £14 million and this is handled by the National Heritage Fund.

For applications that are of local or regional significance, the country is divided into nine regions each with a regional advisory panel and a regional manager. This is to make sure that local circumstances are fully understood. These addresses are all given in 'Chapter information'.

Winning a grant has become more competitive as more people apply; first of all you target one of the 'categories' and contact the office responsible. There are different points of emphasis and subjects within each and applications may have to be made within a specific period. It really is hard work applying for a lottery grant as the long but well-written forms ask for quantities of detailed information; there are 'training days' available on how to apply which can be worth attending.

National industries

Company directories list the annual turnover and the amount dedicated to charity by companies. Most have experienced so many requests that they allocate to a few specific schemes and refuse all others, so look for their 'charity policy' before wasting a stamp. Those that do not limit their benefits in this way can best be approached either because of geographical proximity or the suitability of their product; for example, firms that make fertilisers have sponsored gardens, the manufacturers of women's sanitary wear have paid for a relaxation chamber attached to a labour ward and a water company helped pay for a swimming pool.

National charities

It is a legal requirement (not always honoured) that registered charities submit their accounts to the charity commissioners each year, and this enables a full directory of grant-making trusts to be published by the Charities Aid Foundation. Within this formidable volume are listed hundreds and hundreds of trusts, all with individual aims and rules. How do you decide which to approach?

Anyone can visit the Charity Commission Offices and ask to see the folder of any charity. By reading these folders which contain recent accounts and details of how charities operate, you can select those that are relevant to your schemes; this is hard work and the best short cut is to read instead the Directory of Social Change's two-volume *Guide to the Major Trusts*.

National and local appeals

The BBC broadcasts 'The Week's Good Cause' on Sunday on Radio 4 and the national newspapers print weekly appeals. Depending on how unique your appeal may be, you can ask to be included, and local newspapers and radio and TV stations all have their own schemes.

INTERNATIONAL SOURCES

European grants

This is also an opportunity that is difficult to effect but which can carry substantial gains. Grants tend to be large and for significant national projects; for example, an application was made by one hospital for the restoration of its historic water tower.

The large, metropolitan local authorities have officers for European affairs or you could contact your European MP via the House of Commons. Otherwise, this is the sort of information the Directory of Social Change will supply.

LOCAL SOURCES

Local authority funding

There are often budget allocations in the county and borough authorities that neatly fit specific schemes connected with arts, sport, wildlife and so on. The expertise amongst local authority staff, including the local museum staff, is also well worth using. Some local authorities also have a role to play regarding European money which we dealt with above.

Local industry

There will be business lists either locally compiled or in the business directories and a general mailing can realise (usually small) results. However, 'local industry' is a blanket term covering everything from a small garage run by one person to a vast conglomerate. If you can disentangle and then target those firms that are large enough to have fifty employees or so, or an annual turnover of a certain amount, and perhaps ask for a specific amount – such as 100 firms being asked for £50 – the work involved can be worth while.

Other local sources

The mayor, the scouts, the Round Table and other bodies of dignitaries often have money to dispense and the hospital is usually a popular cause.

Local private finance

Wealthy or well-known people usually keep a low profile because they are constantly approached for donations. However, a personal and appropriate appeal to them as a near neighbour with a promise of anonymity can be successful.

SOURCES PERTAINING TO HOSPITALS

Hospital, NHS funds and affiliated organisations

The average hospital will be likely to have some trust funds, especially if it is an older foundation, as some of these were well endowed. The Regional Offices of the NHS executive may know of funds for specific projects formerly allocated by the Regional Health Authorities. Affiliated organisations such as the WRVS or 'Friends of the Hospital' often have small amounts to offer; it is as well to approach these first as their staff usually have good knowledge of local fundraising possibilities.

Money-raising events

These are events that you run yourself such as sponsored activities, fairs and so on which hospitals and hospices are very successful at running. The amounts raised are usually small but are significant in that they convince those with larger amounts of the commitment of the organisation's staff to the undertaking. These events require well-motivated volunteers and are labour-intensive; they can be regarded as a 'sprat to catch a mackerel'.

SPECIALIST SOURCES

These are organisations set up to benefit some specific undertaking such as the arts, sport and so on. They tend to be precise both in their definition and what they do, but their involvement is often important.

In England, the network of ten arts boards funded by the Arts Council, the Crafts Council and local authorities has money available for the arts and experienced staff to give advice. While it may seem very complex, these bodies then fund 'public art agencies' and 'public arts projects' which themselves do the groundwork of actually making things happen. More details of this are given in Chapter Seven under 'Arts subsidy network' but the first point of call should be the regional arts board for any 'art' element in a scheme. Other specialist bodies, like the Sports Council and wildlife organisations, will also have local representatives.

What can still go wrong?

Many little things can go wrong which are capable of sensible solution, but there are two situations that are especially hazardous.

'NOT QUITE ENOUGH MONEY YET'

Sometimes you simply cannot raise enough money to carry out the scheme. However, you are legally obliged to spend donated money on the promised scheme and not divert it, so if you have raised £35,000 out of £60,000 for a swimming pool, what do you do?

Either write to every donor and ask for authorisation to use the money on something else, or build a smaller pool with a cheaper supplier or try harder next financial year. It is assumed that everything you raise is immediately invested so a small income accrues and this can fund time to try again.

STAFF CHANGES

The second major problem occurs when too many staff change at too many levels. This is another reason to employ a fundraiser and to have a design team of three dedicated people but nevertheless a scheme can have the stuffing knocked out of it if too many of those who were enthusiastic leave. However, the worst situations occur when the higher levels of management change and the new replacements then refuse, through pressure of work or different interests, to defend a scheme on which perhaps years of work have been expended.

AND FINALLY . . . WATCH FUNDING TRENDS

Patterns of funding alter throughout months, let alone years. A hospital will be presenting a very broad spectrum of subjects and these will all need to be handled individually. Events in the political and financial world will affect matters; for example, one spring the budget was beneficial to wealthy landowners so a rural hospital quickly wrote an 'appeal' letter to the five wealthiest

SUCCESS STORY

A garden for handicapped and other children was designed for a hospital courtyard, and the estimated cost was £50,000.

The funding was raised as follows. The safety rubber tiling for the ground was donated by the Sports Council after a visit by the regional representative; the surrounding mural was mainly paid for by the regional arts board via the appropriate public arts agency who increased the allocation from other sources. The Crafts Council paid for a commissioned ceramic-tiled decoration via the arts board, and a fundraising appeal to firms and enterprises within the hospital catchment area raised a third of the overall cost. After taking advice from the Tree Council and Common Ground on planting, the county garden trust gave generously as did a local fertiliser firm. An appeal during the autumn to all the nurseries for their end-of-season stock besides an appeal to all the 4,000 staff in the authority for plant 'bits' from their gardens did very well; to reach all these staff, a bright-coloured 'appeal sticker' was put on all the salary envelopes, two students being employed to undertake this task. The county council and district council both allocated funds, and a local glazier firm made all the surrounding windows shatterproof with transparent adhesive for free. The hospital contributed some money from their trust funds besides the salaries of the people designing and organising the courtyard. It was a complex but successful undertaking.

One lottery grant might have paid for the whole of this and obviated much work. However, an energetic success story like this might suggest that the next hospital project could reasonably be the subject of a lottery application on the strength of this scheme.

landowners within ten miles and their response was generous.

Subjects that are currently 'in the media' can affect events; a scare about meat can influence the demand for allotments for organic cultivation, and a report or TV programme on the benefits of trees, or animals, or fluoride in the water or any one of a number of subjects can influence public perception immediately.

That 'money follows energy' is a truism and success also requires good timing and, of course, luck.

CHAPTER TEN INFORMATION

Fundraising

The 'nuts and bolts' of fundraising, the books, contacts and information generally, tend to be impermanent in that they quickly become out of date. The initial listing we made for this section when we started work on this book contained references, recommended books and suggested procedures which, as time went by, were superseded, went out of print or became irrelevant. We are therefore giving only a few indispensable and stable contacts besides lottery data which promises such large prizes.

On the other hand, fundraising has become so important to so many enterprises that all this information is constantly replenished and up-to-the-minute advice is never hard to find. The internet and the quality of library searches have also altered the situation for the better. That it is important for many organisations to supplement basic funds is due to many factors.

The value of money falling so steadily for so long has coincided with accelerating public expectations in social care, medication, arts, indeed in all aspects of modern life. We take for granted what our grandmothers would only have dreamed of, and to pay for it, we initiate a flurry of activity. The contacts listed below should be of help.

ORGANISATIONS

Directory of Social Change
24 Stephenson Way
Euston Square
London NW1 2DP
(0171 209 4949)

This organisation or, more specifically, its booklist should be the 'first stop' for anyone involved in fundraising. Its primary purpose is to offer information and training to all those in the voluntary sector, but the training courses and booklist on offer extend into business and management. Its publicity specifies that 'voluntary' does not mean 'amateur'.

Its booklist includes guides on the major trusts, on company giving, on setting up a charity, the millionaire givers, the arts funding guide and so on and on. All are excellent and some superb.

The Charity Commissioners
Charity Commission Offices
St Alban House
57–60 Haymarket
London SW1Y 4QX
(0171 210 4477)

They are responsible for furthering the work of the many thousand registered charities by monitoring applications to become charities, overseeing their conduct, giving advice and maintaining a full public register of them for public access.

The offices are open to the public by appointment.

The *Directory of Grant-making Trusts* is published annually but it is a large volume of detailed information and consequently very expensive so is best consulted in a library.

The National Lottery Charities Board
Corporate Office
St Vincent House
16 Suffolk Street
London SW1Y 4NL
(0171 747 5299, enquiries; 5300, reception)

We explained in Chapter Ten how the Lottery works, and these addresses relate to this.

England Office

Readson House
96–98 Regent Road
Leicester LE1 7DZ
(0116 258 7000)

Wales Office
Ladywell House
Newtown
Powys
Wales SY16 1JB
(01686 621644)

Scotland Office
Norloch House
36 Kings Stables Road
Edinburgh EH1 2EJ
(0131 221 7100)

Office for Northern Ireland
2nd floor
Hildon House
30–34 Hill Street
Belfast BT1 2LB
(01232 551455)

Interim England Regional Offices

North East
North Sands Business Centre
Dame Dorothy Street
Roker
Sunderland SR6 OQA

North West
1st Floor
Tannery Court
Tanner's Lane
Warrington WA2 7NR

Yorkshire and Humberside
Prospect House
32 Sovereign Street
Leeds LS1 4BJ

West Midlands
Suite 29
Queens Gate
121 Suffolk Street
Queensway
Birmingham B1 1LA

East Midlands
Office 4
3rd Floor
Sutton Place
49 Stoney Street
Nottingham NG1 1LX

Eastern
Orwell House
2 Cowley Road
Cambridge CB4 4WY

South West
Curzon House
Southernhay West
Exeter EX4 3LY

London
3rd Floor
Whittington House
19–30 Alfred Place
London WC1E 7EZ

South East
3rd Floor
Whittington House
19–30 Alfred Place
London WC1E 7EZ

For arts bodies, the Arts Council, Crafts Council and regional boards, see 'Chapter seven information'.

For the Sports Council and organisations associated with planting, land development and wildlife, see 'Chapter two information'.

Conclusion

And finally . . .

WHAT DO WE THINK OF IT SO FAR?

The publication of this book takes place just as the fiftieth birthday celebrations of the NHS's foundation in July 1948 have quietened down and it is being carried forward into the new millennium. At such a convenient junction of time, if we were a college tutor and the NHS was a student, what would we write for its assessment?

This student has achieved massive popularity and has stayed the course in spite of several disruptions to its syllabus work and many critical attacks. It has demonstrated a lively intellect, ability to absorb and implement far-reaching scientific and organisational changes. It is at its best in times of crisis and, if a missile did hit this country, it would alleviate the resultant disaster with courage and dedication. I and all the other members of this faculty sincerely hope we would end up sharing its bunker.

However, you cannot build an entire reputation on the ability to combat mayhem; like Joan of Arc and Churchill, this student seems to prefer wartime which is all very well but many agencies of the world are trying to instill peace. It is therefore not surprising that it is on the 'daily task, the common round' that this student falters. It maintains that this is due to poor financial support and there certainly seems to be evidence that this may be the case, but this is not the whole picture and some work within the same limited budget has been excellent. We suggest that attention to details such as punctuality and legible writing could be achieved if it so wished. It is generally careless about small matters, but small matters add up into big ones, and it appears to be blithely unaware that many small failures eventually add up into one major failure.

On the question of personal appearance and suitable presentation, we are disappointed; while we do not expect this lovable student to become a 'glamour manikin' it actually undermines its own performance by its unkempt appearance. The same could be said about its cooking and general housekeeping which are notorious on this campus.

Admirable, brave and lovable, this student could do much better and should be encouraged to try harder. Although its admirers and friends continue to support it, they sometimes despair. Now that it is aged over fifty, it can no longer be given the benefit the doubt due to youth and inexperience. We accept that it needs an increase in its grant but recommend that, without quelling its indomitable spirit, it is at the same time given extra tutorials on those instances of failure that we have itemised.

'Do you have something for the human condition?', Mel Calman, 1984

Index

Note on the index
This whole book is about patients in NHS hospitals being cared for by nurses and other staff who are administered by managers. These five salient nouns have therefore been indexed only regarding their most significant discussion. Neither are those subjects listed under 'Chapter contents' individually indexed. All quotations and art works are listed by their originator, not by title.